GERMAN STUDIES SERIES

Industrial Relations in West Germany

Volker R. Berghahn
Detlev Karsten

BERG
Oxford / New York / Hamburg

Distributed exclusively in the US and Canada by
St. Martin's Press, New York

First published in 1987 by
Berg Publishers Limited
Market House, Deddington, Oxford OX5 4SW
175 Fifth Avenue/Room 400, New York, NY 10010, USA
Schenefelder Landstr. 14K, 2000 Hamburg 55, W.-Germany

British Library Cataloguing in Publication Data

Berghahn, Volker R.
  Industrial relations in West Germany.
  1. Industrial relations — Germany (West)
  I. Title   II. Karsten, Detlev
  331'.0943   HD8451

  ISBN 0–907582–64–8

Library of Congress Cataloging-in-Publication Data

Berghahn, Volker Rolf.
  Industrial relations in West Germany.

  Bibliography: p.
  Includes index.
  1. Industrial relations—Germany (West)
  2. Collective bargaining—Germany (West)   I. Karsten,
  Detlev.   II. Title.
  HD8451.B45   1987   331'.0943   87–9359
  ISBN 0–907582–64–8

Printed in Great Britain by Billings of Worcester

Contents

Preface

The Federal Republic of Germany ranks among the major trading and manufacturing nations of the contemporary world and contact between her industrialists and their counterparts in other countries is frequent and close. With the multinationalisation of the Western world economy having advanced at a rapid pace in the past two decades or so, foreign companies and their representatives increasingly find themselves involved in the West German economy. Willy-nilly they will be drawn into the existing system of industrial relations or discover that they require information on its rules and daily practice. Such information is usually found in handbooks or in bulky monographs and anthologies on labour relations in various West European countries. But as far as we can see, a short and up-to-date analysis of industrial relations in West Germany has not been available in the English language. It is in the hope of filling this gap that a political economist and a historian have tried to pool their expertise to produce this volume, which is addressed both to students of industrial relations and to those who need to know something about the West German system for their own daily use as managers, trade unionists or government officials inside or outside the Federal Republic.

This pragmatic purpose has deliberately led us away from long theoretical expositions of the nature of industrial relations in advanced capitalist societies; above all, it has informed the somewhat unusual structure of this book. As a glance at the table of contents will show, it is divided into two main parts. Those who wish to obtain a concise overview of the current organisational framework of West German industry, its main institutional arrangements, legal requirements and recent politics of industrial relations are asked to start with the first four chapters. Here the practical essentials of the West German system are set out and an attempt is made to elucidate what makes it 'tick'. These chapters are also broken down into many

1

sub-headings so that the table of contents may be used almost like an index by those wishing to make quick reference to a specific issue. However, we felt that many readers might like to have an analysis that goes beyond the current framework and practice. To us, one of the striking features of the world economy today is how — notwithstanding the close economic integration and interpenetration which we have experienced since the Second World War — national industrial systems have retained many peculiarities. Despite the hegemonic weight of the United States in the world economy, neither the Europeans nor the Japanese have become thoroughly Americanised in their industrial behaviour. Strong elements of an indigenous industrial culture, which have often grown up over many decades, have survived and proved surprisingly resistant to considerable pressures for adaptation and conformity. As in other spheres of social life, cultural traditions in industry have also been slow to change. This would appear to be particularly true of the industrial relations sphere, where it is not just the entrepreneurs but two or even three parties — the employers, the trade unions and the state — that have become involved in the shaping of a particular national system since the nineteenth century. The interaction between these three forces has resulted in the devising of peculiar rules and institutions which are generally not to be found in other industrial countries. Japan has recently presented an intriguing case in point. But West German industry, too, has developed a number of special features, such as co-determination, works councils and labour courts, which puzzle and fascinate foreign observers to this day. This is why the second part of this book pays attention to the origins of these peculiarities in an attempt to bring the historical dimension back into the study of industrial relations. The reader is therefore invited not to stop at the end of Chapter 4, if he or she is interested in the *genesis* of current theory and practice. And those who are already well familiar with the present, but are inclined to agree with us that history and tradition are important in this area will, it is hoped, find Chapters 5 to 7 illuminating, not least because they point up so many continuities.

The volume is supplemented by a number of important documents and statistical tables designed to reinforce the complex story of industrial relations in West Germany.

Glossary

Allgemeinverbindlichkeitserklärung eines Tarifvertrages (declaration of a collective agreement to be generally binding): The regulations contained in collective agreements apply to the members of the parties to these agreements only. The Federal Minister of Labour and Social Affairs can — on request of one of the parties to the collective agreement — declare the contents of a collective agreement to be binding for all work contracts of the industry concerned in a certain bargaining area. A precondition is that this measure is called for in the public interest, for example to avoid a decline of working conditions to socially unacceptable standards.

Arbeitsdirektor (labour director): Member of the management board with a special responsibility for personnel. All co-determined companies have a labour director, but only in the mining and the iron- and steel-producing industries can the appointment be vetoed by the employees' representatives.

Betriebsvereinbarung (plant agreement): Written agreement between the works council and the employer regulating plant issues of concern to the employees, in particular those where the works council has participatory rights.

Bundesanstalt für Arbeit (Federal Labour Institute): The institute which administers the Employment Promotion Act and conducts labour-market policy. It is a self-governing body with the state, employers and labour representatives participating in its decision-making. It is the head institution of the local and *Länder* labour offices.

Einheitsgewerkschaft (unitary union): A labour union which accepts members regardless of their ideology or religious denomination and which is independent of political parties, although not necessarily without preference for a certain political party. The DGB unions define themselves as unitary unions.

3

Einwirkungspflicht, Durchführungspflicht (obligation to strive for compliance): The obligation of the parties to a collective agreement to induce its members to abide by the agreement.

Friedenspflicht (peace-keeping obligation): During the currency of a collective agreement, no party to the agreement is allowed to take industrial action to change the agreement. A violation of this obligation may result in a conviction to damages due to the other party.

Gemeinwirtschaftliches Unternehmen (co-op enterprise): Co-op enterprises are companies which — unlike capitalist firms — do not primarily strive for high profits but aim for the provision of particular needs. Typical examples are public-utility companies. The DGB advocates a wider application of this principle.

Gewerkschaftliche Vertrauensleute (union shop-floor representatives): Honorary elected trade-union representatives in companies who were created to improve communication between ordinary members and their trade union. Unlike the works councillors, they are not obliged to cooperate loyally with the employer, and can therefore take a stand in labour dispute.

Industriegewerkschaft (industrial trade union): A principle of organising labour where all workers of an industry, irrespective of their profession or position in working life, belong to the same industrial union. In a pure industrial union system only one union would be represented in a company. In the Federal Republic of Germany, the seventeen DGB unions are industrial unions.

Institut der Deutschen Wirtschaft, IDW (Institute of German Private Enterprise): Economics and social-science research institute set up and supported by the Confederation of German Employers' Associations (BDA) and the Federation of German Industries (BDI).

Kurzarbeitergeld (short-working subsidy): A subsidy paid by the Federal Labour Institute which supplements the wages of short-time workers. The purpose is to avoid dismissals in periods of sluggish business.

4

Land: State within the Federal Republic of Germany with certain autonomous rights especially in the field of education and culture.

Leitende Angestellte (top executive staff, top managerial staff): Upper-echelon managers with decision-making powers in a company who were identified as a separate group of employees in the context of the debates surrounding the 1976 Co-determination Bill.

Lohntarifvertrag (collective agreement on wages and salaries): Collective agreements on wages and salaries usually have a duration of about one year.

Neue Beweglichkeit (new mobility): A strategy of trade unions in labour dispute where warning strikes are called in a way which is unpredictable for the employers. Often work is stopped for a few hours only and in key firms or individual departments only. These warning strikes are often accompanied by publicity campaigns and demonstrations.

Organisationsgrad (unionisation): Percentage of potential union members who are organised in labour unions. Typically, retired members and unemployed people are counted as full members.

Paritätische betriebliche Mitbestimmung: Scheme for equal representation of capital and labour in the control and management of public limited companies as implemented in the 1951 Co-determination Act.

Paritätische überbetriebliche Mitbestimmung: Schemes for equal representation of capital, labour and state in economic associations and councils at regional and national level debated after 1918 and again after 1945.

Rahmentarifvertrag, Manteltarifvertrag (collective agreement on general conditions of work): Collective agreements with such contents (e.g. regulation of holidays, schemes of wealth formation) have a longer duration (up to five years) than collective agreements on wages and salaries.

Revolutionäre Obleute (revolutionary shop stewards): Groups of radical trade unionists who emerged in 1917 to articulate and

5

organise growing shop-floor protest.

Sachverständigenbeirat zur Begutachtung der gesamtwirtschaftlichen Entwicklung (Council of Economic Experts): Group of academic economists first appointed in 1962/3 to report annually on the present state and future development of the West German economy. Often referred to as the 'five wise men' (*Die fünf Weisen*).

Streikgeld (strike pay): Paid by the labour unions to its members who, as a consequence of a labour dispute, do not receive wages. For a long-term member it amounts to about two-thirds of the (declared) gross wages.

Tarifautonomie (autonomy of collective bargaining): The right of trade unions and employers' associations (or individual employers) to negotiate wages and conditions of work for their members without government interference. This right is protected by article 12 of the Basic Law.

Tarifvertrag (collective agreement): The agreement reached between a trade union and an employers' association (or an individual employer) regarding wages and working conditions. In its obligatory part it is binding for the parties to the collective agreement; in its normative part it determines the contents of the individual work contracts subject to the collective agreement.

Tarifvertragsgebiet (collective-bargaining area): The area to which a collective agreement applies, about the size of a *Land*.

Urabstimmung (strike ballot): A ballot organised by a trade union among its members prior to a strike. Typically, 75 per cent have to vote in favour of work stoppage.

Verhältnismässigkeit (commensurateness): A principle to which both parties to collective bargaining and to labour disputes have to adhere. It excludes 'excessiveness' both in their demands and in their actions and reactions in labour dispute.

Vermögensbildung (wealth formation): Schemes for coordinated employee saving or employee shareholding discussed in the 1960s and 1970s as ways of creating a 'people's capitalism'.

Verrechtlichung der Arbeitsbeziehungen (juridification of labour relations): Detailed legal regulation of all aspects of labour relations including labour dispute with the consequence that it is difficult to break out of this accepted framework.

Wirtschaftsdemokratie (economic democracy): Syndicalist models of grassroots control of economic decision-making first promoted by the unions in the 1920s but revived after 1945 as a way of counterbalancing and/or undermining the traditional dominance of capital.

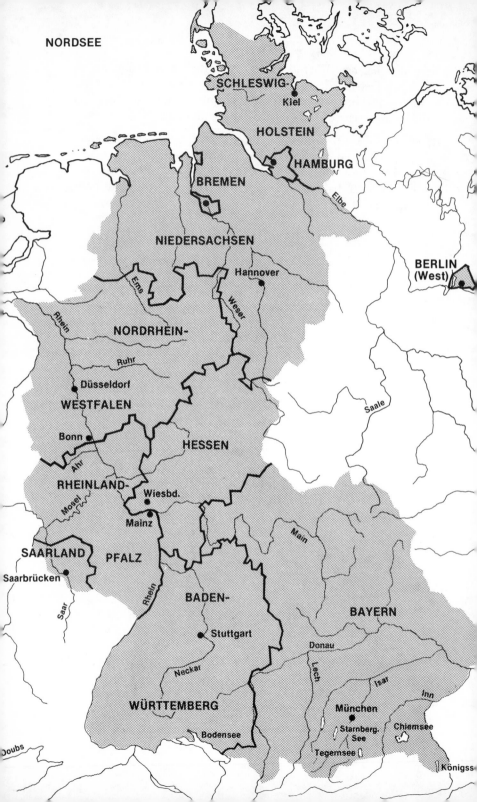

1
Representation of Business Interests

1.1 Introduction

In the Federal Republic of Germany business interests are represented by three different types of organisations:

(1) the chambers of industry and commerce (*Industrie- und Handelskammern*), which are self-governing bodies of the business community of an area and, in addition to an official interest representation, fulfil certain public functions;

(2) the employers' associations (*Arbeitgeberverbände*), whose main field is social policy and — as far as the employers' association of individual branches of industry is concerned — collective bargaining;

(3) the industrial business associations, which represent the economic policy interests of their members and which are pressure groups in the strict sense. This is particularly true for the Federation of German Industries (Bundesverband der Deutschen Industrie — BDI).

All these organisations of business interests are formally neutral in regard to party politics. It is no secret, however, that they and their leading figures are closer to the Christian Democratic Party (CDU) and its Bavarian branch, the Christian Social Union (CSU) — and also to the Free Democratic Party (FDP) — than to the Social Democrats (SPD). In fact, the FDP occasionally behaves like a party specifically catering for the interests of the business community. There are, however, no formal links between the organisations representing business interests and the political parties.

In addition to their external function of representing the economic and social-policy interests of their members, all these organisations have the internal function of supplying information on economic and political matters to their members.

---

opposite **Map of FRG with *Länder* divisions**

(a) *Chambers of Industry and Commerce*

The chambers of industry and commerce are regional self-governing business organisations which by law and as public-law entities represent the overall interests of trade and industry located in their respective districts. Whereas membership in the industrial business and employers' associations is voluntary, all firms are legally obliged to become members of the chamber of their particular region. By law the chambers of industry and commerce must represent the interests of the entire business community of their district with the exception of agriculture and of crafts, which have their own chambers. The chambers of industry and commerce promote the interests of business and, in discharging this function, they must balance and mediate between the interests of individual industries and firms. By submitting proposals, expert opinions and reports to public bodies, they support and advise the government at various levels. They also work towards the maintenance of good and honourable behaviour in economic matters. They are funded by the contributions of member firms.

The chambers of industry and commerce establish and support institutions which serve the interests of the business community at large or of individual industries. They also perform official functions for the government; in particular, they play an active role in vocational training by offering courses and by setting and conducting examinations. They also issue certificates of origin and other papers required for business transactions. By law the chambers of industry and commerce are not allowed to deal with the social-policy or labour-law interests of their member firms.

Together, the regional chambers of industry and commerce have formed an umbrella organisation at the federal level, the Association of German Chambers of Industry and Commerce (Deutscher Industrie- und Handelstag — DIHT). This institution has no status in public law but is a private organisation of the chambers of industry and commerce. According to its statute, it has the purpose of securing and promoting the cooperation of chambers of industry and commerce, of working towards a regular exchange of experience and of representing the common overall view of the business community, in particular *vis-à-vis* official bodies and other institutions in the territory of the Federal Republic of Germany. Because of its comprehensive membership, the official opinion of this institution does not reflect a particular industrial or regional interest, nor is it wedded to a specific ideology. Hence official statements by the DIHT have particular weight in public discussion.

The many international or bilateral chambers of commerce, such as the German/American Chamber of Commerce, are organisations with the specific task of promoting trade relations between the countries involved. They are private organisations and are not part of the self-governing body of the official chambers of industry and commerce, although there are connections with the DIHT.

(b) *Employers' Associations*

The employers' associations represent the social- and wage-policy interests of the entire private business sector; that is, not only those of industry but also of banking, agriculture, insurance, and so on.

There are two types of employers' associations (Tab. 1.1):

(1) industrial organisations comprising employers from the same industry or branch. Usually, all firms active in any given industry within a region will belong to such a regional industrial association. These regional industrial associations make up the *Land* employers' associations (*Landesverbände*) of that industry; the various *Länder* associations together form the federal employers' association (*Bundesverband*) of that industry or branch. The actual collective bargaining takes place for a particular collective-bargaining area, in most cases for a *Land*;

(2) regional organisations of employers, comprising *all* employers in a *Land* regardless of their industry or branch. For administrative reasons there are also sub-organisations at the district level.

Generally, a firm is a member of both types of employers' associations. All the employers' associations — regardless of whether they are organised along industrial or regional lines — belong to the same umbrella organisation, the Confederation of German Employers' Associations (Bundesverband der Deutschen Arbeitgeberverbände e.V. — BDA). In the field of social

11

Table 1.1 Members of the Bundesvereinigung der Deutschen
Arbeitgeberverbände (BDA)

BDA

BRANCH ASSOCIATIONS	REGIONAL ASSOCIATIONS

Industry, including mining
Hauptverband der Deutschen
   Bauindustrie (16)*
Bund. Vereinig. d. Arbeitgeber im
   Bundesverband Bekleid.-Ind. (11)
Wirtschaftsvereinigung Bergbau (15)
Deutscher Braunkohlen-Industrie-Verein
Bundesarbeitgeberverband Chemie (12)
Arbeitgeberverband der
   Cigarettenindustrie
Bundesverband Druck (11)
Wirtschaftsverband Erdöl- und
   Erdgasgewinnung
Bundesverband Glasindustrie und
   Mineralfaserindustrie (4)
Hauptverb. d. Dtsch. Holzindustrie u.
   verw. Industriezweige (28)
Kaliverein
Bundesverband d. Dtsch. Kalkindustrie
   (4)
Arbeitgeberverband d. Dtsch.
   Kautschukindustrie (3)
Arbeitsgem. Keramische Industrie (6)
Gesamtverb. d. metallind.
   Arbeitgeber-Verb. (13)
Arbeitgebervereinigung Nahrung u.
   Genuß (23)
Verband Deutscher Ölmühlen
Vereinig. d. AGV. d. Dtsch.
   Papierindustrie (8)
Hauptverb. d. Papier, Pappe u.
   Kunststoffe verarb. Ind. (12)
Unternehmensverband Ruhrbergbau
Unternehmensverband Saarbergbau
Vereinig. Dtsch. Sägewerksverbände (12)
Arbeitsgemeinschaft Schuhe/Leder (6)
Sozialpol. Arbeitsgemeinschaft Steine u.
   Erden (19)
Gesamtverband des deutschen
   Steinkohlenbergbaus (4)
Arbeitgeberkr.Ges.-Textil i. Ges.-Verb.
   d. Textilindustrie i. d. BRepl. Dtschl.
   (8)
Bundesverband d. Zigarrenindustrie
Verein d. Zuckerindustrie (3)
Banking
Arbeitgeberverb. d. privaten
   Bankgewerbes

Baden-Württemberg
Landesvereinigung Baden-Württbg.
   Arbeitgeberverb. (46)*

Bavaria
Vereinigung d. AGV. in Bayern (83)

Berlin
Zentralvereinigung Berliner
   Arbeitgeberverb. (48)

Bremen
Vereinigung d. AGV. im Lande Bremen
   (14)

Hamburg
Landesvereinigung d. AGV. in Hamburg
   (19)

Hesse
Vereinigung der hessischen
   Unternehmerverbände (49)

Lower Saxony
Unternehmerverbände Niedersachsen
   (52)

Northrhine-Westphalia
Landesvereinig. d. AGV. NRW. (76)

Rhineland Palatinate
Landesvereinig. Rheinl.-Pfälz.
   Unternehmerverb. (13)

Saar
Vereinigung d. AGV. d. Saarlandes (18)

Schleswig-Holstein
Vereinigung d. Schlesw.-Holst.
   Unternehmensverb. (34)

continued on p. 13

12

Table 1.1 *continued*

Commerce
Hauptgem. d. Dtsch. Einzelhandels (12)
Bundesarbeitsgemeinschaft der Mittel- und Großbetriebe des Einzelhandels (12)
Bundesverband d. Dtsch. Groß- u. Außenhandels (12)
Zentralverband d. gen. Großhandels- und Dienstleistungsunternehmen (5)
Crafts
Bund.-Vereinig. d. Fachverb. d. Dtsch. Handw. (51)
Zentralverband des Deutschen Baugewerbes (24)
Agriculture
Gesamtverb. d. Deutschen Land- u. Forstw. AGV. (15)
Transport
AGV d. deutschen Binnenschiffahrt
AGV Deutscher Eisenbahnen
Verband Deutscher Küstenschiffseigner
Verband Deutscher Reeder
Insurance
Arbeitgeberverband der Versicherungsunternehmungen in Deutschland
Others
Deutscher Hotel- und Gaststättenverband (DEHOGA) (14)
Verband privater Städtereinigungsbetriebe
Verband Deutscher Zeitschriftenverleger (6)
Bundesverband Deutscher Zeitungsverleger (9)
Guest members
Vereinig. d. AGV. energie- u. versorgungswirtsch. Unternehmungen (6)

* in brackets = number of member associations

policy the BDA is the counterpart of the German Trade Union Federation (Deutscher Gewerkschaftsbund — DGB), which is the umbrella organisation of the industrial trade unions. Neither takes part in collective bargaining but coordinates and represents the social-policy interests of its members in general. The employers' associations also keep their member firms informed about all important matters of social policy, in particular about recent legislation.

13

(c) *Industrial Business Associations*

Industrial business associations have as their main function the representation of the economic-policy interests of their members. Of all three organisations of business interests they come closest to the concept of a pressure group. This is particularly true of their peak organisation, the powerful Federation of German Industries (Bundesverband der Deutschen Industrie — BDI).

There are thirty-seven industrial business associations organised at national level according to their areas of activity, for example the Association of Automobile Producers and the Association of Chemical Industries (Tab. 1.2). These various industrial business associations represent the specific economic-policy interests of their members; for example, the Association of Chemical Industries may raise its voice in matters of environmental policy on behalf of its members. The Federation of German Industries acts as a lobby for overall industrial interests and makes submissions to political institutions, to the ministerial bureaucracy and to individual politicians. In this way it tries to influence economic policy-making; for example, business typically gives a higher priority to the fighting of inflation than to full employment, and business interests are opposed to what they would call 'excessive' protection of consumers, and so on. There is hardly any aspect of economic policy which does not affect industry in one way or another, and both the individual industrial business associations and the Federation of German Industries use their position to influence political decisions in many formal (e.g. parliamentary committee hearings) or informal ways (e.g. by influencing public opinion through the media). An element in the latter is also the financial support given to influential groups, to political parties and to individual politicians. These activities, which may originate equally from individual firms or from industrial associations, may occasionally border on the illegal, especially in the provision of finances to political parties.

In spite of such occasionally dubious practices, there is no doubt that the representation of interests is legitimate and even vital in a parliamentary-democratic society. To some extent, political decision-making has to rely on the expertise of the firms and

Table 1.2 Member Associations of the Bundesverband der Deutschen Industrie e.V. (BDI)

Verband der Automobilind e.V. (*Frankfurt a. M.*)	Verband der Dtsch. Feinmech. u. Opt. Industrie e.V. (*Cologne*)	Mineralölwirtschaftsverb. e.V. (*Hamburg 1*)
Hauptverband der Deutschen Bauindustrie e.V. (*Frankfurt a. M.*)	Wirtschaftsverband Gießerei-Industrie (*Düsseldorf*)	Wirtschaftsvereinig. NE-Metalle e.V. (*Düsseldorf*
Bundesverband Bekleidungsindustrie e.V. (*Bad Godesberg*)	Bundesverband Glasindustrie e.V. (*Düsseldorf*)	Hauptverb. d. Papier u. Pappe verarbeitend. Ind. e.V. (*Frankfurt a. M.*)
Wirtschaftsvereinig. Bergbau e.V. (*Bad Godesberg*)	Bundesvereinigung der Deutschen graph. Verbände e.V. (*Wiesbaden*)	Verband Deutscher Papierfabriken e.V. (*Bonn*)
Deutscher Brauer-Bund e.V. (*Bad Godesberg*)	Hauptverb. d. Dtsch. Holzindustrie e.V. (*Wiesbaden*)	Vereinig. Dtsch. Sägewerksverbände e.V. (*Wiesbaden*)
Verband der Chem. Ind. e.V. (*Frankfurt a. M.*)	Arbeitsgemeinschaft Industriengruppe (*Nuremburg*)	Verband Deutscher Schiffswerften e.V. (*Hamburg*)
Verband der Cigarettenindustrie (*Hamburg 1*)	Wirtschaftsverband d. dtsch. Kautschukindustrie e.V. (*Frankfurt a. M.*)	Hauptverb. d. Dtsch. Schuhindustrie e.V. (*Düsseldorf*)
Wirtschaftsverband Eisen, Blech u. Metall verarb. Industrie e.V. (*Düsseldorf*)	Arbeitsgemeinschaft Keramische Ind. e.V. (*Frankfurt a. M.*)	Wirtschaftsverband Stahl- u. Eisenbau (*Cologne*)
Wirtschaftsvereinig. Eisen- u. Stahlind. (*Düsseldorf*)	Gesamtverb. Kunststoffverarb. Ind. e.V. (*Frankfurt a. M.*)	Wirtschaftsverband Stahlverformung (*Hagen-Emst*)
Zentralverband der Elektrotechn. Ind. e.V. (*Frankfurt* a. M.)	Verband d. Dtsch. Lederindustrie e.V. (*Frankfurt/M.-Hochst*)	Bundesverband Steine u. Erden e.V. (*Wiesbaden*)
Wirtsch.-Verband Erdölgewinnung e.V. (*Hanover*)	Verband d. Dtsch. Lederw.- u. Kofferindustrie e.V. (*Offenbach a. M.*)	Gesamtverband der Textilindustrie e.V. (*Frankfurt a. M.*)
Bundesvereinig. d. Dtsch. Ernährungsindustrie e.V. (*Bonn*)	Bundesverb. d. Dtsch. Luft- u. Raumfahrtindustrie e.V. (*Bad Godesberg*)	Wirtschaftsvereinig Ziehereien u. Kaltwalzwerke (*Düsseldorf*)
Verb. der Fahrrad- u. Motorradind. e.V. (*Bad Soden i.T.*)	Verein Deutscher Maschinenbau-Anstalten e.V. (*Ffm.-Niederrad 1*)	Verein der Zuckerindustrie (*Hanover*)

their associations, and for implementation it requires their coop-eration. This function is reflected in the standing orders of the federal parliament, the Bundestag, which specifically provide for the hearing of interest groups by its committees. Also, the associations' function of informing members about legislation and other important developments is helpful to the running of the economy. Major problems arise, however, when an interest group becomes so powerful and pushes its case so forcefully that the interests of other groups and of society as a whole are impaired. Occasionally, the activities of the Federa-tion of German Industries and some of its member associations have transgressed this line of public acceptance.

(d) *Common Institutions*

Together with the top organisations of other business branches, these three head organisations — the Association of German Chambers of Industry and Commerce, the Confederation of German Employers' Associations and the Federation of German Industries — have established the Joint Committee of German Trades and Industries (Gemeinschaftsausschuss der Deutschen Gewerblichen Wirtschaft). The Joint Committee is a forum for the discussion and formulation of the common interests of its members; it is not a central representative body of the entire German business sector and consequently does not play a major role in the public discussion of political problems.

The economic- and social-policy organisations, the Confed-eration of German Employers' Associations and the Federation of German Industries, have also set up and support the Institute of German Private Enterprise (Institut der Deutschen Wirtschaft — IDW). Its purpose is to conduct studies on economic- and social-policy developments and to elucidate the common ob-jectives of the private sector, particularly *vis-à-vis* the academic community and the general public. In a way, this research institute is a counterpart of the Economic and Social Science Institute of the Trade Unions.

(e) *Specialisation in the Representation of Business Interests*

In view of the fact that in the Federal Republic of Germany

employee interests are represented by one type of organisation only — the trade union — it is significant that business interests operate through three different organisations with a fairly clear division of functions between the various bodies. There are historical reasons for this which will be explained below (pp. 147ff.).

The chambers of industry and commerce and their head organisations have — due to their special status and also on account of the respectability of their leading spokesmen — an image which gives them high credibility. At times they are not even perceived as interest groups by the general public. On the other hand, the two other organisations are seen as lobbies in the conventional sense. The division of functions has often proven its worth. There have been times when leading figures of industrial business associations and of the Federation of German Industries have engaged in very strong lobbying, articulating interests and opinions which in content and form disqualified them in the eyes of the trade unions as negotiating partners; occasionally, there has even been a touch of personal hostility towards the unions and their leaders. At the same time, however, the representatives of the employers' associations, who are the direct partners of the trade unions in questions of social policy and especially in collective bargaining, have made every effort to maintain at least a working relationship with the trade unions; in fact, representatives of the employers' associations have often expressed their personal respect for individual union leaders. Although this behaviour smacks somewhat of a deliberate strategy, it has contributed to a generally good climate between the employers' associations and the trade unions which has facilitated the forging of compromises in deadlocked negotiations.

In comparison to the labour unions, which represent all the interests of their members, the tripartite division also seems to have some advantages in respect of access to the media; it makes for a higher frequency of appearance and means that the employers' views are presented by a variety of spokesmen. As only the more important issues (where the views of the various spokesmen differ but slightly) are debated by the general public, there is normally no problem of contradictory statements coming from the individual representatives.

1.2 Confederation of German Employers' Associations

The Confederation of German Employers' Associations (BDA) is the umbrella organisation of all employers' associations, be they organised along industrial lines or on a regional basis. The BDA cannot be a party to collective agreements — this function is reserved for the individual industrial employers' associations. The BDA has no power of direction over its autonomous member associations, but it can make recommendations to them, if these recommendations have been unanimously passed by the Executive Board (Geschäftsführender Bundesvorstand). In many respects the position of the BDA is similar to that of the Federation of German Trade Unions (DGB), although it seems to have better control over its members. This, however, results also from the fact that the employers' interests are typically fairly homogeneous in respect of wages and social policy, that the number of persons involved is much smaller, and that the need to maintain solidarity is largely accepted by all employers.

(a) *Functions*

The main functions of the BDA are:

(i) the external *representation* of employers' interests in questions of social policy, in particular to counterbalance the influence of organised labour;

(ii) the *general coordination* of the strategies of collective bargaining pursued by the various employers' associations;

(iii) the *maintenance of solidarity* of the employers, in particular during a labour dispute.

(i) *External Representation*   According to its statutes, the BDA must safeguard the employers' interests in all matters of social policy which go beyond the scope of a particular industry or region and which are of fundamental importance. It is the counterweight to the trade unions in all institutions which provide for a representation of workers' and employers' interests, such as the Federal Labour Institute, the labour courts and the social courts as well as the semi-governmental social-insurance bodies. It also represents the employers' side on bodies where a large variety of groups are represented, such as the Supervisory Boards of the public-law corporations of broadcasting and television. In addition to this, the BDA is mandated to voice the opinions and the interests of the employers *vis-à-vis* the bureaucracy, parliament and the media. It advises legislative bodies in matters of social policy and transmits the opinion of the employers' associations to all concerned public bodies in the shape of expert opinions and position papers.

The BDA also acts as a direct counterpart to the DGB. For example, some elements of the framework for collective bargaining have been agreed upon by the BDA and the DGB and then have been passed on to the individual employers' associations and the industrial trade unions with a strong recommendation to adopt them as a model for their agreements. This is true of the model arbitration agreement of 1954, which — with minor modifications — became the basis of all arbitration procedures in labour disputes.

(ii) *General Coordination*   To some extent, the BDA also coordinates the policies and strategies of the various employers' associations by making recommendations. Although these recommendations are not binding on members, they are usually followed. In this way the BDA acts as a central institution for programming and coordinating the activities of all employers' associations; in other words, it formulates the position of the employers where social policy is concerned — for example, principles of a uniform-wage policy, recommendations regarding the solidarity of employers in labour disputes, suggestions for social improvements on the shop floor, recommendations regarding wealth formation schemes and model schemes for the training and advanced training of employees. A famous example of a recommendation is the 1978 'taboo-catalogue' of the BDA, which defined positions for collective bargaining from which no employers' association was to deviate. One item in this catalogue read as follows: 'After the agreement on the forty-hour week, to be implemented by the end of 1974 for over 80 per cent of the employees, any further curtailment of work capacity through the reduction of the working week below forty hours cannot be justified under any circumstances . . . as it would have a disastrous effect on economic growth and seriously impair

19

the competitiveness of German industry.'[1] This stipulation explains the strong resistance of the employers to union demands of reducing weekly work-time to thirty-five hours and is partly responsible for the length and toughness of the 1984 industrial dispute over this issue.

(iii) *Maintenance of Solidarity*[2]   Firms in the same industry compete with each other. A labour dispute which affects only some firms within an industry can give the non-affected firms an advantage. Also, strike-bound firms may be unable to meet their commitments towards firms in other industries and towards banks. To avoid breaches of solidarity during labour disputes, the BDA has passed a code of conduct which is addressed to all firms. It also encourages agreements of mutual assistance between firms which belong to the same industrial employers' association. The essence of all these arrangements is a temporary suspension of competition and even mutual assistance during a labour dispute.

The general code of conduct contains, *inter alia*, the following provisions:

— firms should not hire striking workers or locked-out workers of another firm;
— firms should tolerate late deliveries if such delays are attributable to a labour dispute;
— firms should defer previously agreed terms of delivery;
— firms should not lure customers away from strike-bound firms;
— no firm should accept an order which was previously placed with a strike-bound firm without the consent of that firm;
— firms should pay previously agreed on-account instalments even if delivery is delayed because of labour dispute.

There are also many mutual assistance agreements between ordinarily competing firms which provide for reciprocally granted

---

1. Confederation of German Employers' Associations, 'Guidelines for the Coordination of Policy on Collective Bargaining Issues', compiled on 12 October 1961, revised on 15 February 1968, 6 May 1975 and 16 March 1978, published in English in I.G. Metall, *The Strike in the Iron and Steel Industry (1978/1979)*, Frankfurt, n.d., p. 53.

2. This section is based on K. Bertelsmann, *Aussperrung, Eine Untersuchung ihrer Zulässigkeit unter besonderer Berücksichtigung ihrer geschichtlichen Entwicklung und Handhabung in der Praxis*, Berlin, 1979, pp. 287–91.

help to bridge delivery problems resulting from a labour dispute, for example direct delivery of products to the strike-bound firm or to a third party, temporary taking over of orders of these strike-bound firms by mutual consent and provisions of production and transport facilities. In these agreements, the scope of and remuneration for such assistance — for example, remuneration for such services at cost price — are regulated in detail. All this helps to minimise the disadvantages of strike-bound firms. To some extent, even foreign firms cooperate in these matters.

The individual firm can be further compensated for the disadvantages it suffers from a labour dispute by payments made out of a common fund, to which all firms make regular contributions. Such common funds have been established by most industrial employers' associations. Also, compensatory payments are effected between the various industries. The payments made to strike-bound firms can be compared to the strike money paid to their members by the trade unions. Although some of these arrangements are confined to individual employers' associations, the BDA has often initiated and helped in the realisation of such schemes.

(b) *Structure*

The BDA is made up of forty-six industrial employers' associations together with the regional employers' associations. Only private employers can be members. Although no exact figures are available, it is assumed that about 80 per cent of all firms comprising about 90 per cent of the total workforce, are members of employers' associations, which points to a certain dominance of large firms.

Although no studies on the actual decision-making procedures within the BDA are available, it is generally assumed that the honorary officials, and among them mainly the people coming from large firms, define the interest and determine the strategy of the federation. Unless they come from very big companies and have a lot of clout, there is little chance for ordinary members to influence overall policy.

If the employers occasionally compare the large administrative apparatus of the labour unions with the smaller bureaucracy of the employers' associations, this is somewhat unfair because work for the employers' associations is often done by member firms. Moreover, the size of the bureaucracy of the various industrial interest groups is considerable. According to estimates from the 1970s, about 12,000 people were permanently employed by employers' associations.[3]

(c) *Programme and Strategy*

As they understand it, the employers' associations in general, and the BDA in particular, are the defenders of free enterprise and the market economy both against the expansion of the state and against the allegedly socialist ideas of the trade unions. They also reject in principle all attempts at restricting the freedom of entrepreneurial decision-making. In this respect they see workers' participation as a threat. Every expansion of the welfare state is resented. The BDA propagates the predominantly conservative views of its members on all issues of social policy, mostly in open opposition to the views expressed by the DGB.

In the important field of wage demands the BDA usually takes a 'rational' position which is backed by scientific arguments and which can count on support of the majority of the media. The following excerpt from an official document reflects this reasoning:

The BDA has always been of the opinion that, in the interest of national economic aims — price stability, a high level of employment and external trade balance, combined with constant and reasonable economic growth — total labour costs should in principle not be increased at a faster rate than national economic productivity, expressed in terms of gross national product per worker/hour. It has, however, never considered this principle of non-inflationary wage policy as a rigid rule; it should rather be considered as a flexible rule of thumb, open to modification, as changes in the national economic situation dictate. The most important criteria for such modifications are: significant upheavals in the labour market situation, consumer demand, utilization of capacity and price trends.

While taking these market indicators into consideration, care must be taken to avoid a situation where increased wages have an adverse effect on price trends, employment stability and hence on economic

3. V.R. Berghahn, *The Americanisation of West German Industry, 1945–1973*, Leamington Spa–New York, 1986, p. 183.

growth. The BDA therefore rejects any programmed wage formula containing provisions for cost-of-living increases over and above expected productivity growth.

Wages cannot be treated as isolated elements in these considerations. The cost of improving working conditions must also be borne by the national economy, and therefore such improvements must be kept within the limits imposed by general economic trends.[4]

Beyond such basic disagreements with the trade unions, the officials of the BDA try to maintain a good working relationship with the trade unions, whose right to exist and whose important role for the functioning of a market economy have not been questioned during the past twenty-five years or so. Together with the trade unions, they have often confirmed the need to keep the autonomy of collective bargaining intact. The BDA has suggested that before a labour conflict everything possible to reach a peaceful settlement should be done; therefore, it is in favour of an extension of voluntary arbitration. Although it aims at peaceful settlements, it encourages the fighting of 'excessive demands' of the trade unions, and it tries to prevent too much willingness to compromise on the part of some of its member associations.

1.3 Federation of the Metal Trades Employers' Associations in Germany

Collective agreements are concluded for individual industries and, with few exceptions, also for certain regions rather than for the Federal Republic as a whole. To understand the actual procedure of collective bargaining it is necessary to look into the structure and the decision-making process of industrial employers' associations.

Although there are significant differences in organisational structure and decision-making, the influence of these differences on overall labour relations in the Federal Republic does not justify a detailed analysis of all the employers' associations. The Federation of the Metal Trades Employers' Associations (Gesamtverband des metallindustriellen Arbeitgeberverbände

4. I.G. Metall, p. 48.

e.V. — Gesamtmetall) is chosen as an example because the relationship between the employers and the trade unions in the metal industry is in many respects the most important field of labour relations. It is the weightiest single industry in the Federal Republic because this industry comprises engineering as well as the automobile and electronics industries; altogether about 54 per cent of all industrial employment is in the metal industry. Also the size of the employers' association makes it the most influential member of the BDA. Moreover, the situation in this industry is not only an example but also acts as a model: collective agreements reached in this industry for a particular collective-bargaining area have often set the pace for other regions and for the other industries. This, incidentally, has often limited the confrontation to one industry and one region only, and consequently reduced the frequency and extent of actual labour disputes. Finally, it is often said that the Metal-Workers Union (Industriegewerkschaft Metall — I.G. Metall) is the most radical of all German trade unions, hence the position of the opposing side must be particularly relevant as a gauge of employers' attitudes.

(a) *Functions*

Although formally the autonomy of collective bargaining rests with the thirteen regional employers' associations of the metal trades, the influence of Gesamtmetall has been growing continuously over the years. Out of the original functions of representing the interests of its members on issues of social law and social policy, of promoting the exchange of experience and information in respect of social and collective-bargaining policy issues and of ensuring a common policy on all questions of general interest, the latter has become the most important. By now the main purpose of Gesamtmetall is to formulate a common strategy for collective bargaining and to secure the unity and the strength of the metal industry employers' front in collective bargaining and in labour disputes. Very often the individual regional employers' associations commission the experienced specialists of Gesamtmetall to conduct wage negotiations on their behalf. Even when the regional association is formally the negotiating party, Gesamtmetall is still represented on the negotiating commission.

Apart from its role in the actual process of collective bargaining, Gesamtmetall has also concluded agreements with I.G. Metall on the framework of this bargaining. The two most important agreements are:

(1) an extension of the peace-keeping obligation (see below, pp. 82f.) to the first four weeks after the previous collective agreement has expired. This extra period should cover the period of negotiating the new agreement;

(2) a procedure for arbitration in case of a breakdown of the negotiations.

Another important function of Gesamtmetall is to secure the solidarity of its members. First of all the normally competing firms have to adhere to the code of conduct described above (see p. 20). If and when it comes to an actual labour dispute, Gesamtmetall often responds to selective strikes called by the trade union with a lock-out of workers of other firms. This is the real test of solidarity; most of the member firms which are not affected by the strike could continue production and could accept orders which their competitors cannot carry out. Moreover, the employers often feel obliged towards their non-unionised workers who do not want to strike and whom they are expected to lock-out as well. The fact that these workers do not get strike pay may induce them to join the trade union — a side effect of a lock-out which is obviously undesirable for the employers. It is the recognition of the long-term advantages of solidarity which induces these firms to forgo the possible short-term advantages resulting from breaking the ranks. So far very few cases where individual firms have violated this solidarity are known, and those were not in the metal industry. These firms were subsequently expelled from their employers' association.

Solidarity among firms is also fostered by providing financial support for the companies affected by strikes and lock-outs. Gesamtmetall has established funds for this purpose. At present between 80 and 90 per cent of the wage and salary bill lost through a strike will be reimbursed through this fund; it is assumed that this covers the fixed costs of the firms affected. During the labour dispute of spring 1984, companies received about DM650 million from this fund (as compared to DM450 million which I.G. Metall paid to its members as strike pay).[5] But such a fund works only on the basis of mutual insurance — that is, this money first has to be raised by the member firms.

As regards concessions at plant or company level, Gesamtmetall sees certain dangers here for the solidarity of its members, if individual firms try to win special advantages by making such concessions to a trade union or the works council, the representation of workers at plant level (see pp. 106ff.). These misgivings are shared by the trade unions, which also prefer regulation via collective agreements to be decisive for wages and working conditions.

(b) *Structure*

Organisationally, Gesamtmetall is the umbrella organisation of thirteen autonomous regional associations of metal industry employers. The regions of these associations are by and large identical with the territories of the *Länder*. There is no direct membership of individual firms. Although membership is not compulsory, most firms and all the large firms of the metal industry are members of their regional employers' association. The only important exception is the Volkswagen Company, where traditionally a plant has agreement applied. The regional associations belong almost without exception to Gesamtmetall.

Because of its small membership of thirteen regional associations, Gesamtmetall has only two organs: the General Assembly (Mitgliederversammlung) and a Management Board (Vorstand). In the annually convened General Assembly, the representatives of the regional employers' associations decide mainly on the formal aspects of business such as changes of the constitution, passing of the budget and the acceptance of the accounts of the Management Board.

The members of the Management Board are the chairmen of the thirteen regional employers associations; Northrhine Westphalia, which is by far the largest association, is represented by two members. More members may be co-opted. In addition, the thirteen regional associations also delegate one deputy each; these deputies may participate in a consulting capacity. The members of

5. V. von Wangenheim, *Industrial Relations in West Germany* (published by the Engineering Employers' Federation), London, November 1984.

the Management Board elect the president from their midst. They also elect up to five vice-presidents and a treasurer to form the Presidium. If possible, the president should not be the chairman of a member association. The Presidium dominates the decision-making process, looking after all matters except those which by law or by constitution are reserved for the General Assembly.

Apart from casting their vote in elections, there is little opportunity for the ordinary members to influence the decision-making of the Presidium. In the elections the General Assembly normally confirms candidates whose nomination for certain posts has been negotiated before and usually endorses the actual policy of the Presidium. The discharge of these functions is almost a ritual. For the rest, the General Assembly provides the chance for a social gathering.[6]

Both formally and in reality, the Presidium is the decisive body because in most cases initiatives originate here. The chairman also has the right to nominate the prospective secretary-general (*Verbandsgeschäftsführer*), who is the head of the Secretariat. The influence of this apparatus, however, is restricted mainly to auxiliary work, such as the supply of data and legal advice, although this can carry important power in itself.

In addition to these two organs, the constitution provides for the appointment of committees. At present, there are nine committees dealing with the following special areas:

(1) collective-bargaining policy;
(2) coordination and negotiation;
(3) pay schemes;
(4) common anti-strike fund administration;
(5) public relations policy;
(6) vocational training;
(7) employment conditions at sites;
(8) international social policy;
(9) economic policy.

These committees play an important role both in practical work as well as in the development of principles and expert decisions on all subjects of common interest. The ordinary committees — other than the Collective-Bargaining Policy Committee — consist of one delegate from a company and one member of the

---

6. See W. Simon, *Macht und Herrschaft der Unternehmerverbände*, Cologne, 1976, p. 86.

professional staff of Gesamtmetall, as well as of a small number of experts.

By far the most important committee is the Collective-Bargaining Policy Committee (Tarifpolitischer Ausschuß). Its main function is the formulation of a strategy for collective-agreement negotiations. The members of this committee are the chairmen of the negotiating commissions of the thirteen regional employers' associations, plus the president of Gesamtmetall, even if he is not the chairman of the negotiating commission of a regional association. This latter provision was introduced in 1971 to improve coordination and to foster the unity of all official bodies of Gesamtmetall. The deputies of the chairmen of the negotiating commissions of the member associations and the permanent secretaries (*Geschäftsführer*) of the regional employers associations participate in a consulting capacity.

To allow Gesamtmetall a hand in the coordination of collective bargaining, the individual regional associations have to forward all relevant information to Gesamtmetall's Collective-Bargaining Policy Committee. This applies in particular to the termination of wage agreements and demands for a new agreement as well as information regarding the beginning and progress of negotiations on collective agreements. Also, the results of negotiations and new agreements on wages and salaries have to be reported.

The final decision on the strategy to be followed in collective-agreement negotiations is taken jointly by the Management Board and the Collective-Bargaining Policy Committee. The theoretical maximum size of this decision-making body of more than sixty participants is reduced in reality by the double membership of several persons. This rather unwieldy body is required to secure the full cooperation of the member associations and their member firms.

There are two more permanent committees which are involved in collective bargaining. The Public Relations Policy Committee (Ausschuß für Öffentlichkeitsarbeit) coordinates the public relations of the various regional employers' associations, in particular in the preparation of publicity campaigns launched on the eve of collective-agreement negotiations. The Pay Schemes Committee (Ausschuß für Fragen der betrieblichen Leistungsentlohnung) deals with technical details of collective agreements, such as the classification of wage groups and the respective wage differentials.

Under the constitution the autonomy of the regional associations is not to be interfered with by measures taken by Gesamtmetall or its organs, unless decisions to this effect are taken unanimously: since all the regional associations are represented in the organs of Gesamtmetall, no regional association can be compelled to any action. However, to improve the coordination of collective bargaining, the Management Board can pass, by a qualified majority, guidelines which are binding upon its members. Prior to the 1971 change of constitution, this would have required unanimity. At any rate, reaching a consensus in Gesamtmetall is much easier than it is in I.G. Metall, because:

(1) the office holders of the regional associations also hold official positions in Gesamtmetall;

(2) the common interest is usually well defined, and there is rarely a disagreement between the members and the leadership;

(3) all members acknowledge the need to build up a united front against the trade union.

The bureaucracy of Gesamtmetall is fairly small, which is not surprising in view of the low number of members. A good deal of the work is also done within the firms whose representatives are the honorary officials of Gesamtmetall and of the regional associations. Altogether there is no doubt that the important decisions are in fact taken by honorary officials whose main occupation is the management of business firms, and not by full-time functionaries, though often with their expert advice. Furthermore, all evidence points to a decisive influence of the representatives of large firms, even if the interests of smaller firms are specifically protected by the statutes of the regional associations. To state a decisive influence of the representatives of the large firms does not necessarily imply that the interests of big business prevail; it means, rather, that these representatives formulate a strategy which satisfies all the member associations and is also in line with the interests of the vast majority of the firms. Anything else would endanger the unity of the employers' associations, which is an important factor in determining their strength at the collective-bargaining table.

(c) *Regional Associations*

The members of the regional metal industry employers' associations are firms located in that area. The regional associations have a formal structure which provides for participation of all members and ensures that the minority interests of certain branches and of small and medium-sized firms are protected. But in reality the above-mentioned principles apply: usually a relatively small group of honorary functionaries who often come from large firms dominate the work of the associations.

Most collective agreements are concluded for a particular collective-bargaining area. Even the fact that Gesamtmetall has a strong influence over the preceding negotiations does not mean that all collective agreements are uniform; regionally varying situations are frequently reflected in the agreements. For the employers the decisive advantage of centralisation is that on certain essential points the employers' position cannot be compromised. Also, without such centralisation the individual employers' associations might make differing concessions to the trade unions. Centralisation and the implied loss of autonomy seem to be the price which the regional employers' associations have to pay for the strong bargaining position of Gesamtmetall.

The growing centralisation was also a reaction to the equally centralised strategy of I.G. Metall, which usually concentrates its attack in labour disputes on certain key areas where its position is strong due to a high degree of unionisation and where the industry concerned is prospering. Here I.G. Metall tries to achieve a breakthrough which could serve as a model for the other areas. Therefore centralisation may also be interpreted as a protection of firms in less prosperous areas against a breach of solidarity, which is what an early surrender of the employers' side in a prosperous area would amount to.

(d) *Goals and Strategies*

The main objective of the employers is to avoid a change in income distribution to their disadvantage. Consequently, the employers' associations are opposed to anything that would increase their costs, be it wage increases or expensive improvements in working conditions. Since the employers usually defend the existing conditions, they are much less in need of a programme and of well-defined objectives than the trade unions, who have to convince their members, the non-unionised workers and the general public that their demands — which aim for changes — are fair and justified.

Thus the usual line of the employers is to concede as little as possible, but enough to avoid a major labour dispute. Since one of their tactical moves is to get the support of public opinion, they try to define a position which, they claim, is the maximum concession to the unions that can be made without exposing the whole economy to serious risks. This position is often supported by economic research institutes and other reputable bodies, such as the official Council of Economic Experts (Sachverstän-digenrat). In the past there has always been a tendency to base possible wage increases on 'objective' guidelines. For example, the percentage growth of productivity plus the rate of inflation would amount to an average figure for the wage increase which would maintain the given distribution of income between the employers and the workers. During the period of full employment this reasoning was also widely accepted by the trade unions because they realised how difficult it was to achieve a long-term redistribution of income by means of wage increases; after all, if higher wages only lead to more inflation, then in the long run nobody stands to gain.

With persistent unemployment, however, the situation has become more complicated. Both sides are in basic agreement that the fighting of unemployment is the top priority, and the trade unions have often expressed their willingness to contribute to an improvement of the economy by means of moderate demands, provided that this actually promised a reduction of unemployment. The difficulty is that nobody knows the right means to accomplish such a reduction. Not surprisingly, the employers favour moderate wage increases to make for improved international competitiveness and to allow for higher profits, which eventually are supposed to lead to more investment and employment. The trade unions, on the other hand, favour a combination of an increase in purchasing power, which requires wage increases, and of a reduction of a weekly working time below the level of forty hours; the metal industry reached a settlement of a 38.5-hour working week in 1985. The trade unions

31

hold the opinion that unemployment can be fought successfully only by a redistribution of work.

There seems to be a tendency on the part of the employers to give more room to the working-out of the details of regulations at the level of the firm. This, they claim, would make it possible for the details of individual situations to be taken into account. For the trade union, however, this practice amounts to a shift of power and influence from the trade unions as an institution to the works councils.

The trade-union strategy of calling selective strikes has been answered by the employers with lock-outs. The employers claim that in this way a fast escalation of the conflict is accomplished which increases the pressure to find a compromise and thus shortens the actual labour dispute. (The lock-out is discussed on pp. 96ff.)

2
Representation of Workers' Interests

2.1 Introduction

In the Federal Republic of Germany the representation of workers' interests rests on three pillars: the trade unions, the system of workers' participation and the desire of the political parties to win the support of this electorally important group.

(a) *Trade Unions*

There are several trade unions or similar organisations which represent the interest of employees. Most important are the seventeen industrial unions which belong to the German Trade Union Federation (Deutscher Gewerkschaftsbund — DGB). The trade unions perform two main functions:

(1) the individual industrial union, or formally its regional sub-division at district level, is the counterpart of the employers' association in collective bargaining over wages and conditions. In this capacity the trade unions enjoy a particular legal recognition and protection (see Ch. 3);

(2) the individual industrial unions, but even more importantly the DGB, also act as pressure groups which try to influence economic and social policy. In this capacity they are legally on equal footing with other interest groups.

The workers' interests are also represented officially in a number of public bodies. In most such cases the trade unions either have a right to nominate representatives or, if there are formal elections, trade-union representatives tend to be elected. Thus trade-union representatives sit on the controlling body of the Federal Labour Institute and its regional sub-divisions. Workers are also members of the Supervisory Boards of the semi-governmental social-insurance institutions. In labour courts and in the courts dealing with social affairs, workers act as lay judges; again, qualified people are put forward by the trade unions. Trade-union representatives are also delegated into the supervisory bodies (Rundfunkrat and Fernsehrat) of those Broadcasting and Television Corporations, which are self-administered corporations under public law; on these supervisory bodies, all important social groups are represented to prevent blatant bias in the media.

(b) *Workers' Participation*

Within firms, the interests of workers are formally looked after by bodies of workers' participation, notably the works council and the workers' representatives on Supervisory Boards (see Ch. 4). In principle this representation of workers is largely independent of the trade unions because it is geared more towards the articulation of the interests of workers employed in the firms than towards the interests represented by the trade unions, be they the interests of the union members or of the institution. *De facto*, however, the trade unions play an important role because most elected workers' representatives are union members. In addition, the trade unions' role is also codified at this level in the sense that the law assigns to them the task of safeguarding the workers' interests against an employer who does not comply with the legal provisions regulating workers' participation.

(c) *Workers' Interest and Political Parties*

Today, both the Social Democratic Party (SPD) and the Christian Democrats (CDU/CSU) define themselves as 'people's parties' encompassing a wide range of interests and social groups. They try, therefore, to cater specifically for the interests of the electorally important group of dependent workers.

In this respect the Social Democratic Party has a long tradition because, prior to its Bad Godesberg Programme of 1959, it specifically defined itself as a 'workers' party'. There is a long-established affinity between the trade unions — today mainly the DGB unions — and the Social Democratic Party which dates back to the origins of both these organisations in the nineteenth century (see pp. 143f.). Membership in a DGB union, however, does not necessarily imply allegiance to the Social Democratic Party, let alone membership. On the contrary, in order to demonstrate its party neutrality, the DGB always has two members of the Christian Democratic Party on its nine-person Executive Board.

The Christian Democratic Party is basically more orientated towards the middle classes. But within the party its left wing, which is moderately social reformist, plays an important role, and the workers' interests are specifically articulated by an important and well-organised group within the party, the Social Committees (Sozialausschüsse).

More than half the members of parliament belong to a trade union. Such simple membership does not mean that the person will always defend the trade union's views. Only trade-union officials who are members of parliament can be assumed to do so.

2.2 Associations of Workers in the Federal Republic

(a) *German Trade Union Federation and Its Member Unions*

By far the most important organisations representing the workers' interest are seventeen industrial trade unions (Fig. 2.1) for membership figures, see pp. 236f.) and their umbrella organisation, the German Trade Union Federation (DGB). Real power rests with the individual unions and, most importantly, with the largest individual union, the Metal-Workers Union (I.G. Metall). Its 2.5 million members (1985) account for one-third of DGB membership and make I.G. Metall the largest single trade union in the Western world.

The industrial union concept along which the trade unions are organised means that ideally all employees of a plant belong to the same trade union. In principle the idea of 'one plant, one union' should have the effect that all workers, regardless of profession or rank in the hierarchy, whether they are manual wage labourers or white-collar salaried employees, are members of the same union. The DGB unions are also 'unitary unions', which means that they are neutral with regard to party politics and religious denomination. In spite of fairly close connections between these trade unions and the Social Democratic Party, there are no formal links between them and the party, either

Figure 2.1 Members of the Deutscher Gewerkschaftsbund

IG Metall		Textiles and Clothing
Public Services and Transport		Food and Restaurants
Chemicals, Paper, Ceramics		Education and Science
		Policemen's Union
Construction		Woods and Plastics
Postal Workers' Union	**DGB**	Printing and Paper
Union of Railwaymen		Leatherwares Union
Mining and Energy		Union of Artists
Banking, Commerce and Insurance		Market gardening, Agriculture and Forestry

financially or through automatic membership affiliation.

The DGB unions comprise altogether 7.7 million members (1985), 83 per cent of all organised labour and roughly 33 per cent of the total number of employees in the Federal Republic of Germany.[1] One can observe some fluctuation of membership in line with the ups and downs in the economy. Recently, however, structural changes, in particular the declining importance of the manufacturing sector *vis-à-vis* the service sector and the growing proportion of white-collar employees in the workforce, have been affecting the membership of industrial unions.

In view of the overwhelming importance of the DGB unions the discussion that follows, after a brief mention of the other associations of workers, concentrates on DGB unions.

(b) *German Union of Salaried Employees*

The German Union of Salaried Employees (Deutsche Angestelltengewerkschaft — DAG) to some extent competes with the DGB unions. A professional union, its target group is the white-collar workers who, following the industrial union principle, have the alternative of joining their respective industrial union, and a good number of white-collar workers have done

---

1. *Statistisches Jahrbuch für die Bundesrepublik*, Wiesbaden, 1986, p. 583, p. 102.

so. The German Union of Salaried Employees is a true labour union in so far as it participates in collective bargaining for wages and conditions and is also prepared to strike.

The German Union of Salaried Employees comprises 501,000 members (1985), or 5 per cent of organised labour and 5 per cent also of all salaried employees.[2] It is most prominent in the public services, where it directly competes with the Public Services and Transport Workers' Union (Gewerkschaft Öffentliche Dienste, Transport und Verkehr — ÖTV). Several attempts to incorporate the German Union of Salaried Employees into the DGB have failed, although there is hardly any disagreement over general objectives. Also, technical and organisational developments in the firms as well as efforts of industrial unions to improve the position of manual workers have by now to some extent blurred previously existing differences between blue- and white-collar workers.

(c) *German Civil Service Federation*

In the Federal Republic of Germany the concept of civil servant (*Beamter*) is broader than elsewhere. Civil servants may come from various professions because the concept also encompasses persons who do not exercise narrowly defined sovereign functions of the state. Consequently, the membership ranges from train drivers to judges, and from school and university teachers to hospital doctors. Civil servants may be employed at the federal level, with *Länder* administrations or with local authorities.

The German Civil Service Federation is not a true trade union because — on account of their special status as civil servants — its members are not allowed to strike. But as it tries to protect the interests of its particular clientele, it has some similarity with a trade union, and in international comparisons (e.g. of the degree of unionisation) this federation has to be taken into account. Many civil servants, however, are organised in DGB trade unions. In particular, many teachers are members of the Education and Science Union (Gewerkschaft Erziehung und Wissenschaft — GEW), and many members of the police force

2. Ibid.

are organised in the policemen's union. Total membership of the German Civil Service Federation was 796,000 in 1985, which represents 8 per cent of all organised labour and 36 per cent of all civil servants.[3]

Civil servants are greatly overrepresented in the Bundestag because parliamentary parties have a disproportionately high number of civil servants among their deputies. This is no doubt one of the reasons why it is apparently difficult to bring about changes that are disadvantageous to the group interests of civil servants.

(d) *Federation of Christian Trade Unions*

In the mid-1950s some members of trade unions who were closely related to the Christian Democratic Party were dissatisfied with the rather close relationship between the DGB and the Social Democratic Party. They first organised within the DGB a Christian Democratic branch opposed to the majority which was leaning towards the Social Democratic Party. In 1955 the two groups split, and in 1956 the first individual Christian Unions were founded; they were organised along vocational lines. The Christian Unions are true trade unions; they engage in collective bargaining and — at least theoretically — they are also prepared to strike. Although they had some local success, they never gained a major influence, because the membership remained low. Total membership was 307,000 in 1985, which is 3 per cent of all organised labour and 1.3 per cent of the total number of employees.[4]

(e) *Degree of Unionisation and the Representativeness of Union Membership*

The overall degree of unionisation is about 40 per cent in the Federal Republic. This is fairly low for a highly industrialised country (Table 2.1). West Germany's low degree of unionisation impairs the claim by trade unions that they speak for all workers. Although the DGB has by far the best justification for its claim to represent the workers' interests, the argument of legit-

3. Ibid.
4. *Zahlenbild Nr. 240 110* (6/86), (Erich Schmidt Verlag).

Table 2.1 Degree of unionisation in some countries of the European Community and some Western industrial nations (%)

	1970	1985
Belgium	66	73
Denmark	65	80
Federal Republic of Germany	37	39
Greece	25	35
France	23	22
Ireland	50	47
Italy	50	40
Luxemburg	55	50
Netherlands	37/36	30
United Kingdom	46	50
Sweden		
manual workers	95 (1979/80)	
white-collar employees	75 (1979/80)	
Austria	60 (1978)	
Japan	32 (1978)	
USA	22 (1978)	

Note: Only approximate percentages of questionable comparability value are available.

imacy is sometimes used against the trade unions by their opponents. But the issue is somewhat more complex than appears from simple figures. A good many workers support the cause of the trade unions, especially of the DGB unions, although they prefer not to join the union and so assume a 'free-rider position'. Apart from opinion polls, this support can be deduced from the fact that in labour disputes the vast majority of the non-unionised workers act in solidarity with organised labour and that in elections, for example for the works councils, most workers vote for the members of these unions. The popularity of the free-rider position is at least in part attributable to the fact that there is little individual incentive for a worker to join a union because the unions can offer only very limited specific advantages to a member.

This is the consequence of the legal principle of the 'negative freedom of association' (see pp. 71f.), which makes the securing of specific advantages for organised labour difficult at least for as long as the employer volunteers to grant the non-unionised workers the same wages and conditions as the unionised ones.

As a result of this principle, 'union shop' and 'closed shop' practices are illegal in the Federal Republic, making it difficult for the unions to make membership attractive. The main individual advantage of being a union member becomes apparent in industrial action when the union grants strike pay (roughly two-thirds of the gross wages for a long-term member) to its members; this is financed mainly from previously accumulated membership dues, since a member has to pay about 1 per cent of his gross wages. In this context a particular problem results from the fact that labour disputes are much more frequent in some industries and some areas. For example, the metal industry in Nord-Württemberg/Nord-Baden has often been the arena for labour disputes. The pioneering function of I.G. Metall in this area is attributable to the fact that very prosperous firms which are also highly export-orientated (e.g. Daimler Benz) are located there; also, the degree of unionisation is high. As a consequence of the relatively frequent strikes in this region, union members have to make use of strike pay more often than union members in other areas. Therefore in such areas it is attractive to be a union member and to pay the membership dues for an honestly declared income, because the strike pay is based on this figure.

The main appeal used by the unions in recruiting new members is to worker solidarity and the granting of extra benefits such as legal aid for members in labour and social courts. There is also the organisation of leisure activities such as subsidised holiday tours.

Regarding membership of unions, one has to remember that official figures include retired and unemployed workers. Also union membership is not representative of all workers; it is highest in large firms, with their dominance of skilled workers. By implication, workers from smaller firms, unskilled workers, females, part-time workers, foreign workers and the very young are underrepresented in the unions. In other words, the labour unions tend to have a bias towards workers in large firms and also towards the 'core segment' of the workers of an industry.

A particular difficulty for the unions is persistent high unemployment, which has been plaguing the German economy since the mid-1970s. In itself this weakens the position of the unions, particularly in collective bargaining. It requires a fair amount of altruism and solidarity on the part of the employed workers to take care also of the interests of the unemployed — whether union members or not — who, as members, pay only minimum dues.

2.3 Industrial Union Principle and Its Consequences

The fact that the unions are organised as industrial unions has three important consequences:

(1) the absence of rivalries between competing unions has contributed to long periods of industrial peace;

(2) because collective agreements on wages and working conditions normally apply to a number of firms, a 'wage drift' results;

(3) occasionally, there is an identity of interests of trade unions and employers.

(a) *No Competition between Industrial Unions*

The fact that in each firm only one union is represented avoids rivalries between competing unions. It also has the consequence that wages and working conditions are laid down in one set of collective agreements arrived at by negotiations between one single trade union and one single employers' association. Consequently, the employers' association — or the individual employer — is faced with one fairly strong union. There is no room for a strategy of playing off one union against another.

On the other hand, the trade union is burdened with the sometimes difficult task of integrating all the interests of the various groups of workers. There may be divergencies in the interests of highly skilled workers from those of unskilled workers; workers with different professional backgrounds may have different interests; there may be a conflict of interest between the core labour force and marginal workers; finally, workers may adhere to totally divergent ideologies. The industrial union principle also puts a high responsibility on the trade union because its actions will be decisive for the overall wage level in the industry and will therefore affect the competitive position of firms or of the whole industry.

The legal provisions applying to collective agreements specify a 'peace-keeping obligation' (*Friedenspflicht*); that is, no party to the collective agreement can take industrial action to change the agreement unless the previous collective agreement has expired or has been terminated (see pp. 82f.). Combined with the representation of all workers of the plant by one union only, this reduces the times during which labour disputes are possible. As long as a valid collective agreement exists, striking is illegal, and the unions have to use their influence on their members to induce them to refrain from striking ('duty to strive for compliance' — *Einwirkungspflicht* — see pp. 83f.).

(b) *Industry-wide Collective Agreements*

In the Federal Republic of Germany collective agreements normally apply to all firms of an industry in a collective-bargaining area; collective agreements for individual firms are the exception. The wide coverage of collective agreements makes it impossible for the union to exhaust the potential for wage increases. In the group of firms to which a collective agreement applies there are invariably both prosperous and rather weak firms. In collective bargaining the unions must be careful not to overburden the weak firms, because this might endanger jobs. Consequently, the union has to settle for an 'average' wage increase, which then allows the more prosperous firms to pay higher wages and to grant better working conditions than specified in the collective agreement. The resulting 'wage drift' means that often the terms of a new collective agreement only confirm and legalise what has already been granted by individual employers. This has the consequence that a new collective agreement does not necessarily result in a substantial improvement for the workers who already enjoy above-average collective-agreement conditions. If the individual employer nevertheless increases wages — as he normally does — he does this voluntarily, although the works council may exert some pressure in this direction. It also means that workers in the same industry who belong to the same union and work in the same town (but in different companies) may have fairly sizeable wage differentials.

Both these effects tax the solidarity of the union members —

in the first case the solidarity of the workers with the union from which they seemingly have little benefit, and in the second case the solidarity with fellow union members who are worse off. In the extreme, this solidarity could compel a worker to strike for better wages and working conditions for his fellow workers — wages and conditions which he himself already enjoys and hence without being able to better his own position by this industrial action.

(c) *Identity of Interest of Workers and Employers?*

An industrial union must be interested in the prosperity of 'its' industry because this is the basis for higher wages and better working conditions. Such an interest is more strongly pronounced if there is one union rather than a whole host of them represented in the firm. It also happens that a union and an employers' association act together and jointly apply pressure on legislators and the administration to make special concessions and grant subsidies to that industry. Although this is rarely done openly, and then usually in a crisis when numerous jobs are at stake, there are instances of this. Such cooperation is only possible in a situation where both parties to a collective agreement act at least temporarily as partners: a behaviour which is incompatible with a conflict model of industrial relations.

2.4 Unitary Union Principle and Its Consequences

The fact that the unions are 'neutral' with respect to ideology and religious denomination has integrating effects at two levels.

(a) *Integration of Diverging Views of Workers*

On the one hand, an individual industrial union has to integrate the many divergent views of its members into a single union position. In this process radical stances must be watered down to arrive at acceptable compromises. This happens in all industrial unions. In performing this aggregating function the unions act as agents which reduce the tremendous variety and complexity of individual positions to politically manageable 'bundles' — rather as political parties do.

Until now, this procedure has been widely accepted by the members. The pressure on individual members or groups of members stems from the fact that they have to accept the resulting moderate position in which their own views may be only slightly reflected. This position is then represented by a strong union. The alternative for dissenters would be to consider splitting the union. The risk that a more radical union would fail was apparently too high even for persons and groups who were very dissatisfied with the way the top union officials discharged their functions and who therefore contemplated a split. In the end the vast majority of dissenters invariably took the decision to work towards their objectives within the union rather than to weaken the union movement as a whole and, in all likelihood, be condemned to a short-lived existence as an almost sectarian group outside the established trade-union movement. At the same time the industrial unions themselves are quite strict with members who support what — in particular from the viewpoint of the trade-union officials — are politically radical views. The unions were and are quite ready to expel both right-wing as well as left-wing extremists and they have never tolerated the emergence of groups suspected of failing to support the democratic order of the Federal Republic of Germany as enshrined in the Basic Law.

On the other hand, the unions have tried to appease less radical leftist views through a rhetoric which might suggest that the unions still adhere to Marxist ideas of class conflict, even if these ideas have little relevance for their practical politics. This rhetoric has helped to maintain solidarity among the membership. In a way, the full strength of the trade unions becomes visible only when their existence is threatened by outside forces, or the loyalty of the members and the supporting outsiders is called into question.

(b) *Integration of Diverging Positions of Individual Unions*

The main agency for influencing general economic and social policy-making in the workers' interest is the DGB. Since this is the umbrella organisation of the industrial unions, the strength of the DGB on issues of economic and social policy, but also on more general questions which are dealt with in the programmes of the industrial unions as well as of the DGB, results from its capacity to integrate the sometimes divergent positions of the seventeen industrial unions. Accordingly, the DGB represents a middle-of-the-road position. Both for the government and for business it is of tremendous advantage that on most contested issues they have to take into account no more than one widely accepted union position. It is possible to claim that the unions have performed the socially necessary task of integrating widely divergent interests, and in this way have contributed to the smooth functioning of the existing economic, social and political order. They have done this although they themselves have suffered in the process: they have occasionally been shaken by internal conflicts and they have lost their specific character — and, with some people, their credibility — in their search for compromise. It has to be appreciated that trade unions see themselves — and, even more, are seen by some social groups outside the trade-union movement — not just as simple functional elements of an essentially capitalist economy; they are also perceived as the main hope in the quest for change towards a fairer and juster society. The fact that the unions have taken a cooperative position is a remarkable act of self-denial and public responsibility, because it has meant 'betraying' or postponing the traditional aspirations of the trade-union movement and thus disappointing many of their more ideologically committed followers. It has also exposed them to international criticism from less cooperative unions in other countries.

To secure a minimum ideological uniformity and continuity, the leaders of the DGB and the leaders of the individual industrial unions also apply a certain pressure from above. Cases where this has become known have triggered off a general discussion raising questions about the democratic nature of the decision-making process within the unions. Every now and then, people who want to see ideals of grassroots democracy applied to the decision-making processes, raise their voice. But reforms to this effect would be against the interest of the established officials and are also incompatible with the existing constitutions, which in general institute a system of indirect representation; finally they might also endanger the unity of the unions, which is the very basis of their power. As a result, such opposition — in particular from people pursuing older syndicalist models of democracy (see pp. 170ff.) — has failed to change the situation decisively.

That the unions have performed a politically very important role in securing the relatively smooth functioning of a parliamentary-democratic system has been recognised not only by most German governments but also by the employers' associations who see the advantage of a system which produces uniform positions on the labour side, even though minority views are not silenced altogether. The employers' associations evidently prefer a strong trade-union movement with reformist ideas to a potentially fragmented and divided one in which at least some groups could be expected to hold revolutionary ideas and become a source of trouble both in politics and in the firms. This interpretation is supported by the fact that recent plans to reform the Works Constitution Act with the aim of giving more protection to the rights of minority groups of workers, were attacked by the DGB as an attempt to weaken the trade unions, and that in this rejection of government plans they were supported by the employers!

The moderate position of the German Trade Union Federation had a feedback effect on the positions of the individual industrial unions: the appeal to overall solidarity of the trade-union movement has often induced the individual union to modify its previously more radical position.

2.5 Cooperative Behaviour of the Trade Unions

It has often been observed that German trade unions tend towards cooperation. This cooperation means first and foremost that the unions in general do not pursue a class-struggle strategy that tries to drive society towards a socialist transformation. It does not necessarily mean that the unions have given up their opposition to the existing capitalist system. In the long term they still aspire to change the capitalist economy and society into a more humane system, whose general structure and most details, however, remain quite vague. The transition is to be effected by a gradual change in which the labour movement is the main agent of change. In the eyes of the trade unions the labour movement represents a progressive force, whereas the capitalist Establishment is seen as the conservative defender of the existing system. All the small improvements which have been accomplished are seen as the fruits of this continuous striving for a better society. What these views add up to in reality is that the trade unions work within the given system and do not incessantly challenge its existence. Although there has never been an explicit decision by union leaders to behave cooperatively, their actual political conduct suggests basic agreement on this point. The reasons for this consensus are manifold. Important in this context was the all-pervasive drive to reconstruct Germany after the lost war. The union leaders took a positive attitude towards the state because they knew that outright opposition by some trade unions had contributed to the collapse of the Weimar Republic. Moreover, the existence of a socialist/communist state in East Germany served as a deterrent to socialism. There is finally also a self-reinforcing element: the fact that trade unions accepted their role within the system has given them recognition and success and has enabled them to effect gradual changes. This, in turn, has confirmed them in their position and reinforced their collaboration. Meanwhile the internal structure of the trade unions has also adapted to foster this strategy.

2.6 German Trade Union Federation

(a) *Function*

The task of the German Trade Union Federation (DGB) is to formulate a workers' position on all societal issues, in particular regarding economic, social and cultural policies, and to represent this position towards the outside world. Workers' interests are to be represented not only *vis-à-vis* employers and their organisations, but also *vis-à-vis* legislatures, administrations and other institutions. The general public is reached mainly through the media; therefore a good relationship with these target groups is also important. Since there is hardly any political decision which does not affect the dependently employed in one way or another, the DGB addresses itself to almost all political problems, even if the main emphasis is on questions of social and economic policy.

In addition to this external function there are also internal tasks. The DGB attempts to bring about a certain amount of coordination of its member unions and their policies and tries to secure a minimum of unity and solidarity at least in programmatic statements. In this process it also provides opportunities for discussions among the industrial unions. Other tasks include training and education for unionists and the operation of legal-aid services.

In partnership with the industrial unions the DGB operates some major cooperative-type enterprises, among them:

(1) the Bank für Gemeinwirtschaft, which ranks fourth in size among the joint-stock banks in the Federal Republic (the majority ownership in this bank was sold to a private insurance company in November 1986);

(2) the Neue Heimat group of urban construction and housing companies (this group is — mainly due to mismanagement — in serious financial difficulties at the time of writing, November 1986);

(3) the Volksfürsorge insurance and home-savings group;

(4) the Beamtenheimstättenwerk building society;

(5) the Beteiligungsgesellschaft für Gemeinwirtschaft AG, the holding company for trade-union co-op enterprises.

The DGB also operates research and cultural facilities — for example, the Economic and Social Science Institute of the Trade Unions (Wirtschafts- und Sozialwissenschaftliches Institut der Gewerkschaften), the Ruhr Festival of Arts Company (Ruhrfestspiele GmbH), the Bund-Verlag (publishing house) and enterprises dedicated to educational and vocational training purposes, (e.g. a correspondence course institute and a vocational retraining programme).

(b) *Organisational Structure*

The formal structure of the DGB, as well as the structures of individual industrial unions, more or less parallel the administrative structure of the Federal Republic. There is a federal level (*Bund*) and there are state districts (*Landesbezirke*) which are by and large identical with the *Länder*. Finally, there are county districts (*Kreisverbände*), which roughly correspond to areas of local government jurisdiction.

As we have said, the DGB is the umbrella organisation of its seventeen members; but the industrial unions are autonomous both in respect of collective bargaining and of finances. Their membership in the DGB implies the acceptance of, and adherence to, the DGB constitution. In this way the DGB works as a coordinator, and its programme amounts to providing a general guideline for the activities of the industrial unions. The DGB depends for its finances on the industrial unions from which it receives 12 per cent of their membership revenues plus DM0.30 per quarter for each individual member. The industrial unions send delegates to the Federal Congress (Bundeskongress), which is the supreme organ of the DGB. The number of delegates from each union depends on the number of members for whom dues are remitted to the federation. Some 500 members of the Federal Congress are convened every four years. The Federal Congress lays down guidelines on trade-union policy, decides on basic programmes, on constitutional changes and elects members to the Federal Executive Board (Bundesvorstand) and to an Auditing Commission (Revisionskommission). The Federal Executive Board consists of the presidents of the seventeen member unions and of the federation officers running affairs on a day-to-day basis, that is the president of the DGB, two vice-presidents and six other elected officials, making up the Federal Executive Committee (Geschäftsführender Bundesvorstand).

The highest organ in the period between Federal Congresses is the Federal Executive Council (Bundesausschuss), comprising 135 members. These include the Federal Executive Board (twenty-six members), the nine state district presidents (*Landesbezirksvorsitzende*), and 100 delegates from member unions. Each union has at least three delegates, the rest being allocated according to the number of members for whom funds have been remitted to the federation. The Federal Executive Council meets regularly every three months. Its main tasks are the monitoring of trade-union policy, organisational matters and decisions concerning the federation budget. It is also empowered to pass 'action programmes'.

This 'political' structure is backed up by administrative staff; a total of about 3,000 persons is employed by the DGB at all levels. Also, and in particular at the lower levels, many voluntary helpers can be relied upon.

(c) *Programme*

The DGB has, in its own understanding, an all-encompassing claim to represent workers' interests. Its ideas regarding society and culture and its demands in the field of economic and social policy have been laid down in three basic programmes (1949, 1963, 1981) and four action programmes (1955, 1956, 1972, 1979). The early programme emphasised the notion of central planning of the economy, nationalisation of key industries and union co-determination (see below, pp. 176ff.). The realisation that a rapid change of the social and political system in the Federal Republic was impossible and also the increasing integration of the trade unions into the existing socio-economic order have induced the unions to shelve the issue of the nationalisation of firms and of key industries and to pursue — together with their traditional aim of raising living standards — a strategy of extending the position of worker and trade-union control instead. The 1981 Basic Programme reflects the experience of the economic crisis, of widespread unemployment and of an uneasiness with the rapid intrusion of new technologies into production and administration (see excerpt, pp. 239ff. below).

After a preamble which emphasises the important role of the trade-union movement for human progress, the 1981 programme deals with thirty topics. They range from the rights of workers to demands on the economic system; from ideas on public finance, environmental protection and energy policy to views on cultural policy and the media. All-pervading are the demands to restore full employment, to improve social protection and to enlarge participatory rights of workers. Altogether it is a moderately reformist programme and very few ideas can be considered radical.

2.7 Metal-Workers Union as an Example of an Industrial Union

(a) *Introduction*

The various industrial unions are similar in their formal structure. But their attitudes differ widely, particularly as regards cooperation with the employers and role of unions in a market economy. The style and behaviour of the more important industrial unions have also been moulded by strong personalities whose names were for many years almost synonymous with 'their' union. Consequently, it would be misleading to talk about a 'typical' set of positions. Rather, the most fruitful approach for an understanding of German labour relations seems to be to describe the policy of the largest and most radical union — the Metal-Workers Union (I.G. Metall). It is also significant that this union has often assumed a pioneering role. In many of the annual rounds of collective bargaining it has taken the lead. Similarly, its demands regarding 'new' elements of collective agreements — for example, in the field of improving working conditions and protection of workers against the consequences of rationalisation — have set the pace for other unions. The following discussion focuses on I.G. Metall and uses it as an example for identifying some of the problems of industrial unions in general.

(b) *Functions of an Industrial Union*

The most conspicuous function of industrial unions is their role in collective bargaining and, as a consequence, in labour disputes. In their function of negotiating for wages and conditions the industrial unions are also legally recognised and specifically protected, because this activity is subsumed by the concept 'autonomy of collective bargaining' (see pp. 70f.).

In their role as interest groups the industrial unions could, theoretically, be the counterparts of the business associations of the industry concerned with all questions of government economic and social policy which affect this industry. However, since both the business association and the industrial trade union are interested in the well-being of the industry, there is usually no major disagreement on fundamentals, although their priorities are often different. Overall, the role of the industrial trade unions as industrial interest groups is overshadowed by their role as parties to collective bargaining; as an interest group which articulates the workers' interest in general, the DGB would seem to be the more important.

The industrial union is also the direct partner of the individual worker because it establishes a presence in the firms and because workers are members of industrial trade unions. This is also the source of power for the industrial unions, which depend both on membership and financial strength. The power of the DGB is only derived from that of the industrial unions.

(c) *Organisational Structure of the I.G. Metall*

(i) *Formal Structure* Formally, the organisational structure of the I.G. Metall is based on the democratic idea that all power originates with the members.

The membership is organised in various local units, which are the basic elements of the organisation. Each local unit elects its leadership — the local-unit administration (*Ortsverwaltung*) — by secret ballot for a three-year term. This election is carried out by an Assembly of Member Delegates (Vertreterversammlung). The elected local-unit administration which has to be confirmed by the I.G. Metall Executive Board (Vorstand) is bound by decisions and directives of the Executive Board. It is responsible for all daily business at that level. In particular, it has to organise the election of union shop-floor representatives (*gewerkschaftliche Vertrauensleute*) who take care of the problems of members in the firm. The local-unit administration collects dues, out of which — depending on membership — it retains between 22 and 38 per cent for its own purposes. The remainder is forwarded to the national union treasury. The decision-making body of the local unit is the Assembly of Members' Delegates; all the rulings of this body are binding on the members of the local units, except when such actions contradict the decisions of the Union Congress (Gewerkschaftstag), the Advisory Council (Beirat) or the Executive Board.

The administrative activity of the Metal-Workers Union is handled by regional organisations which have jurisdiction over districts (*Bezirke*) of roughly the size of a *Land*. A district director (*Bezirksleiter*) is in charge of these district administrations (*Bezirksleitungen*). He is an appointee of the Executive Board and has to follow the directives of that body in dealing with the problems of collective bargaining, administrative matters and inter-local disputes. A five-man District Commission (Bezirkskommission) elected at annual District Conferences (Bezirkskonferenz) by delegates from the local units assists the district director. The other function of the District Conference is to support and advise the district director, to approve his accounts and to confirm appointments for various commissions, among them the Collective Agreements Commission (Tarifkommission).

The Union Congress, held every three years, is the most significant body of the organisation. The delegates to the Union Congress are elected by secret ballot at local Assemblies of Member Delegates. The Union Congress elects the Executive Board and approves the accounts. It is empowered to change the constitution of the union. It also discusses the general situation of the union and all motions brought forward. In addition, it elects the five-man Control Commission (Kontrollausschuß), which ensures that the Executive Board abides by the constitution and carries out the decisions of the Union Congress and of the Advisory Council; it also deals with complaints regarding the activities of the Executive Board. The Executive Board coordinates all the activities of the I.G. Metall. Its duties include:

— the external representation of the Union;
— watching over the observance of the constitution and implementing the decisions of the Union Congress and of the Advisory Council;
— deciding on whether to give notice of termination of collective agreements, and on strike ballots and work stoppages;
— giving directives to the local administration;
— the appointment of personnel or the confirmation of such appointments;
— editing of union publications.

The officers of the Executive Board, the district directors as well as representatives elected at annual District Conferences work together in the Advisory Council which is the highest decision-making organ in the period between Union Congresses.

Almost without exception, the members of the administration of the local unit and of the district administration are professional full-time functionaries. The Executive Board is composed of eleven full-time functionaries, who conduct the daily affairs, and nineteen honorary members, who are still on the shop floor.

(ii) *Formal and Practical Decision-Making Power* The structure described above reflects only the formal arrangements. In reality, however, there are also elements of the structure, some of which can be found in the constitution, but some of which have also become established by daily routine and tradition, which to some extent modify the formally democratic egalitarian principles. In particular, there is a concentration of far-reaching decision-making powers and rights of control and intervention vested in the Executive Board and its administrative apparatus. This restricts the individual members' chances to participate in the formulation of overall policy. Such oligarchical tendencies of trade-union leaders were perceived by Robert Michels many years ago when he analysed the bureaucratisation and oligarchisation of pre-1914 trade unionism.[5]

A specifically German element results from the existence of works councils. Formally, works councils act as autonomous agents of the workers' interests and do not depend on trade unions. In reality, however, there are close links, and works councillors strongly influence decision-making processes in the trade unions and *vice versa*.

The Dominant Position of the Executive Board: The powers of the Executive Board include, on the one hand, the external relations of the union (i.e. policy-making on collective bargaining and on industrial disputes) and, on the other hand, internal relations (i.e. administration, finances and the appointment of personnel).

According to the constitution of I.G. Metall, collective bar-

---

5. R. Michels, *Political Parties: A Sociological Study of the Oligarchical Tendencies of Modern Democracy* (1915), New York–London, 1962. The question of the power and influence of permanent officials in both private and public bureaucracies was, of course, also a major concern of Max Weber's. For a good introduction, see W.J. Mommsen, *The Age of Bureaucracy: Perspectives on the Political Sociology of Max Weber*, Oxford, 1977.

gaining is the task of the districts. The district directors, how-ever, are given their position by the Executive Board and are bound by their orders. The intention to give notice of termina-tion of a collective agreement has to be reported by the district director to the Executive Board, which has the final decision. Strikes and lock-outs in the district have to be reported immedi-ately to the Executive Board. All bodies representing member-ship interests at the district level have only advisory functions. At the local level the executives have to carry out the decisions of the upper levels. In this way the Executive Board has the final decision as regards giving notice of a termination of collective agreements, the conduct of strike ballots and work stoppages. The powers of the Executive Committee are merely limited by decisions of the Union Congress and, in the case of a strike, by the outcome of a strike ballot.

The concentration of decision-making powers in the Executive Board on all issues relating to collective bargaining may be explained in part by the need to pursue a uniform strategy and the need to minimise the financial, legal and organisational hazards of a strike. The trade unions have to observe factors beyond their control, in particular the legal framework for la-bour disputes as well as the strategy of the employers' associa-tion. They have to ensure that the individual collective-bargaining areas cannot be played off against each other and that no individual group embarks on work stoppages which could entail financial and legal risks for the whole union. Moreover, in situations of acute confrontation, fast and well coordinated action may be necessary. Consequently, the need for a uniform strategy of collective-agreement negotiations which also mini-mises risks is undeniable, and this reinforces the tendency towards a centralisation of decision-making authority in respect of external relations, in particular in collective bargaining.

The counterweight to the centralisation of decision-making powers *vis-à-vis* the outside world, — that is, an internal demo-cratic structure — is but weakly developed. According to the constitution, members can directly influence the policy of the Executive Board only by their vote in strike ballots or by actually going on strike. But even in these cases members' participation is fairly limited. According to the constitution, and as laid down in the standing orders relating to the Collective Agreement

55

Commission of I.G. Metall, it is the Executive Board which decides whether and when a strike ballot is to take place. As a rule the Executive Board follows in its decisions the vote of the Collective Agreement Commission. If it pursues a different strategy, however, it does not have to overturn that vote openly; it can simply postpone a decision. There seems to be a tendency to delay strike ballots and the beginning of a strike. In order to call a strike, at least 75 per cent of the members concerned must cast a positive vote in a secret strike ballot. But whether and when the strike is called is again decided by the Executive Board, which acts on the recommendation of the Collective Agreement Commission. Thus it is possible to resume negotiations after a positive strike ballot but before the actual beginning of the strike. According to the constitution, the Executive Board can, on recommendation of the Collective Agreement Commission, approve the result of collective-agreement negotiations without obtaining the consent of the members in a fresh vote. The guidelines do not prescribe another ballot; in reality, however, a fresh vote of the members has always been called. A strike in progress, however, can only be terminated by a second strike ballot. The strike can only be continued if at least 75 per cent of the members concerned vote in favour, thus rejecting the proposed settlement.

In the regulations regarding strike ballots and strikes, members have no autonomous right to articulate initiatives themselves. They can only express their opinion by voting to strike or to accept a compromise reached in negotiations.

The actual work at the various levels of the organisation requires professional full-time staff. Expert knowledge is required, for example, for collective bargaining, for the application of the collective agreements to varying conditions in firms, and for advising members of works councils, union shop-floor representatives and union members on all aspects of labour law. Consequently, in the recruitment of staff, professional qualifications are more important than political views — even if the latter are not considered insignificant.

The constitutions of all unions give the Executive Board a far-reaching influence on personnel decisions at all levels of the organisation. A consequence of this is that the appointment of politically dissenting persons as union officials becomes rather unlikely and ensures that day-to-day work is carried out in a climate of basic consensus. The actual process of appointing personnel is a combination of election plus confirmation by the Executive Board and other bodies.

The need to secure the loyalty of the officials to the cause of the labour movement in general and to the trade union as an institution in particular, may justify the Executive Board's strong influence. The other side of the coin, however, is that the Executive Board may also use its rights to confirm appointments to exercise control over the paid officials with respect to their loyalty to the policy of the Executive Board. Generally, a career within the union is possible only for persons who share the Executive Board's views. This does not necessarily imply that officials attach more importance to their own career than to the interests of the union members, but it is likely to encourage behaviour which does not antagonise the higher echelons.

Nevertheless, both the mechanism of selection as well as their own interests ensure that the functionaries at the lower levels of the organisation adhere to the political principles of the Executive Board. Consensus with the local representative bodies and the honorary functionaries is apparently not a major problem. Opposition to the views of the Executive Board on basic issues of union policy and also regarding collective bargaining has been very rare in the past and was possible only when the functionaries at the lower levels were strongly supported by active members.

In addition to the final decision-making power in matters of collective bargaining and in addition to their influence on the selection of staff, the position of the Executive Board is further strengthened because:

— the Executive Board is entitled to spend the major part of the revenue from membership dues;

— the Executive Board directly employs most of the qualified personnel and has access to outside experts on matters of economic and social policy. It is hence much better informed than people at the lower levels;

— the Executive Board has supervisory rights over the union's official paper, and practically all printed material published by official bodies of the union has to be approved by the Executive Board. Again, this is not conducive to the open discussion of opinions which are in opposition to the views of the Executive Board;

— finally, the day-to-day work of the organisation is steered by direct orders and guidelines addressed in particular to the local-unit administration.

The System of Delegates: The concentration of decision-making powers, of rights to intervene and to exert influence which the Federal Executive Board has, is not balanced by powers of the lower-level organs, which are closer to the members. Their rights of control and participation are poorly developed; moreover, they can be almost completely neutralised by the standard operating procedures. The constitution gives such rights of control to the assemblies of delegates at the various levels. By far the most important of these bodies is the Union Congress, which has to approve all initiatives from below if they are to become official elements of the union's policy.

According to the constitution, the Union Congress is the supreme organ of decision-making. It has the right to control and to revise all decisions, orders and guidelines of the Executive Board. It can also shape future activities by giving directives. In reality, however, these powers are not particularly relevant. So far, Union Congresses have always confirmed Executive Board policy, even if there was violent criticism in the preceding discussion. The reasons for this lie in the organisation of the Union Congresses and in the composition of the body of delegates. The fact that discussions in Union Congresses hardly ever bring about changes is attributable to particular organisational arrangements.

First of all, because of a certain ceremoniousness, the atmosphere at Union Congresses is not conducive to discussion. Important barriers for an open discussion are also presented by the Constitution Committee (Satzungskommission) and the Advisory Committee on Motions (Antragsberatungskommission). Both committees have great influence on what will be debated in plenary session, and they practically also predetermine the results. In these committees the members of the Executive Board have a strong influence.

The climate of opinion at Union Congresses is also consensus-orientated. Very few issues are discussed in detail; after those issues have been voted on, votes on the other motions are passed without discussion and with big majorities. Once the 'voting machinery' gets going, attempts to start discussions are considered a disturbance. Also, the obvious presence of the mass media prevents harsh criticism of officials and of union policy. Consequently, the Union Congress does not really work as a control organ but is manipulated by the Executive Board to confirm its policy. Criticism and dissatisfaction become visible occasionally in elections to the Executive Board when some people lose support.

The mechanisms by which the delegates to the Union Congress are selected favour members who are in agreement with existing policy: they are elected by the Assembly of Member Delegates at the local level. Typically, the majority of the delegates are functionaries from the various levels and, at any rate, in the selection of delegates criteria such as loyalty and past merit play an important role.

One of the most important reasons why the Union Congress cannot properly discharge its control function is that the majority of union members do not actively participate in the union: only about 10 per cent of the members maintain regular contact with the organisation. Only this minority participates actively; these, however, are likely to be members of works councils or they are union shop-floor representatives or members of some special committee. Any radically new proposal would have to mobilise at least parts of the so far silent majority, and this is not very likely. As long as the majority remains silent, its attitude is interpreted by the power elite as support for its policy. This is not completely unjustified. Since the majority of workers are not sufficiently knowledgeable about the often complicated issues, they accept the definition of the workers' interest by the union leaders.

Collective Agreement Commission: The internal regulations on strike ballots and on strike procedures contained in the constitution and in the guidelines suggest a key role of the Collective Agreement Commission. Here the objectives and strategies of the policy to be pursued are formulated. This crucial function is, however, not matched by the commission's position in the organisation because the Collective Agreement Commission is no more than a standing committee of the District Conference.

The guidelines of I.G. Metall give much room for discretion in the formation of these Collective Agreement Commissions. The number of members and their origin from the various administrative units is determined by the district director together with the District Commission. Decisive for the size of the Collective Agreement Commission — usually between fifteen and 100 members — is the coverage and relevance of the collective agreement. The selection of actual persons is done by the local-unit administration, but the appointments have to be confirmed by the District Conference. Each local unit is represented by at least one full-time official; the other representatives from the local units are either members of works councils or union shop-floor representatives. Typically, Collective Agreement Commissions are dominated by works councillors from large firms. The union shop-floor representatives constitute another important element, but they are usually a minority. The Collective Agreement Commissions of I.G. Metall have no formal powers of decision; they can merely pass resolutions and make recommendations which refer to all questions of collective bargaining — demands in the field of wages and conditions, termination of collective agreements, approval or rejection of bargaining results, strike ballots and strikes.

Although the Executive Board is autonomous in its decisions, it usually follows the recommendations of the Collective Agreement Commission. Apart from the rare case of a strike ballot, the recommendations of the Collective Agreement Commission constitute the democratic legitimation for the decisions of the Executive Board.

Decision-making on the central issue of demands in collective bargaining takes place as follows: the Executive Board passes its ideas together with the supporting views of the experts on to the Collective Agreement Commissions of the individual districts and in this way maps out the field. Usually, the Collective Agreement Commissions make only a few changes. Nevertheless, the resulting recommendations to the Executive Board have the appearance of being democratically sanctioned, and the Executive Board accepts them formally. In the rare case of widely diverging demands, the Executive Board may ask for a revision of the proposal to avoid interference with the union's overall strategy. In reality, therefore, the Executive Board ratifies the concept which it originally formulated itself.

On account of the obvious advantages of a uniform strategy of negotiation, and also because the Executive Board has many ways of influencing the Collective Agreement Commission, there is hardly ever any disagreement in this process. On the other hand, members have no control over the Collective Agreements Commission: Collective Agreement Commissions are not obliged to inform union members or to justify their actions to the members. This formal detachment of the Collective Agreement Commission can be interpreted as a reservation against the ability of the members to evaluate properly the situation faced in collective bargaining. But it is also true that this mediation of the members' interests is a prerequisite for a cooperative policy of the union *vis-à-vis* the employees; this cooperation could be endangered by excessive demands of some group of members.

For practical reasons, the Collective Agreement Commission selects from its midst the actual Negotiation Commission (Verhandlungskommission) which carries out the negotiations with the representatives of the employers. This Negotiation Commission of about ten persons is normally chaired by the district director. The Negotiation Commission is fully responsible to the Collective Agreement Commission.

Special Position of the Works Councillors: Formally, there is no connection between the members of the works councils and the trade union. In reality, however, most works councillors belong to the trade union, and very often they are among the active members who play an important role in the union organisation.

The works council is the legally recognised representation of the workers' interests at plant or company level (see Ch. 4). As the conditions laid down in the collective agreements are geared to the average or even to the marginal firms of an industry in a collective-bargaining area, there is — in firms with an above-average economic standing — some room for wage increases beyond the level of the collective agreement. This results in the widespread phenomenon of wage drift. Since negotiations for these extra wages are conducted by the works councils, their members can establish their own political base among the workers of the firms. This is important because it secures the re-election of the works councillors. Altogether, works councillors are not interested in a very militant wage policy: in less

61

profitable firms they know the economic situation of their company well enough and do not want to endanger jobs, and in a prosperous firm they do not want to reduce the room for firm-specific wage increases which will be credited to them.

In the individual firm the works councillors and not the trade-union representatives are the partners or opponents of management. This stems from the Works Constitution Act. Particularly in a situation of a sizeable wage drift, the efforts of the trade union are not perceived as very effective by the workers at large.

In spite of the works councils' interest in the maintenance of some room for firm-specific wage increases, one cannot speak of a competitive relationship between works council and the trade union. The overwhelming majority of works councillors are loyal trade-union members who know very well that their position in the firm also depends on the strength of the union in general. But their position remains autonomous, and to some extent the union has to rely on the cooperation of the works council. As a result of its legally established status in the firm, it has regular contacts with management and determines the influence of the union in the firm and also the room for union activities: the work of the union shop-floor representatives, the access of functionaries to the firm, canvassing for membership, distribution of union papers, and so on. In reality the works councillors are in a better position than the union shop-floor representatives or the full-time functionaries to canvass for membership and to organise the collection of membership dues. This gives them a key position and explains their overwhelming influence at the local level of organisation, which is also transmitted by the system of election of delegates to the higher levels. As a rule, therefore, works councillors have at least a relative majority, if not an absolute majority, not only in the local-unit administration but also in the Assembly of Member Delegates, in the Collective Agreement Commission and in the Union Congress. This, however, does not imply a one-sided dependency of the unions on the works councillors. They are elected in the firm, and union shop-floor representatives and the full-time functionaries of the union exert decisive influence in the establishment of list of candidates. To work successfully, works councillors also need expertise, which they obtain in special union training courses; often they also have to rely on the expert knowledge of the full-time functionaries. Finally, active union shop-floor representatives can put pressure on the works council by mobilising workers.

But there is no question that the legally secured position in the firm and the loyalty of the workers in the firm, which does not depend on the union, give the works councillors a relative autonomy which makes for a special position in the organisational structure of the union. This may contribute to increased realism in union policy, but it also raises the danger that the interest of the works council, which are not directly concerned with the problems of the unemployed, may bias the whole activity of unions towards plant-worker interests as opposed to the interests of the workers at large.

Position and Function of the Union Shop-Floor Representatives: The initiative for the creation of a body of honorary functionaries in the firm came from the top of the union hierarchy. The intention was to have a group of active members who were independent of the works council and who would help to reduce the distance between the union as an institution and the reality of working life. Two major things were expected from the union shop-floor representatives. On the one hand, they were to have close contact with the union members and explain the policy of the union to them. On the other hand, they were to keep a critical watch over the activities of the works council. They were also to canvass for new members, spread information and actively cooperate in labour disputes. The idea was that through the body of shop-floor representatives a permanent presence of the union would be established in the plant.

Although the constitution of I.G. Metall gives no specific rights to union shop-floor representatives, their importance has increased. At the beginning they were less a control organ of the works council than its extended arm and also a reservoir of future works councillors. But gradually they became more independent. Especially in large firms, where the works council developed a bureaucratic structure and had a tendency to cooperate closely with management, the union shop-floor representatives became important for the union. In labour disputes they activate members and alert them to the union's demands. This growing importance is evidenced by clauses in collective agreements which specify that union shop-floor representatives should not be disadvantaged by their work for the union. Although this does not give them the legal protection enjoyed by the works councillors,such clauses help to reduce fears and increase member readiness to take on this function.

The position of the union shop-floor representatives in the I.G. Metall is ambiguous. On the one hand, and in particular in large firms, they perform the important function of informing and activating the union members, which is necessary for the maintenance of the union's power. This function cannot be performed by the works councillors because of their small number and also because the Works Constitution Act obliges the works council to cooperate loyally with the management. On the other hand, the union shop-floor representatives have little formal influence on the decision-making process in the union.

(iii) *Deficient Representation of Members' Interests?* The crucial question for a cooperative trade union is how to organise decision processes in such a way that members can participate but do not take decisions which would be incompatible with a basically cooperative approach. A long-term solution to this dilemma could be to educate the members to get their support for the cooperative policy. Indeed, the trade unions offer educational programmes for their members which aim at a better understanding of economic and social policy, and they also support the idea that basic economics should be an element of general education. But at present the unions also secure continuity of policy by a formal structure which ensures that new ideas of individual members or groups of members are filtered, mediated and transformed in such a way that interference with the basically cooperative attitude of the institution is avoided. In doing this they can even claim adherence to democratic principles: about 90 per cent of union members can be considered a silent majority, which in all likelihood could be activated by an appeal to solidarity, in particular if there is a need to defend the unity of the labour movement against outside threats, but also against radical ideas from within.

In theory and according to the constitution, there is always a chance for the rank-and-file member to launch initiatives aiming at better control of the governing bodies and at a change of union policy. But these initiatives are transmitted by delegates to the Union Congress where the final decision is taken. In reality the chances for an effective control and for the exertion of real influence are very limited; as a consequence there is hardly any opposition.

In this system the range of actual and possible interests is reduced. Interests are filtered and modified according to criteria of compatibility with the basic decision to accept, in principle, the existing economic system and to cooperate with the employers towards maintaining its smooth functioning.

So far this state of affairs has been lamented more by outside, mainly academic, observers than by a sizeable number of union members. There is no doubt that the vast majority of union members support the basic decision to cooperate. On some other issues, however, one may observe a certain alienation of the grassroots from the top, because the top seems to attach more importance to some goals than do the members. This seems to be particularly true for the issue of co-determination at company level, and it may also be true of the idea of wealth formation (see pp. 198ff.). Both objectives are pushed by some unions, but the individual members seem to be more interested in immediate wage increases and in improvements at the workplace, which is more an issue of participation at plant level. But no one can really say that the priorities of the union are not acceptable: the rank-and-file attitude could also be interpreted as a short-term perspective on strategy whereby the individual members cannot really see the long-term benefits due to their incomplete understanding of the working of a complex national economy.

It seems remarkable how the legally protected participatory rights as exercised by the works council affect the trade unions. The works councillors are well informed about the situation of an industry and, as a rule, are not given to dogmas. Their legal recognition makes for their strong position in the union structure. In this way workers' participation not only affects the firms but also makes for a realistic union policy.

(d) *Aims and Strategy of I.G. Metall*

The general aims of I.G. Metall are laid down in its constitution (see Appendix B, Document II, pp. 245f. below). There a general claim to be concerned with promoting the economic, social and cultural interests of its members is established. In particular, the union strives for more workers' solidarity, for better pay and working conditions, for more workers' participation and for better social security.

Regarding the direct goals of collective bargaining there is a certain tendency for I.G. Metall to diversify its demands by including qualitative elements rather than to limit itself to demanding regular wage increases. The following aspects, in particular, are of increasing importance:

(1) reducing working time with the aim of 'redistributing' work to create additional jobs for the unemployed;

(2) protecting workers against the consequences of technological and organisational innovations, including structural changes;

(3) using some of the potential productivity gains to 'humanise' the workplace to reduce the 'intensity' of work.

Contrary to some other industrial unions, in particular the Building and Construction Workers' Union, wealth-formation schemes do not play a role in the demands of I.G. Metall.

As an example of the range of demands which I.G. Metall wants to put forward in collective negotiations, a resolution of the 1977 Congress is reproduced in Appendix B (Document III, pp. 246ff.).

Decisions in all matters relating to collective bargaining and to labour disputes are centrally coordinated for the whole industrial union. There may even be some informal consultation between the various industrial unions; the increasingly frequent practice of 'sympathy strikes' in support of labour disputes in other industries seems to point in this direction.

Before and during negotiations the trade union wants to put pressure on employers by demonstrating the 'unrest' among the rank-and-file membership and their willingness to strike. Members express their discontent by short work stoppages and occasional walk-outs or warning strikes, which are sometimes labelled 'spontaneous'. These actions are typically accompanied by mass demonstrations, protest actions and publicity campaigns: all this is intended to impress the employers, to mobilise the trade-union members and to win the support of the non-unionised workers as well as to convince public opinion of the legitimacy of the union's demands. Unions call these largely unpredictable work stoppages and protest actions the 'new mobility'. Although these work stoppages could also be interpreted as a violation of the peace-keeping obligation, the Federal Labour Court has ruled them to be legal.

The actual labour dispute begins after the breakdown of negotiations with the strike ballot. After a positive strike ballot the typical procedure is to concentrate the strike on the most prosperous firms with a high degree of unionisation. The union hopes that a direct strike of this kind will also result in work stoppages in related firms which either run out of supplies or cannot dispose of their products.

The idea of this strike strategy is that with a minimum of workers officially on strike, a maximum of effect on the employers can be accomplished. This has the advantage that the trade union has to grant strike pay only to those members who are on strike and to those who — as a consequence of this primary strike — are out of work for technical reasons in the bargaining area directly affected. In this situation, workers who cannot work in other collective-bargaining areas can claim unemployment benefit or short-working subsidies from the Federal Labour Institute provided that the demands of the union in the other bargaining areas are not identical to the demands of the union in the area of the primary strike. This point, however, is highly controversial at the moment, and the employers' associations argue that the payment of unemployment benefit and short-working subsidies violates the obligation of the Federal Labour Institute to keep neutral in labour disputes. If the Federal Labour Institute did not pay, the financial burden born by a labour union in a labour dispute would increase enormously because the trade union would have to grant strike pay to all its members who are out of work regardless of the bargaining area. It would also result in strong pressures from all non-unionised workers because they do not get any support, unless, in case of proven need, they are eligible for the rather lower social welfare payments. The issue remains open right now; the Bundestag's recent (1986) definition of the 'neutrality' of the Federal Labour Institute contained in article 116 of the Employment Promotion Act has been taken to the Federal Constitutional Court.

The strategy of the trade unions to call selective strikes has been approved by the Federal Labour Court. However, it allows the employers' association to react by calling a defensive lock-out (for details, see pp. 88ff.). In this way the employers can extend the scope of the labour dispute and exert counterpressure on the trade unions. Again, it is controversial whether the locked-out workers are entitled to payments from the Federal Labour Institute; if not, the trade union has to pay strike money to its locked-out members, and the non-unionised workers who are out of work on account of the labour dispute get nothing.

2.8 Appraisal

Contrary to the sometimes belligerent rhetoric of the trade unions and their leaders, their actions confirm their character-isation as 'cooperative trade unions'. All unions take the situation of the economy at large, the specific situation of their industry and that of individual firms into consideration when they formulate their demands. Such a 'realistic' attitude is partly attributable to the insight the trade unions have into the econ-omic possibilities which — at the level of the firm — results partly from workers' participation; works councillors, especially in smaller firms, are aware of the fact that the power of the trade union ends when a firm goes bankrupt. A symptom of this integration of the trade unions into the economic structure was also their readiness to participate in the 'concerted action' from 1967 until 1977 (see pp. 205ff.).

The organisational structure of the trade unions is adapted to this general attitude. So far the trade unions have managed to maintain the occasionally precarious balance between the expec-tations of the workers (to which the propaganda of the trade unions may have contributed) on the one hand and capacity of the national economy on the other. In this process the interests of the trade unions as institutions and the power interests of the union officials together with an unavoidable conflict between long-term and short-term interests of workers, also play a role, which, for example, prevents the trade unions from pursuing a collective-bargaining policy that aims at individual companies rather than at the whole industry. Although such a policy may be more advantageous for workers in some firms, it would endanger the solidarity of the workers in general and thus reduce the power of the unions.

3
Legal Aspects of Industrial Relations

3.1 Introduction

The legal aspects dealt with in this chapter pertain to three subject areas:

(1) the recognition of the autonomy of the parties in collective bargaining which is derived from Article 9 of the Basic Law;

(2) the rules pertaining to collective agreements; this issue is mainly regulated in the Industrial Agreement Act (*Tarifvertragsgesetz*) 1949, amended on 25 August 1969 and 24 October 1974.

(3) the rules pertaining to labour disputes (*Arbeitskampfrecht*). These rules are — atypically of the German legal system — not to be found in a specific law, but are in the form of case law developed by the labour courts, most importantly by the Federal Labour Court.

All these aspects will be dealt with here, although no attempt will be made to elaborate all the legal details; rather, we will concentrate on issues which are considered relevant to the general question of the impact of law on labour relations. The very elaborate and detailed nature of these regulations is an important element of the situation, which must be reflected in the discussion. The final section of this chapter explores the impact of the legal regulations on the behaviour of the trade unions and employers' associations. This discussion has two aspects. One is the actual content of these rules and the general concepts and principles governing them; the other relates to the very fact of the detailed legal regulation of the labour relations, often referred to as 'juridification'.

3.2 Autonomy of Collective Bargaining and the Parties to Collective Agreements

The autonomy of collective bargaining is defined as the right of associations of workers and employers to determine wages and conditions in bilateral negotiations without state interference. This autonomy of collective bargaining is derived from Article 9 of the Basic Law, which reads as follows:

> (1) All Germans shall have the right to form associations and societies.
> (2) Associations, the purposes or activities of which conflict with criminal laws or which are directed against the constitutional order or the concept of international understanding, are prohibited.
> (3) The right to form associations to safeguard and improve working and economic conditions is guaranteed to everyone and to all trades, occupations and professions. Agreements which restrict or seek to impair this right shall be null and void; measures directed to this end shall be illegal. Measures taken pursuant to Article 12a, to paragraphs (2) and (3) of Article 35, to paragraph (4) of Article 87a, or to Article 91, may not be directed against any industrial conflicts engaged in by associations within the meaning of the first sentence of this paragraph in order to safeguard and improve working and economic conditions.

The measures mentioned in paragraph 3 (sentence 3) are special emergency provisions applying in time of war or during natural and other emergencies. They are not to be applied to lawful labour conflicts.

(a) *The Individual's Right to Form Associations*

Article 9 of the Basic Law is interpreted to guarantee to everyone the following rights:

(1) to found an association, in particular a trade union or an employers' association;

(2) to take part in the founding of such an association;

(3) to join an existing association;

(4) to choose freely the association he/she wants to join;

(5) to stay in an association;

(6) to leave an association.

All arrangements which restrict an individual's freedom to join an association are null and void (positive freedom of association). This would apply, for instance, to a contractual obligation of the worker not to join a trade union or to join only a union which is already represented in the firm. It would apply, likewise, to a clause which obliges an employer not to hire workers who belong to a union or to hire only union members. It also forbids discrimination against union members; hence, a dismissal based on the reason that the worker is a union member is null and void. The fact that by law workers should not suffer any disadvantages from their membership of a union, particularly that the employer should not discriminate against union members, does not mean that all employers welcome union membership among their workers. In smaller firms in particular, the employer may consider the joining of a union to be disloyal and ultimately directed against him. Should he then use other means to discriminate against a worker who is a trade unionist and even find a pretext for dismissing him, it may be very difficult to prove that the worker's membership of a trade union is the underlying motive for that dismissal.

The freedom of association also covers the right of the individual to be active as a union member. This means, in particular, the right of the union member to participate in a lawful labour conflict. But it also gives the union member the right to canvass for union membership. Not even the fact that a worker is a member of the works council or of some other representative organ of the firm excludes him from such activities. What is required, however, is a clearly visible distinction between his work for the firm and his activities for the trade union.

A somewhat more controversial issue than the positive freedom of association is its counterpart, the 'negative freedom of association'. It is the question of whether article 9 of the Basic Law also protects the individual's right *not* to join an association. This issue is important because trade unions have often been trying to solve their 'free-rider' problem by putting pressure on workers to induce them to join. They have attempted this, for example, by confining certain benefits gained in collective bargaining to union members only. Such practices have always been ruled to be illegal by the courts.

(b) *Rights of the Association*

The Basic Law not only guarantees the rights of the individual, described above, but also protects the existence and the activities of associations which have been formed to safeguard and to improve the material and working conditions of their members. These associations — trade unions and employers' associations — are protected in their existence, in their organisational autonomy and in all activities which serve their underlying purpose. Such protection exists in the associations' relationship with the state, which can restrict the activities of these associations only to prevent an infringement of the rights of others. Furthermore, this protection forbids third parties from taking actions that interfere with the continued existence of an association. Finally, an association is also protected against its own members. In particular, these associations have the right to establish a constitution which imposes membership dues, determines reasons for the expulsion of members, and lays down regulations to secure the loyalty of its members as well as terms of notice for leaving the association. The expulsion of a member can be reviewed by a regular court.

The safeguarding and improvement of economic conditions by concluding autonomously negotiated collective agreements is derived from the freedom of association which is protected by the Basic Law. The Federal Constitutional Court has elaborated on this by stating that the autonomy of collective bargaining is meaningful only if the state provides a legal framework for such agreements. This framework is the Industrial Agreement Act.

The Basic Law also guarantees the right of an association to embark on industrial action if this is necessary in the pursuit of its objectives of safeguarding and improving material and working conditions. This is implied in article 9, paragraph 3 (sentence 3) of the Basic Law, which specifies that emergency measures cannot be applied to a labour dispute which is conducted by the associations in the pursuit of their main purpose. What remains controversial, however, is whether this extends only to the trade unions' right to strike or whether it also protects the employers' associations' right to lock out workers.

The constitutionally guaranteed protection of associational activities also implies the right of trade unions to canvass for membership, to spread propaganda in election campaigns for the works council and other representative organs and to have both workers as well as union members who do not belong to the firm distribute information pertaining to the purposes of the association on the premises of the firm as long as this is not done during work hours. A trade union can also use the bulletin boards put up by the firm for information purposes. The employer must tolerate such activities and cannot — except for reasons of security — prevent persons who have been commissioned by the unions from entering the premises and rooms of the firm, provided there has been prior notification. So far, however, the courts have ruled against the holding of elections for union shop-floor representatives on the premises of the firm and against attaching trade-union emblems to safety helmets which belong to the firm.

(c) *Trade Unions and Employers' Associations*

The protection of the Basic Law is extended to an association formed by either workers or employers to promote their respective interests, if it meets the following criteria:

(1) it must be a voluntary association above the level of the firm. Associations of workers whose membership is restricted to one firm only are not regarded as trade unions. The exceptions to this rule are the railway workers' union and the postal workers' union. Both the Federal Railways and the Federal Postal Services operate nation-wide and have plants throughout the country;

(2) the association must comprise a larger number of members, it must be of a permanent nature and must have a corporate organisation;

(3) the association must define itself as being the counterpart to the other side of industry in collective bargaining. It cannot comprise both workers and employers and cannot in any other way be dependent on the opposing side. Mixed groups of both workers and employers are not associations from this perspective, even if their purpose is the regulation of working conditions;

(4) the associations and their decision-making structures must conform with democratic principles. In particular, the members must have a formal influence on the decisions of the association;

(5) the association must recognise as binding existing legislation on collective agreements. Its purpose must be the conclusion of collective agreements aiming at the improvement of the economic and social situation of its members;

(6) although this view is awaiting confirmation by the Federal Constitutional Court, the Federal Labour Court also stipulates an ability to exert pressure which can be derived from the number of members or their position in working life. This requirement makes it difficult for new associations to become recognised as parties in collective bargaining, and consequently supports and stabilises the status quo. In particular, the emergence of new trade unions outside the DGB is made highly unlikely.

All DGB trade unions, the German Union of Salaried Employees and, on the employers side, the members of the BDA, meet these requirements. They are associations in the sense of Article 9, paragraph 3 of the Basic Law.

3.3 Legal Framework of Collective Bargaining

(a) *Concept of Collective Agreement*

As suggested earlier, the legal basis for collective agreements is the 1949 Industrial Agreement Act. The importance of collective agreements for the daily operation of firms is indicated by the fact that more than 90 per cent of all work contracts are determined in their contents by collective agreements.

(i) *Contents and Functions of Collective Agreements* A collective agreement has two components:

(1) in its *obligatory* part, it establishes rights and obligations of the parties to the agreement, that is between the trade union and the employers' association. The two most important obligations are the peace-keeping obligation (*Friedenspflicht*) and the duty to strive for compliance (*Einwirkungspflicht/Durchführungspflicht*). As long as a valid collective agreement exists, neither party to the agreement must embark on a labour conflict with the objective of changing the provisions of that agreement. Moreover, both parties have the duty to strive for compliance: they have to influence their members to abide by the agreement;

(2) in its *normative* part, it establishes legal norms relating to the content of all the individual work contracts covered by the agreement, in particular on conclusion, conditions and termina-

tion of such contracts. It can also regulate matters pertaining to the organisation of the firm and to the works constitution. The norms of the collective agreement define minimum conditions. The individual work contract may deviate from the provisions of the collective agreement to the advantage of the worker, and in reality it often does.

The collective agreement protects the individual worker against attempts of the economically more powerful employer to dictate the conditions of the individual work contract (protective function). It aims at greater equality in the relationship between worker and employer. For its duration the collective agreement precludes new demands and labour conflicts on matters which have been dealt with in the agreement (peace function).

Collective agreements also make for a standardisation of work contracts which clarify the relationship between employer and worker. This is also a contribution to rationalisation within the firm and ensures that the firm can calculate its labour cost for the duration of the collective agreement (standardisation function).

Collective agreements regulate only relations between employers and workers or apprentices. They can neither establish norms for the relationship with third parties nor regulate the private life of the employees. The latter applies in particular to the manner of spending wages. Exceptions to this principle may be made for schemes of wealth formation and for the raising of contributions for joint projects of the parties to the collective agreement.

The collective agreement is a contract in private law which also binds third parties. If difficulties arise in the interpretation of its provisions, in principle the interpretation which is more favourable to the worker is to be applied.

Normally, regular workers and apprentices can be covered by collective agreements. Since 1974, however, groups of persons who are not regular employees but who for reasons of economic dependency are comparable to employees and who are in need of protection, can also be covered by collective agreements. This applies especially to free-lance artists and journalists who derive most of their income from work for broadcasting and television stations.

(ii) *Types of Collective Agreements*   Collective agreements may be

distinguished by contents:
— collective agreements on wages and salaries (*Lohntarifverträge*). Their main content is the rate of pay. Normally, their duration is about one year;
— collective agreements on general conditions of work (*Manteltarifverträge*), which regulate issues such as terms of notice, working hours, vacation, protection against the effects of rationalisation, wealth-formation schemes and workplace safety. Typically, they have durations of up to five years;
Or they may be distinguished by coverage:
— industry-wide collective agreements (*Verbandstarifverträge*) which are concluded for all the firms of an industry or of a branch of industry in a bargaining area except those for whom individual firm agreements are concluded;
— single-firm collective agreements (*Firmentarifverträge*), which pertain to one firm only.

In the Federal Republic of Germany, the industry-wide collective agreement is the rule, and the single-firm collective agreement is the exception. The best-known example of the latter is the singe-firm collective agreement of the Volkswagen Corporation.

In 1983 about 7,000 new collective agreements were concluded; according to the Ministry of Labour and Social Affairs, the following is an approximate breakdown of this figure:
— 300 collective agreements on general conditions of work with a validity of several years.
— 1,900 agreements in which the two parties mutually agree to supplement or alter such collective agreements on general conditions.
— 4,200 collective agreements on wages and salaries.
— 600 collective agreements on apprenticeship remunerations.

Including the newly concluded agreements, there existed about 43,000 valid collective agreements in 1983. Of those, about 28,000 were industry-wide collective agreements and 15,000 single-firm collective agreements. Between 1949 and 1983 about 201,000 collective agreements were concluded.[1]

1. Data from W. Adamy and J. Steffen (eds.), *Handbuch der Arbeitsbeziehungen*, Bonn, 1985, pp. 228f.

(iii) *Legal Minimum Standards*   The parties negotiating collective agreements act within a framework of existing state regulations. There is a lower limit which is represented by legal minimum standards established to protect the worker against encroachments by the employer, against excessive physical demands and against dangers which result from work. Particularly important are regulations regarding dismissal, vacations, working hours and safety standards. Most conditions laid down in collective agreements are much more favourable to the worker than the legal minimum provisions. These legal minimum standards are relevant in particular to smaller marginal groups of the workforce such as domestic servants, who are not normally covered by collective agreements.

(iv) *Form of the Collective Agreement and Communication to the Workers*   A collective agreement is valid when it is signed by the contracting parties. The conclusion, any alteration, nullification and the declaration of the collective agreement to be generally binding (*Allgemeinverbindlichkeitserklärung*; see below, pp. 80f.) are registered with the Federal Ministry of Labour and Social Affairs. This register is open to public scrutiny. The employer must make all collective agreements affecting the firm accessible to workers.

(v) *Conclusion and Termination of Collective Agreements*   For the parties to a collective agreement the signing of the agreement marks the beginning of their mutual rights and obligations, including the peace-keeping obligation. These mutual rights and obligations end with the termination of the collective agreement, which can take place with the expiration of a period, if the agreement was concluded for a specific period only, or by nullification of the collective agreement through mutual consent of the parties to the agreement, or by the giving of notice for termination of the agreement in compliance with the terms of notice specified in the agreement. It is also possible to give notice of termination at any time if there is an important reason. The conditions under which the parties to the collective agreement may begin industrial action are in most cases specified by separate arbitration agreements between the contracting parties.

(b) *Applicability of the Collective Agreement to Individual Work Contracts*

(i) *Work Contracts Automatically Covered*   Norms of the collective agreement which refer to the individual work contract are binding only for those work contracts which are subject to the agreement. That is, they apply to workers who are members of the particular union which is party to the agreement and who are employed by an employer who belongs to the employers' association which is also party to the agreement. The contracts of these workers are automatically changed by the new collective agreement. Incidentally, when he is hired the worker is not obliged to disclose to the employer the fact that he is a union member. Even if he has deliberately concealed his union membership from the employer, he can still claim the application of the collective agreement to his work contract. At that point, however, he has to produce evidence that he is a union member. In practice this is of little significance because employers usually grant the improved conditions arising from a new collective agreement to their non-unionised workers as well.

If a worker moves from one industry to another, he has to change unions. If employer and worker on conclusion of the work contract were both subject to a collective agreement, this collective agreement has to be adhered to until it is terminated, even if either employee or employer leave their respective association before that date.

The question of which collective agreement is applicable to a particular firm is determined by the industry in which the firm has its main activity, for example chemicals or construction, or if collective agreements exist for branches of this industry, by a branch. The criterion is which work activity predominates in the firm. Since in one firm only one 'set' of collective agreements (collective agreements on wages and salaries and collective agreements on general conditions of work) can be applied, a mason employed in a chemical factory is also subject to the collective agreement of the chemical industry. He has a claim to the wages of the chemical industry's wage group which is equivalent to his qualification as a mason.

The area to which a collective agreement is applicable is usually specified in the agreement. Most collective agreements

79

are negotiated in and apply to bargaining areas which are somewhat smaller than the *Länder*; for example, the metal industry has fourteen separate areas which are covered by particular collective agreements. This arrangement, however, is less chaotic than it looks: normally, one bargaining area takes the lead in the round of collective-agreement negotiations, and once a settlement has been reached there, the other bargaining areas follow more or less along the same lines. Usually, a labour union chooses a fairly prosperous bargaining area for the opening round of collective bargaining. This has the typical consequence of confining a labour dispute in a given industry to the leading area. Although there is no requirement that the other bargaining areas follow suit, the parties to collective agreements in the other bargaining areas orientate themselves towards the agreement reached first. This procedure helps to avoid actual labour conflicts. It is, moreover, not uncommon that one industrial union sets an example and other unions take the agreement reached by this union as a guideline. The collective agreements negotiated by I.G. Metall have often served as models for the other unions.

(ii) *The Declaration of a Collective Agreement to be Generally Binding* Normally, only the organised workers and employers are subject to a collective agreement. Under certain conditions, however, the collective agreement can be made generally binding on all workers and employers of an industry. This is declared by the federal minister of labour and social affairs on the request of one of the parties to the agreement. The federal minister — or the *Länder* authority to which he may delegate this function — can do this only in agreement with a Collective Agreement Committee, which is made up of representatives of the trade union and the employers' association.

The preconditions for this declaration are:
— the employers who are subject to the collective agreement must employ at least 50 per cent of the workers to whom the collective agreement is applicable;
— the declaration of a collective agreement to be generally binding must be called for in the public interest, because without this measure, working conditions in an area would drop below a socially acceptable level.

About 600 collective agreements have been declared to be generally binding. About 4.4 million workers, amounting to about 20 per cent of all workers, are employed in industries which are subject to such generally binding agreements. The affected industries are mainly building, textile and metal crafts in which many small firms exist which are not members of employers' associations. It is not necessary that *all* collective agreements in an industry be declared generally binding. For example, in the building industry only the collective agreements on general conditions which regulate issues such as working time, supplementary pension funds or schemes of wealth formation for workers have been declared to be generally binding, but not the collective agreements on wages and salaries.

(iii) *Application of the Regulations of Collective Agreements by Mutual Consent* In a situation where only one or even neither of the parties to an individual work contract is a member of the associations which are parties to a collective agreement, the employer and the employee may nevertheless agree to apply the regulations of the collective agreement. In such a case the regulations of the collective agreement are not legally binding norms which automatically determine the content of the work contract. They are introduced by mutual consent and on the basis of a private agreement. In consequence, these rights and obligations can also be changed by private agreement later, even to the disadvantage of the worker. In such a case the contents of the individual contract looks identical for union members (for whom the norms of the collective agreement apply by law) and for non-union members (for whom the same norms apply by private agreement); however, the rights of the latter are less well protected.

In theory an employer could introduce differentials in wages and working conditions between union members and non-union members. In reality, however, there is no such discrimination, and the benefits contained in a new collective agreement are extended by the employer to the non-unionised workers. Typically, a clause is added to the individual labour contract referring to the relevant collective agreement. Whenever a new collective agreement comes into force, all individual labour contracts are adjusted accordingly. In this way the employer avoids discrimination between workers who are union members and those who are not.

(c) *Obligatory Elements of the Collective Agreement*

The obligations arising from the collective agreement are binding only on the parties to the agreement and not on the individual worker or employer. Consequently, no direct relationship is established between the trade union and the individual employer (with the exception of the single-firm collective agreement) or between the employers' association and the individual worker. If the employer violates his obligations to his employees as they are specified in the collective agreement, he cannot be taken to court by the trade union but only by the employee himself. Because workers, especially in smaller firms, are reluctant to sue their employer if they want to continue working with him, the effect is that rights to which workers are contractually entitled may not always be granted to them in practice. All the union can do is to complain to the employers' association and demand that it should influence its member to abide by the terms of the agreement.

(i) *Peace-Keeping Obligation* The most important obligation of the parties to a collective agreement is to keep peace on the labour front during the duration of a collective agreement. This means that the parties to the collective agreement cannot make fresh demands concerning issues which are the subject of the collective agreement; most importantly, they cannot embark on industrial action to obtain these demands. On the contrary, the trade unions have to use their influence with their members to induce them to abide by an existing agreement. This is of course also true of the employers' association and its members.

Even a spontaneous strike by a union is unlawful and may make the union liable for damages if the employers can prove that the trade union instigated the strike. A famous case of the breach of the peace-keeping obligation is the 1956–7 metalworkers' strike in Schleswig-Holstein. The I.G. Metall held a strike ballot before the previous collective agreement had expired. This was ruled to violate the peace-keeping obligation, with the consequence that the Schleswig-Holstein I.G. Metall was ordered to pay DM40 million in damages to the employers (see also pp. 187ff.). The fear of the consequences of violating this peace-keeping obligation has the effect that whenever workers embark upon a 'spontaneous strike' to express their dissatisfaction with some issue, their trade union immediately denounces this action and avoids using the term 'strike' in that context. These obligations can put the unions and their officials into odd situations. Even if the workers themselves are ready for a strike and if the union officials personally think that industrial action is justified, the trade union as an organisation is obliged to calm the workers. This means that union officials have to take an action which, on the face of it and in the view of the workers, favours the employer — a practice which is hardly conducive to creating a strong sense of solidarity between workers and trade unions. Recently, however, such stoppages — or spontaneous warning strikes — in the opening phase of collective-agreement negotiations have become accepted as legitimate expressions of the workers' feeling.

The peace-keeping obligation, however, does not prevent industrial action regarding issues not covered in the existing collective agreement. If *any* industrial action is to be excluded (absolute peace-keeping obligation), this has to be specified in the agreement.

The peace-keeping obligation can be extended by arbitration agreements. They play an important role, and arbitration agreements have been concluded in the public services, in the metal industry, in the chemical industry and in food-processing, among others. The typical stipulation in these agreements is that industrial action can be taken only after the failure of an arbitration committee to settle the conflict peacefully. Such arbitration committees are made up of an equal number of representatives from both parties to collective bargaining plus an independent chairman.

(ii) *Obligation to Strive for Compliance* The parties to the collective agreement are obliged to use their influence and all their statutory powers to induce their members to abide by the agreement. They are, however, not obliged to compel every single member to obey the regulations. If, for example, an individual employer who is in financial difficulties temporarily pays a lower wage, this may be acceptable. But both parties to the collective agreement have to support the system in general, and in particular they have to intervene against a systematic erosion of the system.

(iii) *Outsider Clauses and Differentiation Clauses*   The legality of outsider clauses and differentiation clauses is a controversial issue. The outsider clause tries to establish the principle that workers who are not members of the union and to whom consequently the collective agreement does not apply automatically cannot be employed under working conditions which are worse than those of union members. Differentiation clauses, on the other hand, aim at the opposite. They try to secure better working conditions for union members than for outsiders. The Federal Labour Court has declared that both types of clauses violate either the positive or the negative freedom of association. However, this decision has not yet been confirmed by the Federal Constitutional Court, where the issue is pending.

(d) *Normative Elements of the Collective Agreement*

(i) *Norms Pertaining to the Individual Work Contract and General Norms*   The norms of the collective agreement may deviate from legal regulations on the same issue only to the advantage of the worker. This may apply to matters such as holidays, minimum wages and maximum working time. A less advantageous regulation is possible only if the law specifically permits this; examples are the regulations concerning terms of notice and vacations.

In addition to the norms regulating the individual work contracts, collective agreements may also incorporate general norms concerning specific plant matters, like work security, recreation and welfare facilities made available by the firm as well as general rules for the organisation of working life, such as non-smoking regulations, gate controls and sanctions for unruly behaviour. In principle, also, provisions changing the works constitution — for example, extensions of the rights of bodies representing the interest of workers — may be included. But because the Works Constitution Act 1972 has regulated this issue in detail, there is little room for regulation by collective agreement which would apply to all employers of an industry.

(ii) *Direct and Compulsory Validity of the Norms of the Collective Agreement* The collective agreement lays down the norms which have been established by the parties to collective bargaining. Therefore all work contracts which are subject to the collective agreement are automatically altered accordingly.

This applies even if no specific agreement to this effect has been concluded between worker and employer and even if neither worker nor employer knows the collective agreement. For example, a worker has a claim to the wages of the collective agreement even if his individual work contract specifies a lower remuneration. A deviation from the conditions of the collective agreement to the disadvantage of the worker is possible only if the collective agreement itself allows this. This, however, is extremely rare.

On the other hand, deviations from the conditions of the collective agreement which are to the advantage of the worker are permitted both in the individual work contract and in plant regulations (*Betriebsvereinbarungen*). Certain deviations, however, cannot be laid down in formally agreed plant regulations, because matters which are usually regulated by collective agreement, such as wages and working conditions, cannot be made the subject of plant regulations unless a specific clause in the collective agreement allows this (Works Constitution Act 1972, Article 27, paragraph 3).

The decisions as to whether a regulation in an individual work contract or in a plant regulation is objectively more advantageous than the provision of the collective agreement, depends solely on the comparison of these regulations. Other considerations are immaterial; for example, the argument that a work contract with conditions which are inferior to the conditions laid down in the collective agreement is still preferable to no work contract at all because the firm cannot afford to pay the high wages and has to close down, is irrelevant.

It is not unusual to find that the actual wages paid are higher than the wages stipulated in the collective agreement. This is because the industry-wide collective agreements are geared to the average or the marginal firms of an industry. This allows the firms which are better off to pay more to their employees either in the form of generally higher wages or through special bonuses. In the past, unions have often been successful in their attempt to include such extra benefits in collective agreements. Examples are Christmas bonuses, extra vacation money and employers' contribution to wealth-formation schemes, which were voluntary benefits at first granted by individual employers but subsequently became firmly established elements of collective agreements.

If the wages actually paid exceed the wages of the collective agreement, a problem arises later on for the conclusion of a new collective agreement. The problem is eased if the parties to the individual work contract have included a clause to regulate this; they may have agreed, for example, that the wage stipulated in the new collective agreement is to be topped up either by a certain sum or by a percentage of that wage. In this case a new collective agreement with a wage increase will not alter the situation decisively. If, however, the work contract does not contain such a provision, the wage does not increase automatically and the wage stipulated in the individual work contract remains in force until the wage increase of the collective agreement exceeds this contractual level or until the provisions of the individual work contract are changed by mutual agreement.

The consequence is that although their work contracts are subject to a new collective agreement which stipulates a considerable wage increase, workers may not get a higher income. Business may be sluggish and the firm may be trying to cut down on labour costs. In this case the new collective agreement may have no effect on the actual wages paid to the workers. This is a cause of great dissatisfaction among the unions, and they have been trying to introduce a clause into collective agreements which guarantees the worker the existing margin over the wages of the collective agreement for the future as well (*Effektivitätsklausel*). The Federal Labour Court has ruled such clauses to be null and void. The same applies to the opposite, the so-called compensating clause (*Verrechnungsklausel*). Such a clause forbids the employer to increase in individual work contracts the new wage of the collective agreement by the margin which was paid before the new collective agreement. In other words, both attempts by the trade unions to get a better grip on wages by incorporating the extra wages into collective agreements or by forbidding firm-specific payments of higher wages than are laid down in collective agreements, were thrown out by the courts.

The payment of wages above the level stipulated in the collective agreement is the cause of wage drift. If wage drift is sizeable, the worker may not really see any direct connection between the efforts of the trade union and his personal income. It also has the effect that the trade unions lose their grip on the wages actually paid: if wage increases stipulated in a new collective agreement are absorbed to a large extent by reducing the margin of additional wages outside the collective agreement, then the trade union cannot claim to have won a major success. Altogether, wage drift allows the employer a certain arbitrariness in the determination of wages above the level of the collective agreement and it gives the works council a chance to secure extra benefits for the workers of the firm. It also makes for wage differentiation even between workers with the same qualifications in the same industry and in the same location; they are merely working for different companies. Both effects are resented by the trade unions. But since the Federal Labour Court has ruled against the inclusion of a guarantee for wages above collective-agreement level into collective agreements, trade unions are in a difficult situation: either they accept that, because of wage drift their relevance for the determination of the wages actually paid diminishes, hence reducing the inclination of workers to join the unions, and that — due to the diverging pace of wage drift in the different firms — wage differentiation which is not conducive to the solidarity of workers results; or they can try to extract the maximum from individual firms by not aiming at industry-wide collective agreements with the concomitant of 'average' wages, but aiming for more limited coverage. So far, such a policy has been rejected by the unions on the grounds that this would be harmful to worker solidarity: workers in a thriving firm with a special agreement applicable to that firm are less likely to support a fight for a wage increase in a collective agreement covering the remaining firms of the industry.

(e) *Arbitration*

If a trade union and an employers' association have failed to reach a new collective agreement by negotiation, an arbitration process is set in motion which tries to bridge the diverging interests in order to avert a strike. Even when a labour conflict is well on its way it is always possible to attempt another arbitration to end the conflict. The main aim of arbitration is to arrive at a new collective agreement and in this way to preserve or to restore industrial peace.

One can distinguish arbitration by mutual agreement from compulsory arbitration by government intervention. The latter does not play any role in the Federal Republic. The foundation of the arbitration procedure by mutual agreement is a model arbitration agreement which was concluded between the DGB and the BDA in 1954. The two sides arrived at this arbitration agreement because there was a danger that the federal government would regulate the arbitration procedure by law if the trade unions and the employers' associations had not taken action themselves.

Normally, the parties to collective bargaining have agreed by means of specific arbitration agreements that an attempt at reconciliation must be made before the beginning of a labour dispute. The arbitration committees are made up of an equal number of representatives from either side and an independent chairman. If the arbitration committee does not arrive at a proposal for a settlement or if the proposal is not accepted by both parties, arbitration has failed, the peace-keeping obligation ends and industrial action can begin. If, on the other hand, the parties to collective bargaining reach a consensus in the arbitration procedure, the result is a new collective agreement.

3.4 Legal Regulation of Labour Disputes

No legal framework has been provided by legislation for industrial action. The existing legal framework of labour disputes, therefore, is largely based on case law established by the courts. In particular, the Federal Labour Court has rendered a number of important verdicts on basic issues in this field, some of which remain highly controversial.

(a) *General Remarks on Strikes and Lock-outs*

Under an interpretation of the Basic Law the strike is recognised as the collective weapon of the workers. If the parties to a collective agreement cannot reach a consensus either by negotiation or by arbitration, trade unions have at their command the strike weapon to induce the employers to sign a new collective agreement. As the Federal Labour Court stated in its judgment of 10 June 1980, trade unions depend on the readiness of the employers to conclude a collective agreement. They cannot assume that the employers have a comparable interest in the conclusion of a new collective agreement and therefore are ready to negotiate. Generally, the existing situation — continued validity of the previous collective agreement — and possibly even a situation without a valid collective agreement, is more advantageous to the employer than to the worker. Historically, it was always the trade union which had to demand improvements and to fight for them. Ever since the Federal Republic of Germany came into existence, productivity and prices have been increasing. Consequently, trade unions were pressed to demand adjustments even if they aimed at no more than to maintain the existing standard of living of the workers and the given distribution of incomes between workers and employers. Basically, employers have always opposed the workers' demand for wage increments, a reduction of working hours and a slowing down of the process of further automation with the help of policies designed to protect workers affected by rationalisation. In this conflict of interests, negotiations for a new collective agreement without the ultimate weapon of calling a strike would amount to little more than 'collective begging' (Federal Labour Court). In short, there is no controversy over the general permissibility of strikes, although when it comes to particulars the right to strike is in some respects legally restricted.

On the other hand, the main weapon of the employers — the look-out — remains highly controversial. For example, Article 29 of the Constitution of the State of Hesse specifically outlaws the lock-out. But at present the employers' right to lock-out workers is in principle accepted by a ruling of the Federal Labour Court. Previously, the Federal Labour Court had considered both the offensive as well as the defensive lock-out to be necessary to secure the required parity of the parties to a labour conflict. In its judgment of 10 June 1980, however, it recognised that the arguments which justify the strike cannot be applied without qualification to the lock-out. According to this judgment, the employers and their associations depend considerably less than the trade unions on industrial action to press their demands. This, however, does not mean that the employers do not require any weapon and that lock-outs should be forbidden altogether. One can conceive of trade-union strategies which alter the equilibrium in favour of the unions. Strikes which are strategically limited both in space and time (selective strikes) could unleash acute conflicts of interest between employers and in this way endanger the solidarity which the employers' association needs for collective bargaining. In this case the employers' side can only regain parity in the labour conflict if it has a defensive weapon at its disposal. This became the decisive argument in favour of legalising a defensive lock-out. The Federal Labour Court has ruled that a general prohibition of lock-outs as it is written into the Hessian Constitution is incompatible with the general system of collective bargaining. So far the Federal Constitutional Court has avoided taking a position on this issue.

The unions' position is that lock-outs are generally illegal. In their opinion, only the possibility of the strike establishes the parity of the parties in collective bargaining. The employers have control over the means of production, therefore are economically more powerful, and hence can see a labour conflict through without endangering their existence. In particular, during a strike employers do not have to pay wages of workers if production has to be discontinued for reasons attributable to the labour side. This gives the employers a weapon which comes close to a lock-out. This argument is specifically accepted in a judgment of the Federal Labour Court of 10 June 1980. On the other hand, a strike demands heavy sacrifices from the workers and implies a risk to their jobs which endangers the material existence of the workers. Since union members on strike get strike pay from the union, labour conflicts are also financially burdensome for the union. Allowing employers the option of resorting to a lock-out changes the equilibrium to the advantage of the employers. A strategic use of lock-outs by the employers could eventually exhaust union finances, because the union also grants strike pay to all union members who have been locked out. Consequently, the trade union simply could not finance another major labour dispute for several years to come. This, however, would destroy the parity of position of the parties in collective bargaining and would interfere with the autonomy of collective bargaining.

The employers, on the other hand, argue that the lock-out weapon is necessary in order to reach parity of power in bargaining. Only the threat of a possible lock-out would pave the way for a fair compromise within a reasonable time. At any rate, after the Second World War an offensive lock-out has never been used to start a labour conflict.

The recent discussion about lock-outs is the result of the changed strike strategy on the part of the trade unions. Rather than calling a total strike in a bargaining area they call selective strikes in key firms. In these firms production is brought to a standstill. Sooner or later all firms which are connected to the key firms, either before or after in the production process, have to stop production either because essential supplies are not forthcoming or because finished products keep piling up. The more highly developed the specialisation between firms in an economy, the more effective this strategy will be. It has been called a minimax strategy: with a minimum of strikers — and therefore with minimum cost to the union — these strikes have a maximum impact on the employers in the whole industry. The employers' response to these strikes was to lock-out workers in all firms affected indirectly by the strike, resulting in an escalation of the labour conflict. Because unions give financial support to union members who are locked out, industrial conflicts are thus made more expensive for labour.

(b) *The Strike*

(i) *Definition and Types of Strike* A strike is the joint and planned stoppage of work by several workers with the intention of resuming their work once their demands have been met through a new collective agreement. In a comprehensive strike all the employers in an industry are affected by walk-outs of unionised workers and in most cases all workers of a firm stop working. Equally legal is a partial or selective strike in which work in particular departments of a plant or in certain key plants or firms of an industry is stopped. Such a strike decisively affects the working of a firm or even of a whole industry. In a general strike all workers stop working and bring the whole economy to a standstill. Short plant stoppages which are related to collective negotiations in progress (warning strikes) are in principle permitted after the peace-keeping obligation has expired, if they are supported by the trade union.

The DGB unions have agreed on guidelines for the conduct of labour conflicts. Similar guidelines have been adopted by the German Union of Salaried Employees. According to these guidelines, preparatory measures, including strike ballots, are not part of the industrial action as such. The following phases can be distinguished:

— the trade union's decision to commence the strike;
— the trade union's decision to carry out a strike ballot among its members;
— the call upon union members to participate in the strike ballot;
— the strike ballot; according to the constitutions of most trade unions, at least 75 per cent of the participating union members have to vote in favour of a strike;
— the approval of the resolution to strike by the Federal Executive Board of the trade union;
— the issuing of the order to strike;
— the actual stoppage of work.

(ii) *Criteria for a Legal Strike*   The labour courts have developed general legal principles concerning the permissibility of strikes. The most important principle is that the strike must be 'commensurate'. This means that both in its objectives as well as in the procedure followed, the strike must take the economic situation into account; nor is the general welfare of society to be patently violated. The Federal Labour Court has defined certain criteria of a legal strike.

— It must aim at a result which can be made the subject of a collective agreement. What cannot be regulated in a collective agreement, for example entrepreneurial decisions on pricing policy and investment, cannot be made the objec-

tive of a strike. Consequently, the scope of the autonomy of collective bargaining automatically restricts the right to strike; for example, it rules out political strikes or strikes which protest against entrepreneurial decisions in the sphere of marketing.
— The strike must not violate the peace-keeping obligation. During the duration of the collective agreement no strike aiming to alter its provisions is permitted.
— The strike has to be organised by a trade union, or at least the trade union has to support the strike after it has started. Moreover, the company has to belong to the sphere of the trade union.
— The strike must not aim at compelling the state or state authorities to some action. Political strikes are not permitted because in a parliamentary democracy political decisions are to be taken by the representative institutions. Only an unconstitutional exercise of state powers could justify a political strike.
— The strike must not violate the principle of commensurateness, which implies (i) the strike has to be suitable and necessary for attaining legal objectives and subsequent peaceful working relations; (ii) a strike is legal only as a last resort, after all other possibilities of reaching an agreement have been exhausted (therefore, in principle, an attempt at arbitration must precede the actual strike); (iii) measures taken as part of an industrial action must not be excessive, they have to be commensurate to the objective pursued; (iv) after the end of the strike, both parties to the conflict must contribute to a speedy and comprehensive restoration of industrial peace; (v) the common welfare of society is not to be blatantly violated.
— The strike has to be conducted according to the rules of fairness and must not aim at the destruction of the opponent.
— During the work stoppage necessary maintenance work must be carried out to prevent lasting damage to production facilities.
— The strike must not offend public morale.
— The strike must not be in violation of a special interdiction to strike, such as applies to civil servants.
— Strikes which aim at the settlement of conflicts at plant

level, in particular those affecting the works constitution, are also illegal. Such conflicts have to be settled by the appropriate procedures, provided mainly in the Works Constitution Act (*Betriebsverfassungsgesetz*).

— The strike must not aim at an objective which can also be reached by taking the matter to the courts. For example, an unjustified dismissal must not lead to a work stoppage.

— With few rare exceptions, 'sympathy strikes' in support of the demands of another union are also illegal.

Unquestionably legal, therefore, is a strike aiming at better wages and working conditions, provided the demands are moderate and all channels of peaceful reconciliation have been exhausted.

A work stoppage which is not approved and supported by the trade union even after it has taken place, is a spontaneous strike and, as such, illegal. Such spontaneous strikes played a role in 1969 when the collective agreements were based on forecasts predicting much less favourable trends in the economy than actually occurred and workers felt cheated (see pp. 210ff.). The trade unions, however, were bound by their peace-keeping obligation. Spontaneous stoppages of a few hours — usually on the eve of wage negotiations to give weight to the demands of the union — are not classified as strikes by the labour courts.

Usually, pickets are placed at the gates of strike-bound firms. Their presence demonstrates to outsiders that the workers at the plant are on strike. They also have the purpose of preventing people who are willing to work from doing so. Pickets are allowed to convince strike-breakers by argument and persuasion; they may not resort to physical coercion and violence. Illegal actions by pickets do not make the whole strike illegal but result in the personal liability of the pickets. If a strike is called by a trade union, the law assumes that the strike aims at the regulation of working conditions and is legal in all other respects. The onus of proving the contrary rests with the person who claims the strike to be illegal.

What represents an 'industrial action' remains controversial: is it the union's recommendation addressed to its members to vote for a strike in a strike ballot, or is it the order to strike or the actual stoppage of work?

(iii) *Rules Regulating Labour Disputes*   The establishment of rules for the conduct of an industrial action is primarily the business of the parties to the collective agreement. They can be established in the union's constitution; for example, as we have mentioned, a provision that at least 75 per cent of the union members participating in the strike ballot have to vote in favour, is contained in the constitutions of the industrial unions. It can also be done by collective agreement; such clauses pertain, for example, to regulations concerning necessary maintenance and emergency work in plants subjected to a strike and to the question of which plants have to be excluded from a strike to protect the vital interests of society (e.g. hospitals). Also, the guidelines of the DGB specifically include the obligation to carry out such emergency work even during a strike. These obligations are binding on union members, if they are requested to do such work. According to labour court judgments, and following the principle of commensurateness, all work necessary to maintain intact the machinery and the production facilities counts as emergency labour. This ensures that after the termination of the conflict, production can be resumed without delay. Emergency work also includes all work which, if refused, would result in disproportionate damage to the employer or third parties.

(iv) *Consequences of Illegal Strikes*   An illegal strike leads to claims of compensation for damages. A famous case is the Schleswig-Holstein metal-workers' strike of 1956–7, which has already been mentioned (see pp. 82f.).

Whether the participation of an individual worker in an illegal strike justifies his dismissal depends on the particular circumstances. According to the Federal Labour Court, the interests of the opponents have to be considered carefully, in particular the degree of involvement of the worker in the strike, whether the illegality of his action could be perceived by him and whether some unlawful action of the employer had induced the worker's action. An important fact exonerating the worker would be that he could have excluded himself from the action only by breaking ranks with his fellow workers. All this, however, may excuse only the ordinary participant in such an action. If a worker is particularly militant in an illegal strike and even resorts to actions which are banned in an ordinary strike, such as the occupation of a plant, his dismissal may be justified. The participation of a worker in a short-term stoppage does not justify immediate dismissal.

(c) *The Lock-out*

(i) *Definition*   A lock-out is the planned non-admittance of workers to work and the refusal to pay their wages, carried out by one or several employers with the intention of rehiring them after the termination of the labour conflict. A lock-out can involve all the workers of the plant. But it can also be directed against striking workers only. Certain types of workers, such as specialists, or certain departments of the company, may be excluded from the lock-out. It is, on the other hand, illegal merely to lock-out members of the striking trade union and to spare the non-unionised workers, because — according to the Federal Labour Court — this would be a violation of the positive freedom of association.

(ii) *Permissibility of a Lock-out*   The Federal Labour Court has ruled the lock-out to be legal, at any rate in the form of a defensive lock-out in reaction to very narrow partial strikes. According to this judgment, lock-outs are subject to the principle of commensurateness in the same way as are strikes. This means that economic realities have to be taken into account and common welfare is not to be openly violated. It also means that the scale of the lock-out must not be excessive. In particular, the following criteria can be derived from decisions of the Federal Labour Court:

— The lock-out has to be suitable and necessary both for reaching the aims of the labour conflict and for the subsequent period of industrial peace; it is only allowed as a measure of last resort.

— The rules of fairness have to be adhered to; the lock-out should not attempt to destroy the opponent.

— The maximum area to be covered by a lock-out is the bargaining area.

— Especially when a small number of workers in key positions strike and paralyse large parts of the economy, the desire of the employers to widen the scope of the industrial conflict by locking out workers is accepted. However, the number of workers locked out has to be in proportion to the number of workers on strike. If less than 20 per cent of the workers of the bargaining region are on strike, a defensive lock-out is commensurate if it does not extend to more than an additional 25 per cent of the workers — the total of workers who are either on strike or locked out than being less than 50 per cent. A lock-out exceeding that number is not commensurate.

— On termination of the lock-out, both parties to the labour conflict have to contribute to a speedy and comprehensive restoration of industrial peace.

(iii) *Consequences of the Lock-out* Normally the lock-out suspends the work contract so that the main obligations of the work contract — the obligation to employ a worker and to pay his wages — are temporarily in abeyance. Lock-outs resulting in a dissolution of the work contract were previously admissible in particular circumstances; in view of the many restrictions imposed today, even on a 'suspending' lock-out it is highly doubtful that a 'dissolving' lock-out would now be approved by the Federal Labour Court. At any rate, a 'dissolving' lock-out cannot terminate the work contracts of specially protected workers such as pregnant women, handicapped workers and elected members of bodies representing workers' interests, in particular works councillors.

(d) *Consequences of a Legal Labour Dispute about the Work Contract*

(i) *Workers Directly Involved* Participation in an official labour dispute is no violation of the work contract; this applies both to the members of the parties to collective bargaining and to outsiders. Therefore the employer affected by a strike is not allowed to dismiss a worker on account of a breach of contract. Only if an individual worker violates the ordinary strike procedure, for example by physically attacking strike-breakers, may a dismissal be justified.

During an official labour dispute the mutual rights and obligations resulting from the work contract are suspended. This implies that the employees do not have to work; nor do they have a claim to wages. Normally, union members who are on strike and who have been members of the union for at least three months get strike pay from the union amounting to about two-thirds of their gross wages.

Non-union members participating in the strike have no claim to wages nor to support from the union. Neither does the Federal Labour Institute pay any unemployment benefit because this is considered to be an interference in the process of collective bargaining. In case of proven need, striking workers are — like everyone else — entitled to social-welfare payments.

(ii) *Workers Indirectly Affected*   Regulations are similar for workers who are indirectly affected by a labour conflict. If a department of a firm comes to a standstill because the workers in some other department are on strike and the persons who are willing to work cannot be usefully employed, the employer does not have to pay their wages. The same applies to the situation where entire companies which are not subject to the strike have to stop production because supplies are not forthcoming or because they cannot dispose of their products, owing to the strike. This at least is the situation when a company belongs to the same employers' association which is a party to the labour conflict or is organisationally linked to it.

The question of the payments by the Federal Labour Institute to workers from a different bargaining area, who cannot work or cannot work their full hours on account of the industrial action, is controversial, be it unemployment benefit or short-working subsidy. Refusal by the Federal Labour Institute to pay such subsidies means that the union members will have to rely on strike pay from their union. These demands may very soon exhaust the financial resources set aside for the labour conflict. They have the further consequence that the non-unionised members have to rely on their savings and, in case of need, fall back on social security. Non-unionised workers are likely to exert pressure on the unionised members and, through them, the union, to bring the conflict to an end. So far the Federal Labour Institute has refused to pay unemployment benefits or short-working subsidies to persons who are out of work on account of a labour dispute in another bargaining area, if the demands of the unions in both bargaining areas are almost identical. This was assumed to be the case in the labour conflict over the thirty-five hour working week in 1984. Although the demands of the various sections of the I.G. Metall were differentiated in some respects, in the opinion of the Federal Labour Institute they had the same main objective in common, that is to topple the forty-hour working week. For this reason the slightly varied demands of the various sections of the I.G. Metall were considered to be elements of the same labour dispute. Because, according to Article 116 of the Employment Promotion Act, the Federal Labour Institute is not allowed to take sides in labour conflicts, it refused payments to workers who were out of work as an indirect consequence of the strike. This decision, however, was taken to the courts, and the final verdict is still pending.

3.5 Juridification of Labour Relations

Foreign observers have often commented on the impressive detail and thoroughness of the legal regulation of industrial relations in the Federal Republic of Germany;[2] in this connection many experts have spoken of 'juridification' (*Verrechtlichung*).

The existence of very detailed legal regulations gives labour relations a somewhat conservative character because all conflicts have to be argued out within a given framework. This applies in particular to the most important economic and social conflict, the conflict between employers and workers over wages and conditions. The juridification of this relationship has two aspects. One is concerned with the question of what general ideas and ideologies and which concepts of industrial relations are to be found behind the existing regulations. The other has to do with the effect of these regulations on the behaviour of the parties to the conflict.

---

2. See, e.g., P. Gourevitch et al., *Unions and Economic Crisis: Britain, West Germany and Sweden*, London 1984, p. 92: 'The Federal Republic's industrial relations system, an unusually dense web of legal rules and regulations'. Ian Maitland, *The Causes of Industrial Disorder*, London 1983, p. 47: 'In Germany, the state has established a detailed framework of laws for the regulation of labour relations'.

(a) *Principles and Ideologies Governing the Legal Regulation of Industrial Relations*

The entire system of legal regulation — either by law or by jurisdiction — is based on a harmonious view of society and the economy. Conflicts, especially labour conflicts, are considered to be dysfunctional because they interfere with this harmony and the existing order. Consequently, a high threshold is established before the process of collective bargaining can escalate into actual industrial action. This conclusion is derived from the following considerations:

(1) the principle that a strike is only allowed as a last resort;

(2) the idea that all industrial actions are subject to the principle of commensurateness;

(3) the emphasis on the peace-keeping obligation and the narrow definition of the criteria for legality of a strike.

The first priority is to avert industrial action. If it cannot be avoided, at least it is to be confined to quite a narrowly defined setting. In legal terms this means that only trade unions — and an association has to satisfy specific legal requirements to qualify as a trade union — have the right, or rather the privilege, to strike. No informal group of workers can strike legally; it would need the support of a trade union, and the appropriate procedures have to be followed. Any deviation from this approved path may have serious consequences for the individual worker. Even trade unions are, however, only allowed to strike for certain well-defined objectives — to safeguard and to improve their working and economic situation — that is, essentially, for higher wages and better conditions. Even in the pursuit of these objectives they have to consider the general welfare; they are not allowed to try to destroy their opponent, and they are bound by the principle of commensurateness: excessive demands would make a strike illegal. Even a strike for legally approved objectives which is carried out according to the rules can only be begun after the peace-keeping obligation has expired. Violation of the peace-keeping obligation may lead to the payment of high damages to the other side. Even during the strike the union has to be indulgent with the employer: production facilities have to be kept intact and no major lasting damage must be inflicted on the employer. In all its actions the trade union has to keep in mind that the period of industrial unrest will eventually result in renewed industrial peace.

The employers, on the other hand, can only use the lock-out defensively, and they also have to observe comparable legal restrictions. The lock-out is allowed only because it is assumed to bring a labour conflict to an end more quickly. It may also be necessary to maintain the solidarity of the employers, which is essential for collective bargaining. In this way the trade unions and the employers' associations are assigned certain roles in the economic and social structure. Both are made functional parts of the institutional set-up, and it is difficult to make changes to the system. This conservatism is easily acceptable to the employers, who in their overwhelming majority wholeheartedly support the existing capitalist economy. The acceptance of the system by the trade unions, on the other hand, is far less certain. Their traditional role has been to demand reforms of the existing economic and social order. Their support of the system can only be understood in the context of historical developments and as a result of the successes of the trade unions in attaining real improvements in the situation of the worker in the field of both wages and conditions and in the extension of the welfare state; they have also won a partial realisation of co-determination rights. Consequently, the existing legal regulation of industrial relations in the Federal Republic of Germany is, on the one hand, the result of a prevailing spirit of cooperation; on the other, the material substance of the legal regulations makes it difficult for the unions to refuse further cooperation in the field of social and economic policy.

It is symptomatic that the law also supports both the existing position and the given structure of trade unions. This can be deduced from the fact that for the recognition of an association such as a trade union the Federal Labour Court demands an ability to exert pressure; this is a requirement that constitutes a major hurdle for any newly formed organisation of workers and one which protects the dominant position of the DGB trade unions.

On the other hand, the Federal Labour Court's refusal to give the trade unions some means of providing incentives for membership prevents the degree of unionisation from growing. This is not because the court lacks sympathy for the workers' cause;

jurisdiction on problems of the individual work contract tends, if anything, to lean towards the employee. We may therefore interpret the court's attitude as an expression of its satisfaction with the existing strength of the unions.

(b) *Juridification and Social Conflicts in the Federal Republic*

It has often been observed that German society has a longing for harmony and consensus and is 'conflict shy'.[3] Conflicts in general are not accepted as something normal, something without which a modern industrial society could hardly exist, but as an infringement of social harmony and the existing order of things. In such a social setting, legal regulations for the settling of conflicts become even more important than elsewhere. Public opinion is very fast in taking sides if one party to a conflict violates the peace, and even more so if it breaks the law.

Of course, no social group wants public opinion to take the side of the opponent and least of all immediately before or during a conflict. This is particularly important for trade unions, which, for a strike to be successful, have to rely on the support not only of all union members but also of the non-unionised workers, who have to join union members in work stoppages to make a strike effective. The non-unionised workers may vacillate under the impact of public opinion. The importance of public opinion may be one of the reasons why German trade unions are so keen on getting legal confirmation that their strike practices are legal and on getting lock-outs banned altogether.

There is still another aspect to juridification. Juridification means, on the one hand, an official recognition of a social group. In the case of the trade unions and employers' associations, these groups are recognised as agents who, without state interference, are authorised to bargain over wages and conditions. This official legal recognition is an important achievement of the German trade union movement. But the assumption of this role implies an acceptance of the system and its rules. The consequences of this have been pinpointed by G. Teubner who wrote:

> On the one hand, labour law protects and secures certain interests of

3. This point has been stated and discussed many times. See, e.g., Ralf Dahrendorf, *Democracy and Society in Germany*, London, 1968.

workers and guarantees the trade unions' room for action. On the other, however, social conflicts become depoliticised by the 'repressive function' of juridification because the unions' room for acting and fighting is drastically restricted. . . . Juridification therefore enhances a 'cooperative policy' of the trade unions and the cooperative policy enhances juridification.[4]

This argument links the cooperative behaviour of trade unions to the fact and process of juridification: because both parties to the conflict try to avoid a violation of the law, they want clear guidelines as to which behaviour is legally acceptable, and this in turn fosters juridification even further.

Since in collective bargaining the unions tend to take the offensive, we may say that they start with a handicap: in the eyes of the general public they are responsible for a breach of peace and harmony. In launching their attack they can hardly afford to break the established rules of procedure by introducing new forms of industrial action. It could be argued, therefore, that the detailed regulation of these matters — but also the self-imposed restrictions as they are contained, for example, in arbitration agreements between the parties to collective agreement and in the constitutions of these organisations — push the whole process of collective bargaining in a conservative direction. We may also assume that the unions' adherence to these rules works to the advantage of the defending group, that is the employer's association.

In the 1920s juridification of labour relations was opposed by the trade unions and by writers who sympathised with them because it depoliticised what was considered a genuinely political conflict (see pp. 156ff.).[5] If the unions accept juridification today, their attitude marks the transition from ideas orientated towards class conflict to a cooperative understanding of their role within the social and economic system of the Federal Republic.

---

4. G. Teubner, 'Verrechtlinung — Begriffe, Merkmale, Grenzen, Auswege', in W. Zacher et al., *Verrechtlichung von Wirtschaft, Arbeit und sozialer Solidarität*, Baden Baden, 1984, pp. 298f.

5. Ibid., p. 298.

4

The System of Workers' Participation

4.1 Introduction

Workers' participation ranges from the mere right to be informed about certain issues to workers or their representatives playing an active role in all entrepreneurial decisions. It is institutionalised by law both in private companies and in bodies of public administration.[1]

In private firms workers' representatives are involved both at the level of the plant as well as on the level of the company. Workers' participation at plant level is effected mainly through the works council (*Betriebsrat*) prescribed by the Works Constitution Act 1972 (*Betriebsverfassungsgesetz*). Participation at this level pertains essentially to questions concerning the relationship of the workers to the plant in which he or she is employed, and actual co-determination is confined to social problems. Workers' participation under the terms of the Works Constitution Act does not extend to the general policy decisions of the company, such as production and pricing policy, its external relations with banks, and so on. Participation at company level takes the form of the representation of employees or their trade unions in existing decision-making bodies of companies, most importantly the Supervisory Board (Aufsichtsrat) which appoints and supervises the management. Participation at company level applies to the full range of entrepreneurial decision-making. It is regulated in three different forms, depending on the size of the firm, on its legal status and on the industry the firm belongs to:

(1) the Co-determination Act of 1976 (*Mitbestimmungsgesetz*) applies to all limited companies which regularly employ more than 2,000 persons. In such firms 50 per cent of the members of the Supervisory Board are representatives of the employees. The top managerial personnel have their own representative,

---

1. English translations of the relevant laws are contained in Federal Minister of Labour and Social Affairs (ed.), *Co-determination in the Federal Republic of Germany*, Bonn, 1980.

who in some respects must be assumed to be closer to the capital owners; the chairman — who has a casting vote in case of a tie — cannot be appointed against the combined votes of the capital owners. Consequently, this model of co-determination falls just short of full parity between capital and labour;

(2) in all firms which regularly employ more than 500 people but which are not subject to the 1976 Co-determination Act, the employees are entitled to a one-third representation on the Supervisory Board, as stipulated by the 1952 Works Constitution Act, the predecessor of the 1972 Works Constitution Act;

(3) in all firms in the mining and the iron- and steel-producing industries which regularly employ more than 1,000 people, 50 per cent of the members of the Supervisory Board or its equivalent are representatives of the employees. The extension of this model of full parity co-determination to all major companies has been an objective of the unions in their quest for equality of capital and labour.

Participatory rights of civil service employees are regulated in the Personnel Representation Act 1955 (*Personalvertretungsgesetz*). This law provides mainly for consultative participation. It is guided by the principle of cooperation between the staff council (analogous to the works council) and the public employer in question. The federal Personnel Representation Act applies only to employees of the federal government. The various *Länder* have legislated their own personnel representation Acts which follow framework provisions contained in the federal Personnel Representation Act.

Finally there is the concept of participation at the macroeconomic level. It aims essentially at a specific representation of workers' interests in matters of economic and social policy, in particular sectoral and regional policy.[2] Although the idea is still to be found in union programmes, it has increasingly been overshadowed by the issue of workers' participation at plant and at company level and has declined in importance (see pp. 158ff.). However, some elements of this idea exist in the form of an official workers' representation in institutions of the social-

2. In two *Länder* — Bremen and Saarland — 'workers' chambers' (*Arbeiterkammern*) with compulsory membership were created to counterbalance the influence of the chambers of industry and commerce. They failed to gain major influence, and the concept was not adopted by other *Länder*.

security system, either within a tripartite structure or in a bilateral system with the employers.

4.2 Workers' Participation at Plant Level[3]

The legal basis of workers' participation at plant level is the 1972 Works Constitution Act. This act covers mainly matters concerning the organisation of work in the plant, the recruitment and dismissal of employees as well as various rights and obligations. Its regulations are primarily designed for profit-making organisations. In fact, article 118 precludes the application of some of its provisions to ideological establishments and religious communities.[4]

The Works Constitution Act provides for several bodies representing the interest of the employees. The most important of them is the works council, which in larger establishments has its own executive organ, the works committee (*Betriebsausschuss*). The economic committee (*Wirtschaftsausschuss*), the youth representation (*Jugendvertretung*) and the works meeting (*Betriebsversammlung*) are basically institutions which support the works council. A conciliation panel (*Einigungsstelle*) helps to settle conflicts between the employer and the works council. In addition to the granting of 'collective rights' to the body of employees, the Works Constitution Act also improved the legal position of the individual worker, for example by giving a right of access to his or her file.

(a) *Works Council*

(i) *General Provisions* The most important institution through which workers participate is the works council. Works councils are to be elected in all plants that have five or more permanent

3. All quotations of articles in this section refer to the 1972 Works Constitution Act, published in Federal Ministry of Social Affairs, pp. 99–192.

4. 1972 Works Constitution Act, Article 118: '(1) The provisions of this Act shall not apply to companies and plants that directly and predominantly — 1. pursue political, coalition, religious, charitable, educational, scientific or artistic aims; or 2. serve purposes of publishing or expressing opinions covered by the second sentence of section 5 (1) of the Basic Law — in so far as their application would not be in keeping with the specific nature of the company or plant. . . . (2) This Act shall not apply to religious communities or to their charitable and educational institutions irrespective of their legal form.'

Table 4.1 Numbers of members of works council

Employees	Members
5– 20	1 (works representative)
21– 50	3
51– 150	5
151– 300	7
301– 600	9
601–1,000	11
1,001–2,000	15
2,001–3,000	19
3,001–4,000	23
4,001–5,000	27
5,001–7,000	29
7,001–9,000	31

Note: In plants employing more than 9,000 employees the number of members of the works council is increased by two members for every additional 3,000 employees.

employees with voting rights, including three who are eligible. Works councils are not automatically established; either the workers themselves or a trade union represented in the plant have to seize the initiative. For this reason and because the employer especially in small companies is not always happy with the creation of a works council, some workers remain excluded from this form of participation.

The works council is a representative organ whose members are elected by all workers who are eighteen years of age or over. All employees with voting rights who have been employed in the plant for not less than six months are eligible to stand for the works council. No person external to the firm (e.g. a trade-union official who is not employed at the plant) may be elected to the works council. Also, the top executive staff are neither eligible nor entitled to vote (Art. 5). The size of the works council depends on the number of workers in the plant (Table 4.1).

There are specific provisions for the representation of minority groups. Works councillors are elected for a three-year term of office and enjoy a specific protection against dismissal. The Works Constitution Act spells out in detail the electoral procedure. The costs of the election are borne by the employer.

If a works council consists of nine or more members, it sets up a works committee made up of the chairman and the vice-chairman of the works council plus — depending on the size of the works council — additional members of the works council who are elected to this office. The works committee deals with the day-to-day business of the works council.

Normally, the works council meets during working hours. The position of works councillor is unpaid; but the employer continues to pay the regular wages plus normal increases while the works councillors are released from their work duties to the extent that this is necessary for the proper discharge of their functions (Art. 37). This includes attendance at training and educational courses to improve their qualifications as works councillors (Art. 37, para. 6). Over a total number of 300 employees, one or more works councillors are fully released from their regular works duties (Art. 38). All expenses arising out of the activities of the works council are borne by the employer; the employer provides premises, office equipment and office staff (Art. 40).

If there are several plants in a company and consequently two or more works councils, a 'central works council' made up of members of the works councils has to be established (Art. 47). This central works council deals with matters which affect the company as a whole or two or more of its plants and which the individual works councils are generally unable to settle. Similarly, in a combine (*Konzern*), a 'combine works council' may be established by resolution of the individual works councils (Art. 54). This works council deals with matters affecting the combine as a whole or two or more of its subsidiaries, which the individual central works councils are unable to settle.

(ii) *Function of the Works Council*   The works council is there to protect the interests of the workers of the plant. The workers have the right to consult the works council during working hours at a time fixed by agreement with the employer (Art. 39). The general duties of the works council are spelled out in Article 80:

(1) 1. to see that effect is given to Acts, ordinances, safety regulations, collective agreements and plant agreements for the benefit of the employees;
2. to make recommendations to the employer for action benefiting the plant and the staff;

3. to receive suggestions from employees and the youth representation and, if they are found to be justified, to negotiate with the employer for their implementation; it shall inform the employers concerned of the state of the negotiations and their results;
4. to promote the rehabilitation of disabled persons and other persons in particular need of assistance;
5. to prepare and organise the election of a youth representation and to collaborate closely with the said representation in promoting the interests of the young employees; it may invite the youth representation to make suggestions and to state its views on various matters;
6. to promote the employment of elderly workers in the plant;
7. to promote the integration of foreign workers in the plant and to further understanding between them and their German colleagues.

(2) The employer shall supply comprehensive information to the works council in good time to enable it to discharge its duties under this Act. The works council shall, if it so requests, be granted access at any time to any documentation it may require for the discharge of its duties; in this connection the works committee or a committee set up in pursuance of Article 28 shall be entitled to inspect the payroll showing the gross wages and salaries of the employees.

(3) In discharging its duties the works council may, after making a more detailed agreement with the employer, call on the advice of experts in as far as the proper discharge of its duties so requires. The experts shall be bound to observe secrecy as prescribed in Article 79, mutatis mutandis.

The works council has participatory rights in management decisions which are differentiated in the following way. Its maximum power is mainly in the area of social issues, where the works council has a genuine right of co-decision, in the sense that the employer cannot take action without the consent of the works council; the works council can also seize the initiative to bring about changes. To quote Article 87:

(1) The works council shall have a right of co-decision in the following matters in so far as they are not regulated by legislation or collective agreement:

1. matters relating to the order by operation of the plant and the conduct of employees in the plant;
2. the commencement and termination of the daily working hours including breaks and the distribution of working hours among the days of the week;
3. any temporary reduction or extension of the hours normally worked in the plant;
4. the time and place for and the form of payment of remuneration;
5. the establishment of general principles for leave arrangements and the preparation of the leave schedule as well as fixing the time at which the leave is to be taken by individual employees, if no agreement is reached between the employer and the employees concerned;
6. the introduction and use of technical devices designed to monitor the behaviour or performance of the employees;
7. arrangements for the prevention of workplace accidents and occupational diseases and for the protection of health on the basis of legislation or safety regulations;
8. the form, structuring and administration of social services where scope is limited to the plant, company or combine;
9. the assignment of and notice to vacate accommodation that is rented to employees in view of their employment relationship as well as the general fixing of the conditions for the use of such accommodation;
10. questions relating to remuneration arrangements in the plant, including in particular the establishment of principles of remuneration and the introduction and application of new remuneration methods or modification of existing methods;
11. the fixing of job and bonus rates and comparable performance-related remuneration, including cash coefficients (i.e. prices per time unit);
12. principles for suggestion schemes in the plant.

(2) If no agreement can be reached on a matter covered by the preceding subsection, the conciliation panel shall make a decision. The award of the conciliation panel shall take the place of an agreement between the employer and the works council.

Somewhat weaker is the position of the works council in matters where the employer has to seek the consent of the works council. This is true for individual measures of personnel policy such as recruiting, the grading or regrading of workers or transfers within the firm; this co-decision in individual cases of personnel policy applies only to plants with more than twenty employees with voting entitlements (Art. 99). The employer has to obtain the consent of the works council also in respect of general measures in the field of vocational training and the formulation of the personnel questionnaire.

Still weaker is the influence of the works council in all matters requiring mere consultation; this is true for all decisions relating to manpower policy and in the planning of technical production facilities which affect job requirements. The works council is to be heard in the case of dismissals of workers; dismissals where the employer failed to give a prior hearing to the works council have been declared void by the labour courts. The works council has a right to be informed in all matters which are relevant for the proper discharge of its functions, in all matters relating to personnel planning, hiring of managerial employees and — with reference to the economic committee — information relating to the economic situation of the firm.

(iii) *Obligations of the Works Council towards the Employer*
The works council and the employer are expected to work together in a spirit of mutual trust and in cooperation with the trade unions and the employers association for the good of the employees and of the plant (Art. 2). The employer and the works council hold joint meetings at least once a month; they are to discuss matters at issue in the earnest desire to reach agreement and make suggestions for settling their differences (Art. 74). In order to prevent the divulging of business secrets, all members of participating bodies are obliged to keep to themselves all matters which the employer has stated to be confidential; this obligation extends beyond their term of office.

The works council and the employer conclude plant agreements which are binding on both sides. Such plant agreements deal with all issues concerning the workforce. In principle, plant agreements should not cover issues which are typically regulated by collective agreement. In reality, however, the line is difficult to draw, and many plant agreements do in fact regulate issues which are very close to wages and working conditions. Similar to a plant agreement is the 'social compensation plan' (*Sozialplan*), which is an agreement between the employer and the works council with the purpose of minimising disadvantages to the workforce which result from major policy decisions, such as a reduction of operations or the closure of whole departments of the plant (Arts. 111, 112).

(b) *Economic Committee*

An economic committee has to be established in all companies with more than 100 regular employees. This committee consists — depending on the size of the company — of between three and seven members who are appointed by the works council; at least one of the members must be a works councillor. It is convened at least once a month. The employer or his representative must attend the meeting. The economic committee is also to be fully informed, well in advance, of the economic situation of the company and to be supplied with the relevant documentation; the company is, however, not compelled to disclose trade or business secrets. The main purpose is to inform the committee of the possible implications of particular economic developments for manpower planning. In particular, the employer has to provide information on the following issues (Art. 106, para. 3):

1. the economic and financial situation of the company;
2. the production and marketing situation;
3. the production and investment programmes;
4. rationalisation plans;
5. production techniques and work methods, especially the introduction of new work methods;
6. the reduction of operations in or closure of plants or parts of plants;
7. the transfer of plants or parts of plants;
8. the amalgamation of plants;
9. changes in the organization or objectives of plants; and
10. any other circumstances and projects that may materially affect the interests of the employees of the company.

(c) *Works Meeting*

To improve the flow of information down the line the works council should call a works meeting every three months; in fact, it is convened less frequently. This works meeting is made up of all workers of the plant; if a meeting of all employees is impracticable, departmental meetings are to be held. The works meeting is conducted by the chairman of the works council. The employer is invited to the meeting and is notified of the agenda; he is entitled to address the meeting. Work meetings take place during work-time; attendance does not result in a loss of income for the participants. The main subjects to be discussed at works meetings are issues of direct concern to the employees; these include, in particular, questions connected to collective-bargaining policy, social policy and economic matters. The meeting may make suggestions to the works council and can take a stand on its decision. Decisions of the works meeting, however, are not binding on the works council. Delegates from the trade unions represented in the plant are entitled to attend works meetings in an advisory capacity. Similarly, the employer may be accompanied by a delegate of his employers association.

(d) *Youth Representation*

Youth representations are to be elected in plants where five or more persons below the age of eighteen are employed. The youth representation is supposed to defend the specific interests of the young employees. The youth representation has the following general duties (Art. 20):

(1) 1. to request the works council to take action for the benefit of young employees especially in vocational training matters;
   2. to see that effect is given to Acts, ordinances, safety regulations, collective agreements and plant agreements in favour of the young employees;
   3. to receive suggestions from young workers, especially in matters of vocational training, and have the works council act on these suggestions if they appear justified. The youth representation shall inform the young employees concerned of the state of the negotiations and their results.

(2) The works council shall supply comprehensive information to the youth representation in good time to enable it to discharge its duties. The youth representation may request the works council to make available any documentation it may require for the discharge of its duties.

113

Youth representation delegates take part in works council meetings in a consultative capacity whenever issues which are of specific interest to the young workers are on the agenda. The youth representation may also convene works meetings for young employees.

Altogether, the youth representation is a sort of 'works council for the young'. Its suggestions are to be taken up by the ordinary works council.

(e) *Conciliation Panel*

Differences of opinion between the employer and the works council are to be settled by a conciliation panel. It is composed of an equal number of persons nominated by the employer and the works council plus an independent chairman accepted by both sides. If the two sides fail to agree on a neutral chairman, he will be appointed by a labour court.

(f) *Appraisal of Workers' Participation at Plant Level*

Workers' participation at plant level is largely non-controversial,[5] although attempts to extend the rights of the works council — for example, to give the works council effective rights of co-decision in the introduction of new technologies — meet with firm resistance by the employers.

However, the climate between management and works council seems to vary considerably. On the basis of empirical studies, H. Kotthoff has developed the following typology:[6]

(1) the works council which is respected but has an ambiguous position between workers and management;

(2) the works council which is firm in its representation of workers interest and is respected by the employer;

(3) the works council which is cooperative but acts as a countervailing power;

(4) the works council which is an organ of management;

(5) the isolated works council;

5. See, e.g., Der Bundesminister für Arbeit und Sozialordnung (ed.), *Übersicht Recht der Arbeit*, Bonn, 1981, p. 247.
6. H. Kotthoff, 'Betriebliche Interessenvertretung durch Mitbestimmung des Betriebsrates', in G. Endruweit et al. (eds.), *Handbuch der Arbeitsbeziehungen*, Berlin–New York, 1985, pp. 65–87.

(6) the ignored works council.

Types 5 and 6 were encountered mainly in smaller firms. Types 1 to 4 together account for more than 50 per cent of all companies covered by Kotthoff's study. It seems significant that no works council was found which genuinely espoused notions of class struggle.

There is no question that the existence of works councils and their rights of co-decision and information have strengthened the position of labour in the companies. In particular, the implications of all decisions on the workforce are given more emphasis than before. There is also no doubt that the works council is an important institution for the individual worker who has a grievance. Often the works council helps to secure industrial peace in the plant either by effecting changes or by explaining to the workers why a particular problem cannot be resolved; in this respect the works council has occasionally turned into an 'extended arm' of the management.

Although there are cases of irreconcilable conflict between the management and the works council, the rule is that a management which makes an effort to convince the works council by the strength of its arguments usually succeeds in securing its cooperation. And normally the management is well advised to seek the cooperation of the works council because the consent of the works council helps when it comes to the implementation of decisions. On the other hand, if the management tries to impose decisions which were taken against the advice of the works council, it can expect all kinds of trouble. This 'trouble-making potential' of the works council has been put succinctly by the manager of a large German company: 'Without the works council nothing goes, with the works council everything goes.'[7]

Since most works councillors are members of the trade union concerned, the works council could be considered as a channel through which trade unions exert some influence on firms. But this influence is not very strong. In particular, the fact that the works council's main concern is with the well-being of the workers of the plant and not necessarily with workers' interest in general or the interests of the trade unions leads to occasional tensions with the labour union. Especially the peace-keeping

---

7. Quoted in W. Streeck, 'Co-determination: The Fourth Decade', in B. Wilpert and A. Sorge (eds.), *International Perspectives on Organizational Democracy*, London, 1984, p. 406.

obligation of the works councillors prevents them from giving support to the case of the workers or the labour unions in a labour conflict. On the contrary, as the works council tends to be well informed about the overall economic situation of the firm, it often — in its desire not to endanger jobs in the firm — exerts a moderating influence on the trade union. The fact that, due to the loyalty they owe to the employer, works councillors cannot be used for union purposes and do not necessarily take a union view, has contributed to the labour unions' increasing reliance on their shop-floor representatives.

4.3 Participation at Company Level

The principle of securing the participation of the employees at company level amounts to a representation of their interests in the existing decision-making bodies of a company themselves and hence *beyond* the works council framework. It is assumed that this will result in entrepreneurial decisions which serve the interests not only of the shareholders but also of the employees. The various types of co-determination vary in respect of the relative weight given to the interests of the shareholders and the interests of the employees. This is reflected in the composition of the Supervisory Board and the Management Board and in provisions which protect the interests of the labour side against the traditionally more powerful shareholders.

All the firms which are legally subject to participation at the level of the company are also subject to the Works Constitution Act. Consequently, these two forms of workers' participation supplement each other, and an overall appraisal of workers' participation has to consider the combined effect of both.

To understand the system of co-determination one has to know that most larger companies have the legal form of joint-stock companies. By law, joint-stock companies have three organs: the Annual General Meeting, the Supervisory Board and the Management Board.

The Annual General Meeting is the assembly of the share-holders. As a rule, it takes place once a year; voting is by number of shares, not by individuals. Apart from some other matters which are basic to the company — for example, change of purpose, dissolution of the company, distribution of profits — its main function is to elect the Supervisory Board.

In practice, the Supervisory Board has a stronger position than the Annual General Meeting. Its major responsibilities are the appointment and dismissal of the Management Board as well as the supervision of the management. Moreover, the charter of the company or the Supervisory Board itself may provide that certain matters require the consent of the Supervisory Board. For example, it is quite usual that investment and expansion programmes above a certain financial volume, credits and loans above a certain limit as well as the recruitment and dismissal of top managerial staff, require the consent of the Supervisory Board. Altogether the Supervisory Board has considerable influence on major managerial decisions.

The Management Board conducts the day-to-day business of the company under its own responsibility. It has the usual entrepreneurial functions and also acts as the employer of the employees of the company. The functions of the Managerial Board are assigned to the individual members, making each member responsible for a particular field (e.g. technical, commercial, financial) or for a particular division. Irrespective of his special task, each member of the Management Board is also responsible for the overall policy of the company.

Although not all companies which fall under the respective Acts regulating co-determination are joint-stock companies, the vast majority are. For the remaining ones the law has special provisions to allow participation in a comparable way. The following description, however, concentrates on the typical case of the joint-stock company.

(a) *Co-determination in the Mining Industry and in the Iron- and Steel-Producing Industry*

In mining and in the iron- and steel-producing industry, co-determination is regulated by the Act Regarding Co-determination by Employees in the Supervisory Boards and Management Boards of Companies in the Mining Industry and in the Iron- and Steel-Producing Industry, 21 May 1951 (*Gesetz über die Mitbestimmung der Arbeitnehmer in den Aufsichtsräten und Vorständen der Unternehmen des Bergbaus und der Eisen und Stahl erzeugenden Industrie*).[8] This

117

Act was supplemented on 7 August 1956 and further amended on 6 September 1965, 27 April 1967 and 2 May 1981.

The provisions of this Act apply to companies of the specified industries with more than 1,000 regular employees. The particular features are, first, the numerical parity of capital and labour on the Supervisory Board with a neutral chairman and, second, a labour director as a member of the Management Board.

(i) *Composition of the Supervisory Board*   The smallest Supervisory Board is eleven persons strong; for larger companies it may comprise fifteen or twenty-one members. The following description and Figure 4.1 use the eleven-person Supervisory Board as an example. Shareholders and employees appoint five members each. Of the representatives of the employees, at least two must be employees of the company; one of those must be a wage-earning and the other a salaried employee. This is to ensure that both the interests of the staff as a whole and the specific interests of wage-earners and of salaried employees are represented. The employee representatives from among the staff are nominated by the works council after consultation with the trade unions represented in the company and their top organisation. The remaining three representatives do not have to be employed by the company (outside employee representatives): two of them are typically trade-union officials; one is an 'additional' member on the employee side. All three are put forward to the works council by the trade union and their top organisation after consultations with the works council; the official nomination, however, is the privilege of the works council.

Both the employee side and the shareholders' side have one additional member. According to Article 4, none of the additional members may:

(a) be a representative of a labour union or employers' association or of a central workers' or employers' organisation, or be a permanent employee or business agent of such union, association or organisation;

(b) have exercised any of the functions referred to in (a) during the

---

8. Published in English in: Federal Ministry of Labour and Social Affairs, pp. 76–83.

Figure 4.1 Co-determination in the mining and iron- and steel-producing industries

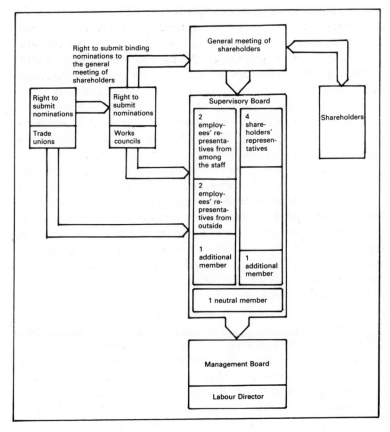

year preceding the election;

(c) belong to the company as employee or employer;

(d) have any considerable financial interest in the company.

(3) All members of the Supervisory Board shall have the same powers and duties. They shall not be bound by mandates and instructions.

The employee representatives must be formally confirmed by the general meeting of the shareholders, but the nominations advanced by the works council are binding.

The neutral eleventh member is expected to overcome a

119

deadlock between the two sides on the board. The candidate has to meet the requirements for the 'additional member' as spelled out in Article 4, above, and is nominated by a majority of the members of the Supervisory Board; at least three members from the employees' side and three members from the shareholders' side have to approve the nomination. This is to ensure that the neutral member has the confidence of both employees and shareholders and is able to reconcile differing opinions. After this, the neutral member will be elected by the general meeting of shareholders.

(ii) *Labour Director* The Act provides for the appointment of a labour director as a full member of the Management Board. This director cannot be appointed against the majority of the employee representatives and is typically responsible for matters such as personnel management, organisation of work in accordance with human needs, performance and remuneration, matters concerning collective agreements, training and further training, labour law and welfare regulations, and industrial safety and housing. These responsibilities require close cooperation with the works council.

(iii) *Supplementary Acts* The original Act has been supplemented mainly in order to secure the continued validity of workers' rights even when a company which was originally subject to this form of co-determination shifted the focus of its activities away from mining and steel as a consequence of structural change and economic concentration (see pp. 192ff.).

(b) *Co-determination under the 1976 Co-determination Act*

(i) *Legal Basis and Coverage* The Act Regarding Workers' Co-determination of 4 May 1976 (*Gesetz über die Mitbestimmung der Arbeitnehmer — Mitbestimmungsgesetz*),[9] is the basis for the participatory rights of workers in all limited companies which regularly employ more than 2,000 persons, except those which are subject to the specific regulations of the mining industry and the iron- and steel-producing industry. The Co-determination Act

9. Published in English in ibid., pp. 48–72.

does not apply to companies in the field of news media and companies with charitable, ideological or religious objectives.[10]

The characteristic features of the Act are, first, the composition of the Supervisory Board and the special position of its chairman and, second, the requirement of having a labour director on the Management Board.

(ii) *Size and Composition of the Supervisory Board*   The size of the Supervisory Board is as follows:

Up to 10,000 regular employees   12
10,000–20,000 regular employees   16
More than 20,000 regular employees   20

Half the members of the Supervisory Board are shareholders' representatives elected by the General Assembly of shareholders. The employees' side is divided into people employed by the company and outsiders (trade-union representatives); Table 4.2 shows the distribution.

Table 4.2 Distribution of members of the Supervisory Board

Size of the Supervisory Board	Shareholders representatives	Employee representatives	
		Staff members	Outsiders
12	6	4	2
16	8	6	2
20	10	7	3

The composition of employee representatives has to reflect the proportion of wage-earners and salaried employees which exists in the company; also, the representation of the salaried employees has to include top managerial staff (*leitende Angestellte*) in proportion to their presence in the firm. However, each of the three groups must be represented by at least one person.

In a company employing more than 8,000 workers, the employee representatives on the Supervisory Board are elected

10. Article 1, para. 4 of the 1976 Co-determination Act reads: 'This Act shall not appply to companies which directly and chiefly serve — 1. political, trade union, denominational, charitable, educational, scientific or artistic purposes: or 2. purposes connected with the reporting of information or the expression of opinions. . . . This Act shall not apply to religious communities and the charitable and educational institutions of such communities, irrespective of their legal form.'

indirectly through delegates; below that level there are direct elections. This rule can be changed by a majority vote of the workers. Normally, the wage-earners and the salaried employees hold separate elections; they can, however, also decide to hold joint elections. The rule concerning the indirect or direct election of the representatives emerged from a highly controversial discussion in which the trade unions were in favour of indirect elections because they assumed that this would reduce the chances of non-union candidates.

The formal election procedure is complicated, in particular in the case of indirect elections through delegates. The underlying principle, however, can be gauged from the procedure for direct elections by groups of employees. In this case the employee representatives on the Supervisory Board are elected through four different ballots:

— Election of the wage-earners' representatives: voting is limited to wage earners.
— Election of salaried employee representatives: voting is limited to the salaried employees, including the top managerial staff.
— Election of the top managerial staff representatives: voting extends to all salaried employees, including the top managerial staff.
— Election of the trade-union representatives: all employees have the right to participate.

Nominations of staff representatives require the support of 20 per cent or a maximum of 100 supporting signatures of the group of either wage-earning or salaried employees respectively; the candidates for the top managerial staff representative are nominated by the group of top managerial staff only and require 20 per cent or a maximum of fifty supporting signatures.

The resulting composition of the Supervisory Board is illustrated in Figure 4.2, showing a twenty-person Supervisory Board. This arrangement gives slightly more weight to the shareholders because the representative of the top managerial staff is likely to be more sympathetic towards the shareholders than towards the interests of the ordinary employees.

(iii) *Chairman of the Supervisory Board* Since the Supervisory Board is made up of an even number, a tied vote is possible. If a

Figure 4.2 Co-determination under the 1976 Co-determination Act: basic model company with more than 20,000 employees

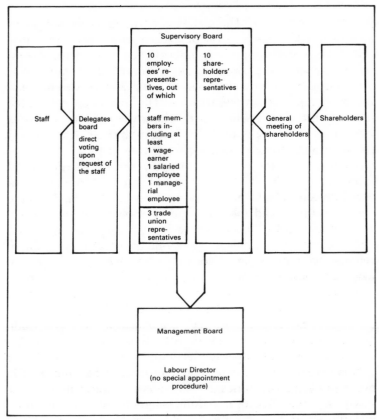

vote has to be repeated on account of a tie and the second vote again results in deadlock, the chairman of the Supervisory Board has a casting vote. This casting vote is a personal privilege of the chairman and cannot be exercised by the vice-chairman.

This makes the election of the chairman most important. In principle the chairman and the vice-chairman are to be elected by a two-thirds majority. If no two-thirds majority is attained in two consecutive ballots, the shareholders' representatives elect the chairman, and the employee representatives elect the vice-chairman from among their members. As a result, the chairman will normally be a shareholders' representative, and the vice-chairman will normally be an employee representative.

(iv) *Management Board*   The members of the Management Board are appointed by the Supervisory Board with a two-thirds majority. Where this majority is not attained, a mediation committee is called upon. This mediation committee is composed of the chairman, the vice-chairman as well as one shareholders' and one employees representative. The mediation committee submits a list of nominations to the Supervisory Board; the list is then subject to majority decisions, and in the case of a repeated tie, the chairman exercises the casting vote.

A labour director with specific powers in staff and social matters is appointed as a full member of the Management Board. In contradistinction to the co-determination model in the mining industry and the iron- and steel-producing industries, he is appointed by the same procedure as the other members. This means, the employee representatives have no right of vetoing his appointment. Normally, however, only a person who has the confidence of the employees is elected labour director.

(v) *Controversy over the 1976 Co-determination Act*   The trade unions were very disappointed with the Co-determination Act because it fell short of their model of full-parity representation of capital and labour on the Supervisory Board like that in the mining and steel industries. Nevertheless, they accepted the Act — which was passed by the Bundestag with an overwhelming majority — as the best they could get in the given political circumstances.[11]

The employers, on the other hand, felt that the 1976 Co-determination Act was a first step away from capitalism and would endanger the entrepreneurial rights. The Federal Constitutional Court had ruled on other occasions that the Basic Law does not guarantee the existing economic and social system, in particular that the 'social market economy' is not specifically protected by the Basic Law. In fact it had even gone so far as to state that the Basic Law is neutral on the question of the econ-

11. The law was passed by a coalition of the Social Democratic Party and the Free Democratic Party; the Free Democratic Party strongly opposed any full-parity model.

omic order. There was hence little chance of the employers succeeding in a suit based on such general issues. They therefore chose to call into question the constitutionality of individual provisions of the law, and on 29 June 1977 nine firms and twenty-nine employers associations lodged an appeal with the Federal Constitutional Court against the main provisions of the Co-determination Act. The employers justified their constitutional appeal as follows:

1. The Co-determination Act contains a provision on the right of employees to an equal say in the Supervisory Board and this will lead sooner or later to an equal number of employees' and shareholders' representatives in management.
2. The provisions of the Co-determination Act and those of the new Works Constitution Act of 1972 mean that the employees' rights will prevail and thus lead to 'supra-parity'.
3. Hence, the Co-determination Act infringes the property guarantee contained in Article 14 of the Basic Law. Shareholders' property is fundamentally affected both in the substance of members' rights as well as in that of the value of their property.
4. The Co-determination Act contains elements of an enforced amalgamation between shareholders and employees and thus infringes the freedom of association pursuant to Article 9, para. 1 of the Basic Law.
5. Furthermore, the Act infringes entrepreneurial freedom as part of the right freely to choose one's trade, occupation or profession (Article 12 of the Basic Law).
6. Finally, the Co-determination Act offends the freedom of association (Article 9, para. 3 of the Basic Law). The employers argued that co-determination in companies makes the employers' associations dependent on the opposing side and thus renders the collective bargaining system unworkable.
7. All things considered, the Co-determination Act results in a reshaping of the structure of the economy and of labour, which would only have been admissible by a law enacted to amend the Basic Law.[12]

This challenge against a properly ratified Act of parliament resulted in considerable tensions between the trade unions and the employers associations and provided the direct cause for the

12. Federal Minister of Labour and Social Affairs, pp. 23f.

withdrawal of the DGB from the 'Concerted Action' (see pp. 205ff.). These tensions were further heightened when some companies took organisational measures to evade co-determination altogether; they did this by changing the legal form of the company, or by splitting a large company into several smaller legally autonomous companies. Also, the employers' associations issued guidelines which gave advice on how to minimise the impact of co-determination, for example by changing the standing orders of the Supervisory Board in a way which reserved vital decisions to committees of the Supervisory Board.

The appeal itself was dismissed by the Federal Constitutional Court on 1 March 1979, when it ruled that the contested provisions of the Co-determination Act were without qualification consistent with the Basic Law.[13] In its judgment the Federal Constitutional Court warned against general inferences from its verdict: 'The subject of our examination is solely the contested provisions of the Co-determination Act submitted for examination; no decision had to be taken on whether other provisions of co-determination for employees are consistent with the Basic Law'[14]

Directly answering the points raised by the employers, it stated that the Co-determination Act established neither legally nor factually full parity for the labour side in the company. In particular, on account of the casting vote of the chairman of the Supervisory Board, the capital owners had the edge over the labour representatives. Moreover, the group of employee representatives in the Supervisory Board is — due to the guaranteed seat for at least one member of the top managerial staff — less coherent than that of the shareholders. This preponderance remained unaffected by the co-existence of co-determination at company level and workers participation at plant level because both forms of participation occur in organs with different functions and by virtue of different procedures. Consequently, there is no accumulation of co-determination powers. Contrary to the hopes of many employers, however, the Federal Constitutional Court did not make the preponderance of the shareholders a

13. The judgment on the Co-determination Act is summarised in a statement from the Public Relations Office of the Federal Constitutional Court of 1 March 1979, reproduced below on pp. 249ff.
14. Ibid., p. 27.

precondition for the Act's constitutionality.

Specifically, the Federal Constitutional Court dealt with the possible violation of the guarantee of private property (Basic Law, Art. 14). According to the judgment, property enjoys a marked degree of protection wherever, as personal property, it forms an element in the safeguarding of individual freedom. On the other hand, the protection of property is becoming less firm, and the dispositive rights of the legislators increasingly extensive, the more the property in question has 'a social relationship and a social function', as is true, for example, of shares in companies. In this case the use of property affects the interest of other parties to the law, in particular the employees, who depend on the shareholdings being used in such a way that their freedom remains ensured. The court emphasised that the cooperation of shareholders and employees is necessary to attain the aims of the company and of the proper use of property. The court rejected the view that a company is simply a matter for the shareholders. Rather the legislator is given a wide scope in regulating and limiting the influence of shareholders in large companies.

Another important point was the question of whether the 1976 co-determination model interfered with the basic right to form associations and hence impinges upon the autonomy of collective bargaining. The court ruled that co-determination does not contain any element of a forced amalgamation between employees and shareholders, nor does it jeopardise the viability of companies and subject companies to directives from outside. The Federal Constitutional Court also argued that the presence of trade-union representatives on Supervisory Boards — which was criticised by the employers — was in fact in the interest of companies because their presence added expertise to the Supervisory Board and helped to counter an excessively 'parochial' attitude. The court disowned the attempt to play off the autonomy of collective bargaining against co-determination. It noted that co-determination and collective bargaining in fact supplemented each other. The court recognised that the simultaneous existence of the collective-bargaining system and co-determination may produce a conflict of obligations which must be resolved; it is the function of the legislator to organise the system of collective bargaining in a way which ensures the workability of that system. There is no question, however, that the system of collective bargaining presupposes that both trade unions and employers' associations are sufficiently independent to be able to represent effectively the interests of their members *vis-à-vis* the other side. The principle of independence also admits to certain restrictions, provided that it remained fundamentally intact. The possibility of the employees exercising an influence on the employers' association under the Co-determination Act did not, in the court's view, challenge this principle. It was assumed that the Co-determination Act does not lead to any lasting functional impairment of the collective-bargaining system as has been asserted by the employers.

(c) *Representation of Employees on the Supervisory Board under the 1952 Works Constitution Act*

Participation of employees on the Supervisory Board of companies had already been provided for in the 1952 Works Constitution Act.[15] It is stipulated in this Act that one-third of the members of the Supervisory Board shall consist of employee representatives. This one-third formula continues to exist in addition to the 1976 Co-determination Act and is applicable to companies with fewer than 2,000 employees.

The 1952 Works Constitution Act provides for this one-third participation for all limited companies which regularly have more than 500 employees. Below that limit it applies to all joint-stock companies and companies with limited-liability shareholding capital (*Kommanditgesellschaft auf Aktien*), with the exception of family-owned companies.

The employee representatives on the Supervisory Board are directly elected in a secret ballot of all the employees of the company. Where only one representative of the employees is to be elected, this must be an employee of the company. If two or more are to be elected, at least two of them must be employees of the company, one of whom must be a wage-earning and the other a salaried employee. Since there are no other provisions regarding further employee representatives, it is possible to elect outsiders, such as trade-union officials. The principle is

15. The relevant passages are published in English in ibid., pp. 96–8.

Figure 4.3 Co-determination under the 1952 Works Constitution Act: model (nine-member Supervisory Board)

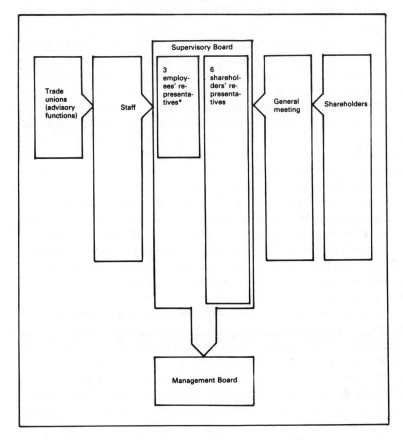

Note: * In this model one employee may be an outside representative

illustrated in Figure 4.3 which assumes a nine-person Supervisory Board.

4.4 Workers' Participation in Retrospect

(a) *Significance of the Various Forms of Workers' Participation*

Since no official statistics are available, the quantitative significance of the various forms of workers' participation can only be estimated. In 1985 H.-U. Niedenhoff published the following figures which, although he does not give a year, convey at least a general idea.[16]

Out of the total of 23 million workers in the Federal Republic of Germany, 3.2 million (13.9 per cent) are without any institutionalised form of participation because they work in institutions to which the relevant laws do not apply. Another 3.4 million (14.8 per cent) are state employees who are subject to the Personnel Representation Act 1955. The remainder — 16.4 million (71.3 per cent) — fall under the Works Constitution Act and could elect works councils. Out of this group, however, 200,000 employees work in 'ideological establishments' with restricted participatory rights. Although Niedenhoff does not mention this point, it may be assumed that not all the remaining 16.4 million workers have their interests represented by works councils; in a good number of smaller companies no works council exists.

Altogether 6.1 million workers (26.5 per cent of all employees) have their interests represented on the Supervisory Board; all these firms also have works councils. Of these 6.1 million, 4.5 million working in 484 companies, fall under the 1976 Co-determination Act; 1 million are covered by the one-third representation according to the 1952 Works Constitution Act, and 600,000 work in large firms in mining and in the iron- and steel-producing industries with full-parity co-determination. The vast majority of the workers representatives in all participatory bodies are members of trade unions. In addition, there are also some firms which, by individual agreement, practise various models of co-determination, often combined with special schemes under which the employees acquire a share in the capital of the company.

(b) *Basis of the Appraisal*

The following appraisal is based on the situation in companies with both workers' participation at plant level and one of the three forms of co-decision by employee representatives on the

16. H.-U. Niedenhoff, *Mitbestimmung in der Bundesrepublik Deutschland*, 5th ed., Cologne, 1985, p. 20. Niedenhoff is head of the Trade Union Policy Department in the Institute of German Private Enterprise (Institut der Deutschen Wirtschaft); see p. 16 above.

Supervisory Board. This is true for most larger firms. But conditions there have an impact on the general atmosphere of relations between capital and labour throughout the economy. After all, even companies with no more than plant-level participation are affected to some degree by attitudes which develop in the leading companies. In the long run, even very paternalistic employers in small firms — who so far have even managed to avoid the establishment of a works council — will not remain untouched by these changes of attitudes.

In companies where both these forms of participation are practised, it is impossible to assess participation at plant level and co-decision at company level separately. The reasons for these difficulties are that regulations are interrelated in their effect and cannot be separated from other factors, such as the attitudes of the people operating the system. Almost all the 'internal' workforce representatives on Supervisory Boards are also works councillors. These interlocking offices render the legally clear separation of functions fictitious. For example, the information obtained by someone as a member of the Supervisory Board will also influence him in his capacity as a works councillor and *vice versa*. The reality is a progressive *de facto* integration of workplace and enterprise co-determination.[17] This development is reinforced by the fact that the decisions taken on these two levels mutually influence each other. The combined effect of both forms of participation and the way the system is operated by the people involved have resulted in an extension of participation beyond the boundaries set by the legal provisions. Referring to this development, E. Witte speaks of 'supralegal co-determination'.[18]

(c) *The Labour Side*

The trade unions have gained several advantages from the system of participation.

(1) The position of the trade union in the works council is strong, and in larger companies works councils have become *de*

17. See Streeck, pp. 404f.
18. E. Witte, 'Klassenkampf und Gruppenkampf im Unternehmen. Abschied von der Konfliktideologie', in *Hamburger Jahrbuch für Wirtschafts- und Gesellschaftspolitik*, vol. 27 (1982), p. 169.

facto union bodies.[19] There is also the labour director, who normally enjoys the confidence of the trade unions, in the personnel department; all this is no doubt conducive to the recruitment of new trade-union members.

(2) The presence of trade-union officials on Supervisory Boards makes for close and continuous contacts between union headquarters, the works council and the trade-union members at the workplace.

(3) The presence of some works councillors on the Supervisory Board strengthens the position of the works council *vis-à-vis* the management. They have improved access to information; and the fact that they also have a say in the appointment of members of the Management Board prevents career-orientated managers from antagonising the works councillors. Moreover, the Management Board tries to avoid taking conflicts to the Supervisory Board and therefore makes every effort to settle controversial points beforehand. As Streeck has put it, 'In effect, this amounted to an extension of works council co-determination to a wide range of subjects not covered by the Works Constitution Act'.[20]

(4) The trade-union officials on Supervisory Boards acquire first-hand information about the economic situation of the company which is useful both for the formulation of a strategy of collective bargaining as well as for their activities as an interest group which tries to influence economic and social policy. This improved access to information is independent of the numerical strength of the representation on the supervisory board.

However, this influence is a mixed blessing for the trade unions. The main problem is a divergence between the interests of the employees of the company and those of the unions as a whole representing the basis of solidarity of the labour movement.[21] The interests of the employees are the main concern of the works council and the internal employee representatives on the Supervisory Board. Not least they depend on the employees of the firm for their re-election. And the employees as individuals are primarily interested in job security, high wages and optimal

19. Streeck, p. 405.
20. Ibid., p. 396.
21. See H. Wächter, *Mitbestimmung. Politische Forderung und betriebliche Reaktion*, Munich, 1983, p. 179.

working conditions. These interests can only be served if the company prospers and maintains its competitiveness; workers in export-orientated firms are particularly aware of this. In this respect the interests of employees, of shareholders and of the management are in parallel.

The trade unions, on the other hand, derive part of their strength from the sense of solidarity of all workers. Their credibility is based on their ability to articulate and to defend overall workers' interests. This general workers' interest includes the interests of the unemployed. Because the possibility of such a conflict was foreseen by the legislator, the 'external' employee representatives on the Supervisory Board — typically trade-union officials — were created. But for a variety of reasons, most of the external employees representatives play no more than a marginal role. If they advocate a position which increases employment in the company at the price of reduced efficiency of the firm, they find themselves outvoted by the other members of the Supervisory Board, including the 'internals'.[22]

This conflict is embodied in the works councillors who by law have to take a cooperative attitude towards the employer in all matters relating to their function within the firm. In fact, there are some people who claim that the works council has to pursue not only the interests of the employees but also of the plant.[23] Consequently, it is hardly surprising that works councillors often exert a moderating influence in their other capacity as trade-union members when radical union demands are put forward. The fact that the union will try to maintain the solidarity of the labour movement by harping on historical achievements brings the works councillors into a precarious position when they have to mediate between the interests of the employees and the employer. Since this is their main difficulty, most of them show little inclination to take the general interests of the trade union, of the economy at large and of the unemployed outside the firm into consideration.

The dilemma of the works councillors and of the other employee representatives is that they are elected by the workforce but their chances of becoming nominated and elected depend

---

22. Streeck, pp. 396f.
23. This is reported by W. Däubler, *Das Arbeitsrecht*, vol. 1, Reinbek, 1985, p. 350.

on the support of the trade union. In fact, the same people who exert the participatory rights have gradually taken over managerial responsibilities. This in turn has contributed to reinforcing a vested interest of workers in 'social partnership' and 'cooperation' in the enterprise.[24]

(d) *Interests of the Employers*

The employers and in particular their associations have traditionally opposed workers' co-decision at company level. They judged this idea to amount to an indirect expropriation which would lead to socialism. At the very least, co-decision was expected to impair competitiveness and the right to manage because it made decision-making more cumbersome. There were also fears that the trade unions could exercise a kind of remote control of private business. This general opposition, however, does not affect the day-to-day operations of the companies. For the functioning of the system it has to be remembered that the interest of the employers' side is not monolithic either. There is the interest of the capital owners who are hoping for high dividends. But there is also the management's interest in the well-being and the growth of the company, which does not necessarily coincide with the payment of dividends. Characteristically, management tends to favour the reinvestment of profits. In this respect, co-determination has strengthened the position of the management *vis-à-vis* the shareholders.[25] Also, the management is interested in a smooth functioning of the company and hence in the avoidance of conflict with the employees and their representatives.

The most important effect of co-determination seems to be the greater emphasis that it has given to manpower-planning. The co-determination of the employees has subjected all manpower policy to co-determination and — fully in line with employee interests — made dismissals even more difficult than they already were.[26] Also, the appointment of a labour director to the Management Board has promoted the issue of manpower-planning

24. See Streeck, p. 391.
25. Ibid., p. 413.
26. Workers in companies of five or more employees are generally protected against unjustified dismissal. Workers who have been employed for more than six months can only

to the same position as, for example, sales, production and finance.

Another aspect is the effect of co-determination on the process of decision-making. There is no doubt that the need to consult with the works council and the need to convince the employee representatives on the Supervisory Board requires lengthy communication. But the need to convince the others also calls for rational arguments, which contributes to a more careful preparation of decisions; this, in turn, requires competent management personnel with a willingness to cooperate with the other groups in hammering out a consensual solution. Moreover, this careful preparation of decisions improves the chances of implementation because the works council will help to convince the workforce. It is safe to assume that the works council could extend its power by obstructing and delaying the implementation of decisions. To avoid this, the management usually secures the cooperation of the works council beforehand. Again, the price for this cooperation is paid by the works councillors: because they are better informed and have a deeper understanding of the firm's economic situation than the rest of the workers, the works councillors often find themselves in the position of having to defend management decisions before their workmates. In some instances works councillors have had to defend the closing down of unprofitable lines of production — resulting in dismissals and early retirements for some of the workers — in order to save the rest of the company. It may therefore be said that co-determination has delayed decisions, but it has also improved the quality of these decisions and contributed to the acceptance of the decisions by the workforce.

(e) *Impact of Workers' Participation on Labour Relations and on the National Economy*

The previously dominant question of whether co-determination would endanger the capitalist system and the competitiveness of companies no longer plays a major role in today's discussions.

---

be dismissed either for personal reasons (e.g. alcoholism), or for reasons of unacceptable behaviour (e.g. stealing of company property) or for operational reasons (e.g. lack of demand). The burden of proving such reasons is on the employer.

One may say, however, that co-determination has changed the system to some extent. The most important elements of this change seem to be the following, which are all interrelated.

First, labour as a factor of production has gained in importance in the planning of private companies. It is in the field of manpower policy that works councils are most powerful, and the institution of the labour director also emphasises the importance of this aspect. All workforce representatives in decision-making bodies have to defend what is the main interest of their electorate, in particular of the core workforce. Although there has never been a climate of hire-and-fire in the Federal Republic of Germany, co-determination added considerably to a company losing its flexibility in respect of manpower management. The works council and the other internal employee representatives have a strong interest in preventing dismissals. Their rights of co-determination give them enough power to stir up trouble whenever the management considers dismissals. The result is an avoidance of dismissals and an almost complete foreclosure of the internal labour market to the outside labour market. Any need for qualitative and quantitative flexibility is first met by a more efficient use of the existing workforce, that is by internal measures of redeployment and training, possibly also by overtime, by short-time working or by early retirement. Temporary employment and manpower-leasing serve the same purpose. The workforce is increased only if a particular need cannot be satisfied by the internal labour market and if prospects for a long-term employment of the newly hired people are good.

Second, this priority for manpower-planning results in the early consideration of all effects of entrepreneurial decisions on the workforce. Since the employee representatives' consent to all measures adversely affecting the workforce is required anyway, it is rational for the management to let them participate in the early stages of policy-formulating and to secure their cooperation in this way. Because there are almost no decisions which do not in one way or another affect the interests of the workforce, this development leads to an extension of the legally prescribed scope of participatory rights. In principle, the increased immobility of the workforce makes planning and particularly a rapid reaction to technological and structural change more difficult and interferes with competitiveness. But careful manpower-planning which finds the full support of the employee representatives in all bodies of co-determination, can help to avoid this pitfall and also to implement the mutually agreed measures; in some instances even dismissals were condoned by the employee representatives.[27] Although co-determination reduces the flexibility of the system, it facilitates the speedy implementation of the necessary measures. This may be a reason why German firms have not done badly in respect of rationalisation and technological innovation. In this way the adverse effects of a stabilised workforce which seems to be dysfunctional in a dynamic market economy have largely been neutralised.

Finally, there is some evidence that the result is a 'productivity coalition'[28] of management, of the internal employee representatives and of the shareholders. Their common interest is the productivity of the company — this, after all, is the basis of job security, of higher wages, of management status and of higher dividends. The consequence in many cases is joint and integrated decision-making and not — as the legislator had envisaged — a limited influence of the workers on certain decisions. In fact, we may say that employee representatives share the managerial prerogatives and responsibilities — a process which, depending on the author's ideological position, has been described either as the 'integration of labour' or a 'colonisation of management'.[29] In many companies this has resulted in the replacement of the them-and-us attitude with a sense of cooperation. Legislation on participation has thus provided a trigger for the development of greater worker–management cooperation.[30]

The result is a 'company egoism'.[31] The legislator was aware of this danger[32] and therefore introduced the external employee representatives. Their position, however, is not strong enough

27. A. Höland, *Das Verhalten von Betriebsräten bei Kündigungen*, Frankfurt on Main–New York, 1985.

28. Streeck, p. 415.

29. Ibid., p. 416.

30. Ibid., p. 417.

31. W. Adamy and J. Steffen (*Handbuch der Arbeitsbeziehungen*, Bonn 1985, p. 203) quote (without a source) the following statement of a worker: 'With competing firms and the workers employed there we have less in common than with "our" company'.

32. In fact, the Commission on Co-determination (often called Biedenkopf-Commission, after its chairman) — which in preparation of the 1976 Co-determination Act had reviewed

to overcome the resistance of the productivity coalition. Moreover, the fact that these 'externals' are elected by the workforce makes it difficult for them to defend larger interests which are at variance with the interests of the workforce. This 'company egoism' influences the decision-making processes of the trade unions. Here the active trade unionists who participate in the company's decision-making act as transmission belts. Together, this is a rather unexpected side-effect of increased participatory rights. It confronts both the trade union and the government with a dilemma, in particular in a situation of widespread unemployment.

The dilemma for the trade unions is that they find it difficult to promote an overall labour interest — which includes the interest of the unemployed — against the interests of those in work. If they emphasise the overall interest too strongly, they run the risk of losing the support of the workers who have jobs. If they do not, they lose their credibility as a defender of larger welfare interests and undermine workers' solidarity. The way out is a return to full employment, which may well be impossible without sacrifices on the part of the job-holders. We may say that the existing system of co-determination is compatible with the market system exactly because the external representatives do not have the power to influence the company in a direction which may be in the general interest but would be harmful to the individual company.

The government is not in an enviable position either. The segmentation of the labour market into an internal and external market with a resulting reluctance of companies to hire new workers is not conducive to a reduction of unemployment. In other words, the high efficiency of individual companies goes hand in hand with adverse effects on the overall productivity of the economy. In this context Streeck warns against a gradual replacement of industrial unionism by company unionism.[33] Worse, the state has high expenditures on unemployment ben-

---

the experience with co-determination in the mining industry and in iron- and steel-producing industry — had already observed a 'certain enterprise egoism'. See Mitbestimmungskommission (ed.), *Mitbestimmung in Unternehmen. Bericht der Sachverständigenkommission zur Auswertung der bisherigen Erfahrung bei der Mitbestimmung* (Bundestagsdrucksache VI/334 vom. 4.2. 1970), Bonn, 1970, p. 58.

33. Streeck, p. 420.

efit, social-security payments and the like — which have to be financed and thus burden the prosperous companies and the job-holders in particular. The state is facing in a new form its perennial task of finding new ways of reconciling strong particularist interests with its overall economic and social objectives.

5

German Industrial Relations
Prior to 1945

5.1 Introduction

The first part of this book has been concerned with the present-day system of industrial relations in the Federal Republic of Germany and with the immediate background to current practice. This system has been examined in its different legal, institutional and political aspects in order to provide up-to-date information for anyone in industry, politics or the academic world who is looking for a survey of recent trends. However, as has been explained in the Preface, knowledge of the legal framework and the organisational structures may not be sufficient for an understanding of the overall picture. There are underlying assumptions, often unspoken, which also determine the theory and practice of industrial relations in contemporary West Germany. These assumptions are related to what we have defined as the 'industrial culture' of that country — a sphere which is more resistant to rapid change. This industrial culture is rooted in Germany's history, which has shaped the attitudes and organisational behaviour, laws and styles of operation on both sides of industry. To gain a deeper understanding of present-day practice and possible future developments, it is necessary to go back into the past and to survey roughly a century of the history of industrial relations in Germany.

5.2 Paternalism and the Beginnings of the Institutionalisation of Industrial Conflict, 1850–1914

If industrial relations is unthinkable without industry, there have of course been industrial enterprises in Central Europe for many centuries and certainly well before the unification of the

140

country under Prussian leadership in 1871. Thus mining went back as far as the Middle Ages in some parts of the country. In the second half of the eighteenth century the regions on the Lower Rhine around Krefeld, the uplands south of Aachen, the villages along the Wupper River valley north-east of Cologne, the Eichsfeld region south-east of Göttingen and the uplands of Silesia and Saxony had seen a flourishing textile and iron industry based on cottage manufacture. The putting-out networks which were similar to the ones in Flanders or those around Birmingham in England were run by merchant capitalists and often comprised several thousand 'protoindustrial' households making cloth or metal household goods for a wider market.

However, it was only in the 1850s and 1860s that Germany experienced its 'First Industrial Revolution' in the strict sense and that a modern factory system emerged on a larger scale. It was also in this period that some of the more successful enterprises faced the task of having to organise several dozen or even several hundred workers under the same factory roof. As elsewhere in Europe this led to far-reaching changes in the daily rhythm and routine of the working population. The approach of the employers to the problems of workforce organisation tended to be similar to that of their British or other foreign counterparts: disciplinarian and, as A.W. Gouldner has called it, 'punishment-centered'.[1] Elaborate factory codes were drawn up which laid down detailed work rules and chains of command. Wage deductions were fixed for such misdemeanours as overstaying in the ale-house during the lunch-hour. Industrial relations, in so far as one can speak of it at all, were autocratic and paternalistic. The owner saw himself as a monarch who knew all his workers and had an oversight over all aspects of production and marketing.

However, after the founding of the German Empire in 1871, industrial capitalism underwent further marked change. To begin with, concentration and merger movements set in, resulting in ever more complex organisations. Capitalism, one might say, became *organised* at all levels. Internally more sophisticated structures of research and development, production, commercial management, financial control and sales were being intro-

1. A.W. Gouldner, *Patterns of Industrial Bureaucracy*, New York, 1954, p. 207.

duced. The workforce became more differentiated. The rise of the white-collar worker began, especially in the new industries of the 'Second Industrial Revolution' — that is, manufacturing, engineering, electrical engineering and chemicals. Industrial associations and lobbies were formed to represent the collective interests of industry and commerce *vis-à-vis* the governmental bureaucracy and the parliamentary assemblies. Company law and commercial law became enshrined in detailed codes. The organising phenomenon extended not only to the German banking system, with important implications for the capital structure and growth of German industry, but also to sales and marketing. Partly promoted by the wave of protectionism during the period of retarded economic growth in the 1870s and 1880s, German industry began to form an elaborate system of cartels and sales syndicates — horizontal contractual agreements between independent firms fixing such matters as production quotas and prices which the Sherman Act 1890 and related Congressional legislation proscribed in the United States. In Germany cartels became a deeply ingrained tradition.

Given the increasing concentration and organisation of German industry since the second half of the nineteenth century, it was to be expected that sooner or later the growing workforces in the factories would also begin to organise themselves. However, unlike in Britain and France, this effort on the part of blue-collar workers was disrupted and hence delayed by Bismarck's Anti-Socialist Laws. For more than ten years, throughout the 1880s, the government banned not only the political organisation of the industrial working class which had come into being in 1875 in the shape of the Social Democratic Party, but also made all trade-union activity impossible. Bismarck's hopes, which were shared by many employers, were that repression would deal a mortal blow to socialist ideas among the working class. But in order to enhance these calculations he adopted a carrot-and-stick approach and also began to introduce a rudimentary programme of social insurance and welfare benefits.

Meanwhile Friedrich Krupp used further means of naïvely paternalistic persuasion. In a speech in 1877 he urged his workers to

enjoy what is granted to you. Your work accomplished, remain in the circle of your family, with your parents, your wife and children, and think upon household matters and education. . . . As for the high politics of the country, do not waste your breath. Higher politics require more time and a greater insight into conditions than are given to the workers. You are doing your duty if you elect candidates recommended to you by those whom you can trust. You will do nothing but damage if you try to interfere with the helm of the legal order.[2]

Unfortunately for Krupp and Bismarck, the workers did not take the carrot. The experience of persecution and police harassment rather increased the feelings of solidarity in the factories and working-class communities in the rapidly expanding industrial centres all over the country. When the Anti-Socialist Laws lapsed in 1890, both the Social Democrats and the trade unions re-emerged with surprising speed. The latter increased their membership from some 350,000 in 1890 to 850,000 in 1900 and to no less than 2.4 million in 1910. Three years later the total figure hovered around three million.

This growth was greatly enhanced by demographic changes. The earlier big waves of emigration came to an end, and the population grew from around 50 million in 1891 to 65.3 million twenty years later. Furthermore, it was in this period that a marked population shift took place away from agriculture towards industry and commerce, from the rural parts towards the cities. Millions of people were on the move in Germany on the eve of the First World War, most of whom tried to escape from the still semi-feudal and restrictive conditions of work and life in the countryside and especially on the large-scale estates of East Elbia. Some cities, particularly in the Ruhr area and in Saxony, trebled and quadrupled their populations within a generation, partly through immigration and partly through high birth-rates.

It is not difficult to visualise what kind of problems this raised for the authorities in terms of housing provision, sanitation and social control. But given the appalling conditions under which millions of Germans were forced to live, it is also not difficult to appreciate why these proletarians were amenable to the arguments of the Social Democrats and trade-union organisers who talked about the blatant inequalities in German society and the injustices of its autocratic system of political domination.

2. Quoted in H. Grebing, *History of the German Labour Movement*, rev. edn, Leamington Spa, 1985, p. 53.

However, these organisers did not speak with one voice. Three columns were in fact marching side by side and to some extent competing against each other. The largest faction from the start were the Social Democratic ('Free') unions which grew from 278,000 in 1890 to 2.5 million by 1913. Initially, the Hirsch-Duncker unions, which were non-Marxist and opposed to the notion of class struggle, were the second largest grouping with 63,000 members in 1890 and 107,000 in 1913. However, on the eve of the First World War they had been overtaken by the Christian trade unions representing Catholic working-class interests. The Christian unions had emerged in the mid-1890s, but counted some 343,000 members by 1913. While the Hirsch-Duncker unions declined further and eventually disappeared, the difference between Free and Christian unions continued and has a political significance to this day (see pp. 38f.). On a number of occasions the two movements combined to affect major changes in the German system of industrial relations; at other times divisions weakened the thrust of the working-class movement as a whole.

Overall it may be said that by 1914 Germany had the largest and best-organised working-class movement in Europe which, through its manifold branches and cultural institutions, tried to influence and represent the growing millions of the country's blue-collar workers from cradle to grave. The pre-1914 period also saw the mushrooming of white-collar unions, which tended to keep their distance from the blue-collar workers and whom the government and the employers tried to keep apart from the Free unions. Thus the difference between being an *Arbeiter* and being an *Angestellter* was not merely psychologically important, but was also reflected in the evolution of the German system of pensions and social security. Meanwhile Bismarck's carrot-and-stick approach towards the blue-collar workers had turned into a disaster in a dual sense: the Anti-Socialist Laws had promoted, rather than destroyed, the growth of unionism, while the introduction of his modest welfare schemes left plenty of room for improvement, and this is what all unions began to push for once they were allowed to operate again after 1890.

The following basic point has to be remembered here: historical research is now generally agreed that even if the situation looked different to upper-class contemporaries, pre-1914 German trade unionism was not particularly radical. Of course, there were differences between individual unions in this respect, as there are today. But their main concern was not the preparation of a violent socialist revolution or fundamental socio-economic reforms, but a gradual improvement of very meagre wages and ungenerous work conditions. The unions fought for the eight-hour workday, better insurance rights and recognition as the legitimate representation of the shop floor. They basically wanted to leave the political and cultural ghetto into which Bismarck had thrust them, and in return for recognition as the bargaining partners of the employers, they were prepared to integrate themselves into the existing order without wanting to turn it upside-down.

The response of the employers to these aspirations was not uniform. Some of them recognised the advantages of introducing collective-bargaining processes and of establishing, through the unions, firm contractual relationships which made production and industrial relations more calculable and reduced the risk of spontaneous strikes or poor morale. Not least, they realised that the unions could act not only as agencies for the focusing of shop-floor demands but also as transmission belts and upholders of the compromises which had been struck across the negotiating table. Some companies, like MAN at Augsburg, Krupp-Gruson at Magdeburg or the Howaldt Shipyards at Kiel tried to establish pliable company unions, the 'yellow' unions, as a counterweight. However, among the first industries to institutionalise and channel labour conflicts by negotiating with the established unions were the printing and the construction industries. Similarly, the Robert Bosch electrical engineering company in Stuttgart recognised the Metal-Workers Union (DMV) and concluded its agreements on wages and working conditions without the institution of a workers' committee.

However, the overwhelming majority of employers remained fundamentally hostile to the regularisation of industrial relations and a recognition of the trade unions. They fought hard to preserve the old patriarchical conditions. Union activities were banned from their premises. 'Troublemakers' were dismissed and blacklisted. Their response to strikes tended to be to lockout everybody. There were also the stipulations of Article 153 of the Prussian *Gewerbeordnung* the interpretation of which effectively restricted the right to strike in Prussia, by far the largest and most highly industrialised state of Germany. The Prussian 'Strike Decree' of 11 April 1886, moreover, instructed the police authorities to see to it that disputes over wages remained peaceful and within the bounds of the law and, if necessary, to provide protection to workers willing to work. Thus the employers could rely on the police and the courts to defend them against strike movements even after the lapse of Bismarck's Anti-Socialist Laws.

Time and again the police and even the Army were drawn into the industrial centres of the Ruhr or of Central Germany to deal with labour unrest in quite uncompromising terms and to protect strike-breakers. After the end of a strike the courts would mete out harsh sentences against workers arrested on various law-and-order charges. In the face of the present-day system of industrial relations in the Federal Republic, it is not always easy to understand just how different the climate was under the Hohenzollern monarchy and how difficult it was even for the most moderate unions to gain some kind of recognition by the employers and the authorities which commanded the repressive instruments of the Prusso-German military state. On the eve of the First World War only a small minority of workers in industry were covered by collective-bargaining agreements. The print unions had made the most impressive advances in respect of agreements together with the construction unions and by 1913 the total picture had developed in the way shown in Table 5.1.

Employers' attitudes remained particularly hardline in industries like mining, where even the idea of company unions was anathema. As American research on the Silesian coal industry has shown, the unions, in advocating institutionalised bargaining, were well ahead of the mine-owners. German entrepreneurs may have been 'modern' in the sense that they were keen to introduce the latest technologies and to imitate American mass-production methods; but as regards the treatment of their blue-collar workers, most of them clung to a traditional authoritarianism, which in many ways matched the autocratic ways of the political rulers of Germany at the Kaiser's court in Berlin. This was also the position of the powerful Centralverband der

Table 5.1 Employees covered by collective agreements in 1913 (000s)

Agriculture	4
Mining	—
Metal-work	207
Woodwork	166
Stone, glass, china	64
Chemicals	6
Textiles	16
Food, drink, tobacco	109
Clothing	143
Building (for 1912)	596
Printing	89
Transport	55
Paper	41

Deutschen Industrie (CVDI), one of the peak associations which considered as 'extremely dangerous for German industry and its continued development' the conclusion 'of collective agreements between organisations of employers and of trade unions'. In this hostile climate cooperation between more liberal companies like Bosch and the DMV also remained precarious and was liable to be replaced by a factory committee, if a serious strike broke out.

The large working-class movement in pre-1914 Germany tended to inspire fear among other classes, and growing social tensions and domestic problems, by which the Hohenzollern monarchy became afflicted in the last years before the war, merely exacerbated the situation. It is a measure of the disaffection of many voters with the existing political system that by 1912, 4.2 million out of 12.2 million adult males eligible under the universal suffrage for Reichstag elections voted for the Social Democrats, which became the largest party in the national assembly, holding 110 seats.

It is against this background of labour unrest that the Vereinigung deutscher Arbeitgeberverbände (VdA), was finally created in 1913 as the peak employers' association, long after industry had organised itself in other spheres. Often starting at local and regional level, industrial associations were founded in the 1870s. Heavy industry was particularly alert and also became instrumental in the creation of the CVDI in 1876. The 1878 election campaign saw the promotion of Reichstag candidates who were to act as spokesmen of industry in parliament. Ultimately, the weight of the conservatives from the big Ruhr combines in the CVDI proved to be too much for the smaller and medium-sized enterprises in light and manufacturing industry. In 1895 they formed their own separate association, the Bund der Industriellen (BdI). Local and regional chambers of commerce had been in existence since well before the unification of Germany. Craftsmen had constituted their own *Handwerkskammern*. The peculiarity of all these chambers was that, though private organisations, they were given certain public-service functions, such as the examining of apprentices in collaboration with the local authorities. A national organisation of the chambers of commerce finally emerged in 1861, known as Deutscher Handelstag (DHT). The DHT, just as its post-1945 successor, the Deutscher Industrie- und Handelstag (DIHT), included individual enterprises among its members, and by 1902 heavy industry had begun to gain the upper hand in this association also. As social and welfare issues were becoming increasingly important in Wilhelmine Germany, the power of the conservative CVDI, originally more concerned with questions of economic policy, also came to bear upon the politics of the VdA.

5.3 Impact of the First World War and Industrial Relations in the Weimar Republic, 1914–30

The fear of the working-class movement among the German middle and upper classes continued to mount well into the last days of peace at the end of July 1914. After the Austro-Hungarian government had handed over its ultimatum to Serbia, it looked as if the diplomatic crisis might escalate into full-scale war. In this situation peace demonstrations were held in various German cities. These demonstrations so worried the local military commanders, who were expecting to receive their mobilisation orders for foreign war, that they began to check their instructions for the eventuality of civil war (which, of course, they all had in their lockers). Seeing the demonstrators milling through the streets, some commanders felt that the time had come to arrest the ring-leaders and to put the 'masses' under the tight regime of martial law. Reich Chancellor Theobald von Bethmann Hollweg was appalled when he learnt of these plans. He felt that becoming involved in a civil war at the same time as the German government began to reckon with the outbreak of a major foreign war was the worst situation imaginable. So he persuaded the 'Red-baiters in uniform' (as Kurt Riezler, his private secretary, called the generals) to desist. Simultaneously, he started negotiations with the Social Democratic leadership, while conducting his diplomacy *vis-à-vis* the other foreign powers in such a way that it looked as if Germany was becoming embroiled in a *defensive* war. As the chief of the naval cabinet, Georg Alexander von Müller, put it in his diaries on 1 August 1914: 'Brilliant mood. The government has succeeded very well in making us appear as the attacked'.[3]

It is only against the background of these developments that we can understand the enthusiasm with which large sections of the German population, many of the allegedly unpatriotic working class among them, greeted the declaration of war and the Kaiser's announcement that henceforth the nation had shelved its differences and combined in a sacred union (*Burgfrieden*) to fight and win this war. On 1–2 August the leadership of the Free Allgemeiner Deutscher Gewerkschaftsbund (ADGB) resolved to support the war effort. No official strikes were permitted, strike pay was cancelled, and the government was to be supported in its attempts to help solve the increase in unemployment resulting from the war-related dislocations in the national economy. The rhetoric which accompanied the proclamation of the *Burgfrieden* was given some organisational back-up. The CVDI and BdI, though not announcing their merger, decided to form a joint War Committee of German Industry. Similarly, the ADGB combined with the Christian trade unions and the Hirsch-Duncker associations to facilitate cooperation with the government and the employers.

Centralisation went further on the government side. When war broke out, the Prussian Siege Law of 1851, a relic of semi-absolutist days, came into force. Under this law the commanding generals in each military district in the Reich became responsible not merely for providing logistical support for the front-line armies, but also for law and order, for censorship and generally

3. Quoted in J. Röhl, 'Admiral von Müller and the Approach of War, 1911–1914', *Historical Journal* 4 (1969), p. 670.

for organising the war effort in the rear. The civilian admin-
istrators were expected to provide support services. While the
state machinery began to coordinate its infrastructure, it is
important to emphasise that it was in fact the old Prussian
military state that took charge — and increasingly so the more it
turned out that, contrary to most people's initial expectations,
this war would not be over by Christmas 1914. As far as social
and labour policies were concerned, this meant that a peculiar
triangular relationship emerged which was fraught with tensions and contradictions and which saw frustrated trade unionists and generals repeatedly confronting obstinate industrialists
who were not prepared to make concessions or conclude
compromises for the sake of the higher national goal of military
victory. It was not difficult to see that this war, which was
turning more and more into a total war, would have a profound
impact on the existing distribution of socio-economic and political power in Germany.

In particular, it was bound to increase the pressure from the
working class (whose members were now bearing the brunt of
the trench-war in the West with its heavy losses) to be given a
more important place in society and politics than had been
granted before 1914. These shifts were recognised from the start
by a prominent industrialist, Alfred Hugenberg, who explained
in November 1914:

> The consequences of the war will in themselves be unfavourable for
> the employers and industry in many ways. There can be no doubt
> that the capacity and the willingness of the workers returning from
> the front to produce will suffer considerably when they are subordi-
> nated to factory discipline. One will probably have to count on a very
> increased sense of power on the part of the workers and the labour
> unions, which will also find expression in increased demands on
> employers and for legislation.[4]

The problem was that industry was not prepared to meet any of
these demands — at least not until the hour of military defeat in
November 1918, when a revolution threatened to sweep away
not only the discredited Hohenzollern monarchy but also the
existing property structures. For the time being the preferred

4. Quoted in V.R. Berghahn, *Modern Germany*, Cambridge, 1982, p. 52.

option was therefore a suggestion with which Hugenberg had concluded his perceptive analysis of November 1914: the employers, he felt, would 'be well advised, in order to avoid internal difficulties, to distract the attention of the people and to give fantasies concerning the extension of German territory room to play'.

In line with this advice, industrialists like Hugenberg could be seen in subsequent years, and in conjunction with the Pan-German League and later the right-wing radical Fatherland Party, to be promoting dreams of territorial annexations and of a German-dominated bloc stretching from the Atlantic to the Ukraine. No doubt the massive war-aims propaganda and the first-stage implementation of an ambitious imperialist programme after the Treaty of Brest Litovsk in February 1918 was also designed to distract the Germans from the deteriorating situation at home and from their demands for domestic reform. Meanwhile, the unions had, not surprisingly, begun to press their case for greater participation and for giving some substance to the slogans of the *Burgfrieden*. Traditionally unsympathetic to working-class aspirations, the military authorities at first also offered words of comfort and no deeds. But as the war dragged on and as the military became increasingly involved in the total mobilisation of Germany's economy and manpower resources for the war effort, social policy came to be seen by them as a promising means of increasing efficiency.

The focus of this activity became the Abteilung für Zurückstellungswesen (AZS) in the War Ministry. Originally concerned with exemptions from military service, the AZS became involved in questions of labour mobility more generally. In this connection it developed the idea of setting up 'arbitration committees' under the military commanders; it also proposed the establishment of 'labour exchanges on the basis of parity' and 'close collaboration with unions and employers' associations'. In order to promote such collaboration, the AZS wanted to avoid all measures that might alienate the workers and the unions, and was therefore also opposed to a general restriction on the right of workers to move to better-paid jobs. Negotiations through tripartite committees rather than compulsion seemed to be a more promising way of securing the cooperation of both workers and unions in manpower-planning. As top AZS officials put it:

151

The workers are now fulfilling their war duty . . . with the greatest willingness. In this they are being strengthened and driven on by their unions. A military or legal compulsion to work will have a laming and destructive effect upon the readiness of the unions to help out. Pointing to the brilliant success of compulsory military discipline in the army misses the fundamental difference between service in the defence of one's country, in which all members work for the common good without personal benefit, and the capitalistic work relationship, in which there is a profit for the employer from the performance of the worker. To intervene in this relationship, which . . . was to be seen as a consequence of the historical development of the workers as a fighting class, in the manner that one group should be forced to perform by *official order*, while the other receives the highest remuneration from the same authority, would be felt by the workers and other classes of people as a partisan stand in favour of the employers and would place at stake the further confidence in the military authorities of a class decisive for the carrying on of the war.[5]

The response of the employers to these arguments was far from uniform. Under the leadership of Ernst von Borsig, the Berlin metal manufacturers became convinced that the creation of a negotiating machinery was in their interests, and in February 1915 the Kriegsausschuß für die Metallbetriebe Gross-Berlins was formed on which the employers, the Berlin Metal-Workers Union and a delegate from the Ordnance Master's Office were represented. As Borsig reported in November 1916, 'in so far as the unions are concerned . . . I can only say that they have worked hand in hand with us during the war'. They could, he felt, be used to have a restraining influence on the demands of the rank and file. Such experiences did not move the majority of Borsig's fellow industrialists to abandon their anti-unionism and to heed government exhortations to cooperate with the unions. The most some of them were prepared to contemplate was the creation of arbitration committees on which individual workers, but not union officials, would have a seat. Above all, industry never forgot that the '*consequences* of the intervention of the military authorities in the relationship between employers and

5. Quoted in G.D. Feldman, *Army, Industry and Labor in Germany, 1914–1918,* Princeton, 1966, p. 75.
6. Quoted in ibid., p. 79.

workers will also remain when those authorities are no longer competent after the end of the war'. Ewald Hilger, a hardline conservative and spokesman for Silesia's heavy industry, put it even more bluntly: 'I see in these arbitration agencies an extraordinarily great danger. They will not be terminated after the end of the war. That is a belief in miracles. I am completely convinced that when we once have them we will never be rid of them, and then a breach is shot through our social position.'[7]

What ultimately put the brakes on the War Ministry's experiments in tripartist industrial relations was less the employers' opposition than the increasing manpower shortages. By December 1916 these shortages had become so acute that the government was forced to introduce the Patriotic Auxiliary Service Law which obliged all men between the ages of seventeen and sixty to render labour service. Although workers in principle retained the right to move to better-paid jobs and the machinery for the settlement of labour disputes was incorporated in the law, the strains of total war could by now be felt everywhere. Rising inflation and food shortages triggered demonstrations and strike movements which the union leaders desperately tried to contain. What made their task more difficult was that the army leadership, with Erich Ludendorff now at the helm, like the employers, adopted an increasingly uncompromising and repressive stance. In the spring and summer of 1918 workers, exhausted by the war and round-the-clock production, demanded a reduction of weekly hours from sixty to fifty. Spontaneous strikes broke out over this issue. But Ludendorff insisted that 'when the workers try to shorten working hours by strikes, they work directly against the patriotic interest'.

Then, in the autumn of 1918, came the hour of defeat and panic. The High Command declared that the war was lost and that Germany must sue for peace. With the threat of a 'revolution from below' increasing, it suddenly seemed wiser to the hitherto recalcitrant employers to try and draw the unions into politics, as they seemed to be the only organisations which still had an influence over the workers in the factories. The hope was to find, through consultations with them, a joint solution to the problems of demobilisation and of restarting peacetime pro-

7. Quoted in ibid., p. 91.

duction in a defeated country.

Negotiations were opened on 22 October, which were attended by the most prominent names of German industry: Hugo Stinnes, von Borsig, Carl Friedrich von Siemens, Walther Rathenau, Felix Deutsch, Hans von Raumer and others. The ADGB leader, Carl Legien, acted as one of the spokesmen for the union side. From these talks emerged the famous Stinnes–Legien Agreement. In it the employers recognised the right of association for all workers and promised to stop supporting all 'yellow' unions. They also agreed to take all measures to speed up the re-employment of returning soldiers and to support the introduction of a jointly administered system of labour exchanges. Works Committees were to be formed in firms with more than fifty employees, and there would be an arbitration system for the settlement of disputes. Finally, the employers pledged to introduce the eight-hour workday. In return the unions promised to put on ice all demands for a nationalisation programme and to cooperate with industry and the government to keep the country from slithering into a social revolution of the kind which had taken place in Russia in the previous year.

With the Hohenzollern monarchy having collapsed and Germany in turmoil, Legien's cooperation with the new revolutionary government remained initially without a firm constitutional base. The trade-union leader supported the aims of those Social Democrat politicians who had been catapulted into positions of power in November 1918. These were to roll back the extreme Left and the Workers' and Soldiers' Councils which had cropped up all over the country and to bring about early elections for a national assembly to approve the establishment of a parliamentary system and a constitution. Cooperation with the employers, on the other hand, became institutionalised at an early stage. Under the leadership of von Borsig and in the wake of the Stinnes–Legien Agreement, sealed at the beginning of November, the so-called Zentralarbeitsgemeinschaft (ZAG) was formed between employers and unions on 15 November 1918.

Borsig's role in the ZAG is important for two reasons. In 1916, as we have seen, he had been instrumental in setting up the Arbeitsausschuß which united the local DMV and the Berlin metal employers around the negotiating table in the presence of an army representative. But just like most of his fellow industrialists, he had never been in favour of a governmental presence and a *trilateral* relationship. To them this was an outgrowth of the wartime emergency to be abandoned as soon as the war was over. Industry was to be left to deal with the problems of postwar economic reconstruction free from government interference and, should this prove unavoidable, in cooperation with the workers and their representatives. In this sense Borsig, who remained the leader of the employers in the ZAG until its collapse in 1924, was a protagonist of the *Arbeitsgemeinschaft* idea. He saw this 'work community' as an antidote to the notion of class struggle and to the conflict model of industrial relations which was advocated — albeit from the opposite end of the ideological spectrum — by the right-wing hardliners in the employers' camp on the one hand, and by radical trade unionists on the other.

Borsig's approach must also be differentiated from that of Rathenau, another prominent industrialist involved in the November compromise. His colleagues suspected Rathenau of being a socialist; but on close inspection it turns out that he was in fact an advocate of wartime *tripartism*. Given the experience of the war and the huge problems of postwar reconstruction, he believed that the task could not be mastered without an involvement of the state. To Rathenau some macro-economic planning seemed inevitable and even vital. As he put it in November 1918 with reference to industrial relations, 'the function of the state should not be to possess and to suppress free initiative, but to regulate and to balance'.[8] Rathenau therefore aimed at a more organised capitalism than did Borsig and his colleagues. There is a further point concerning Borsig's position: while he was not opposed to trade unions in principle, and was prepared to talk to them at a higher level within the framework of the ZAG, he preferred a concept of cooperation lower down the scale, and especially at company level, with workers' representatives who had been elected from among the workforce. This was his notion of *Gemeinschaft* and he was no friend of *außerbetriebliche Einflüss* exerted by union officials from the outside. All these differences in attitude and position have to be borne in mind for our discussion of German industrial relations in the late 1920s

8. Quoted in H. Pogge von Strandmann (ed.), *Walther Rathenau: Notes and Diaries, 1907–1922*, Oxford, 1985, p. 20.

and early 1930s later in this chapter. And they also have a long-term significance for the reconstruction period after 1945.

While the Stinnes–Legien Agreement and the creation of the ZAG reflected major shifts in the balance of power between the two sides of industry, if compared with the Wilhelmine period, similar shifts can also be discerned in another sphere. As early as the second half of the war, workers' committees had been formed in a number of industries which tried to represent the interests of the workforce *vis-à-vis* the management. Moreover, in the context of the proliferating strike movement, so-called Revolutionary Shop Stewards' Committees had sprung up in a number of places. These developments at grassroots level, together with the influences coming from revolutionary Russia, served as models for the workers' and soldiers' councils which emerged all over Germany in November 1918. However, the constitutional structure of these councils was virtually irreconcilable with the parliamentary-representative system which the moderate Left, in alliance with the Liberal Democrats and the Catholic Centre Party, were hoping to institute. This explains why the council movement, which frightened many contemporaries because of its apparent similarities with the Russian soviets, was rolled back and ultimately destroyed with the help of paramilitary units, the Free Corps.

However, the fathers of the Weimar Constitution did take on board the idea of *factory* councils. Thus Article 165 stipulated that 'the wage-earning and salaried employees are called upon to cooperate, with equal rights and in community with the entrepreneurs, on the regulation of wages and working conditions and on the total economic development of the productive forces'. The Reichstag was moreover called upon to draw up legislation, which was finally ratified in February 1920 in the shape of the Works Councils Act (*Betriebsrätegesetz*). This law required companies to have an elected committee which was to act as the voice of employee interests. Paragraph 70 of the Act provided for one or two members of the works council to sit on the company's Supervisory Board (see p. 117). The details of the selection of these employee representatives were regulated by a further law in February 1922.

The fact that it took the Reichstag some time to ratify the Works Councils Bill points to difficulties which it encountered on its passage through the legislature. Borsig, as we have seen, might have been prepared to deal with the unions at national level; but he, like many other industrialists, did not favour the idea of a union involvement at company level. Nor did they support the *Tarifvertrag* principle — that is, the idea that agreements on wages and conditions were to be hammered out in collective bargaining with the unions on the basis of branches and regions. There was a growing trend towards the promotion of pliable company unions to be used as a counterweight to the ADGB, the Catholic and the Hirsch-Duncker unions. The employers invoked the constitutional right of the freedom of association, which, they argued, also covered their own right to bargain with whoever they saw fit. This was no doubt a violation of the aims and the spirit of the Stinnes–Legien Agreement, indicating that the conservatives in industry were gaining the upper hand and that the post-revolutionary balance of power between employers and unions had begun to swing back in favour of the former. Indeed, the conservatives had never regarded the November accords as being more than a temporary alliance forced upon them by military defeat and the threat of revolution. Nor did they see the ZAG as a finely balanced instrument for achieving social-political compromises. Rather, they wished to reassert the primacy of economic considerations and to roll back many of the advances which the working class had made in 1918.

The position of the conservatives in the VdA had been strengthened in 1919 by the founding of the Reichsverband der Deutschen Industrie (RDI), which was in effect an amalgam of the pre-1918 CVDI and BdI. The division of labour between the VdA and RDI was officially the same as it had been before 1914; but after 1918 more than ever before the growing interconnections between economic and social policy made it virtually inevitable that the basic positions of the powerful and conservative RDI began to impinge upon those of the VdA, the more so since heavy industry, supported by the anxious cohorts of medium-sized enterprises, soon exerted a dominant weight within the internal power structure of industrial lobbyism.

Meanwhile mainstream opinion in the trade unions was moving in the opposite direction of tripartism. Like Rathenau, the outsider, the moderates among them believed that the state must continue its commitment to the management of the economy. Otherwise the social and economic problems of demobilisation and reconstruction would not be solved. It should be emphasised that these moderates did not take this view because they were hoping to transform the economy into a socialist one. What they wanted was a viable and expanding economy operated on the basis of compromise and consensus politics through which it would be possible to expand the net of welfare measures. For the same reason the ADGB was also keen to retain and reinforce another gain of the Revolution of 1918, that is the system of arbitration of labour disputes. Under this system either side to a dispute could submit the case to a public arbitrator if the counterpart blocked the conclusion of a new wage agreement or if negotiations had become so deadlocked that only an intermediary appeared to be able to break the impasse. The system was designed to induce employers to live up to their promises of November 1918 and to conclude collective wage agreements. Overall it was an aspect of the 'juridification' of the German industrial relations structure with its hierarchy of labour courts and similar institutions (see pp. 99ff.). Yet in view of the gradual dissociation of the employers from the Stinnes–Legien Agreement and their continued insistence that the principle of contractual freedom must not be undermined, arbitrations often went against them and became in their eyes compulsory (*Zwangsschlichtung*). Finally, there was the eight-hour workday, another fruit of the 1918 accord, which the employers found more and more distasteful. The crisis of 1923 provided the opportunity to abolish this cornerstone of the Stinnes–Legien Agreement. Under the leadership of the Ruhr iron and steel industrialists, Germany moved back to the traditional two twelve-hour shifts. Exposed to such strains between the two sides of industry, the ZAG became an empty shell and finally fell apart in January 1924.

The frustration and disappointment over these developments among the unions, and in the ADGB in particular, surfaced soon thereafter. At the ADGB Congress at Breslau in 1925, a more detailed debate took place on the concept of 'economic democracy' (*Wirtschaftsdemokratie*) and the concomitant demand that parity between capital and labour be established at all levels of the economy. Similar demands appeared in the programme of the Social Democratic Party, ratified at Heidelberg during the same year. However, at this stage the debate still revolved mainly around the 'defensive variant' (R. Kuda) of *Wirtschafts- demokratie*. It was only in 1928 and under the impact of further union setbacks and a more polarised industrial relations picture that the 'offensive variant' (R. Kuda) was unveiled.

What prevented further radicalisation and deeper rifts be- tween the employers and the unions in 1925 was the temporary rise of a liberal-capitalist faction in both the RDI and the VdA — a development related to the ephemeral stabilisation of the domestic economy between 1924 and 1928 and Germany's re- turn to the world market. Once the reparations problem had been settled with the help of the Americans, US investments began to pour into the industries of the Second Industrial Revolution. The boom in the consumer goods and export- orientated branches which this engendered also resulted in a power-political shift within the peak associations. In the VdA Presidium, Borsig replaced Kurt Sorge, a director of Krupp, and true to his earlier belief he repeatedly voiced an interest in a revival of the ZAG. Meanwhile, in the RDI Carl Duisberg, one of the key figures of the chemicals industry and founder of the I.G. Farben trust, was elected president. Ludwig Kastl, another moderate, became executive director of the association. Other prominent faces were Hermann Bücher of the AEG electrical engineering firm and the lignite industrialist Paul Silverberg.

At the RDI annual meeting in September 1926, Silverberg made a speech which was much commented upon at the time. He called for a recognition of the Republican order and for support of the pro-Western diplomatic strategy of the foreign minister, Gustav Stresemann, himself a former BdI official in the Wilhelmine period. Above all, Silverberg urged his fellow in- dustrialists to resume the postwar dialogue with the trade unions at all levels. As regards collective bargaining, this liberal-capitalist group did not, apparently, wish to dismantle the system of arbitration as the conservatives had been aiming to. Nor was it opposed to the policy of Heinrich Brauns, the Reich Labour Minister. Being connected with the Catholic labour movement, Brauns pursued a policy of compensations in the field of welfare which had the situation of the labouring masses very much at heart and saw the state, in tripartist fashion, as the guardian of social peace and liberal-corporatist cooperation. Disagreement continues among historians as to how committed the 'liberals' in the RDI and VdA were to their conciliatory line. Borsig certainly continued to insist that the idea of 'community' at company level was compatible with formal contacts with the ADGB at the top.

However, the more crucial point is that all the time Borsig and his colleagues in the RDI had to look over their shoulders and to take account of the views of the conservatives in heavy industry and the medium-sized enterprises. Although those who upheld their fundamental hostility towards the unions had lost the initiative in intra-industry politics after 1924, they and the Ruhr managers in particular still possessed enough 'veto-power' (B. Weisbrod) to undermine a more flexible approach to industrial relations. By 1928 they felt strong enough again to flex their muscle when they provoked a lock-out of 250,000 metal-workers. Significantly, this action was not merely directed against the wage demands of the DMV, but also against the system of arbitration and more generally against the social policies pursued since 1918. In this sense the *Ruhreisenstreit* was also an attack on the government and the politics of cooperation with the unions. Thus the reassertion of the hardliners in the entrepreneurial camp occurred well before the outbreak of the Great Depression. Meanwhile, the unions came under pressure from their left wing. At the Hamburg Congress of the ADGB, Fritz Naphtali and a number of other theoreticians submitted their concept of *Wirtschaftsdemokratie*. Unlike the earlier variant, it aimed at a gradual transformation of the capitalist system. As Naphtali put it, capitalism was to be 'twisted before it was broken'.[9]

5.4 Industrial Relations of a Special Kind, 1930–45

If the Weimar system of industrial relations with its many 'modern' features suffered an eclipse in 1928, the years of the Great Slump after 1929, with mass unemployment, dwindling industrial output and general austerity, exacerbated by the

---

9. F. Naphtali, *Wirtschaftsdemokratie*, Frankfurt, 1966, p. 19.

orthodox financial policies of the government of Heinrich Brüning, dealt a mortal blow to all industrial relations in the strict sense. The welfare state collapsed and open class warfare broke out. At the beginning of the crisis the moderates in the RDI still made attempts to continue the dialogue with the unions and to formulate a common platform in matters of general economic policy. Later, three trade-union leaders developed a proto-Keynesian plan for a reflation of the German economy; but all these moves came to nought. As the depression hit harder, the power of the unions weakened. Many leaders took up an attentist position, believing that capitalism had reached its terminal crisis and that they merely had to await its collapse. Although the rank and file may have been prepared to stage a general strike, no orders to come out were given even when the Social Democratic government of Prussia was illegally deposed by the Reich government on 20 July 1932. For the employers the problem was increasingly not how to generate a consensus with the unions and the working-class movement as a whole against the rising Nazi Party, but how to integrate Hitler's mass movement into an authoritarian right-wing government which would replace Brüning and curb the unions. After various other alternatives appeared to have petered out by the end of 1932, the appointment of Hitler to the chancellorship looked like the only viable solution in the eyes of those who had been moving the octogenarian Reich President, Paul von Hindenburg, slowly in this direction. Industry's contribution to this outcome remains controversial and ambiguous. However, there is general agreement among historians that, even if the major employers were not directly and openly involved in the backstairs intrigues of the winter of 1932/3, they contributed indirectly to the destruction of the Weimar Republic by refusing to support it and link up with those political forces that could have been rallied in the Republic's defence. These reservations also explain why the employers did not oppose Hitler when he took swift action against his erstwhile Republican opponents. On 2 May 1933 the new Reich chancellor also banned the trade unions. Thenceforth, industrial relations in Germany took on a shape which was fundamentally different from that of the 1920s.

Following the brutal repression of the entire working-class movement during the first months of 1933, the Nazi regime began to draft a 'Law Concerning the Ordering of National Labour' (AOK) which finally came into force on 20 January 1934. This Act annulled the Works Councils Act of 1920 and the supplementary legislation of 1922. Above all, it established the Führer principle in industry and obliged the workforce to keep the social peace. Meanwhile, the employers were given a free hand in all company matters. Whether one defines the conditions established by the AOK as a relapse into a nineteenth-century paternalism or calls them a twentieth-century-style industrial autocracy, two points should be noted. To begin with, many industrialists did not find it difficult to adopt the new system. They had always preferred an authoritarian approach to team-work and participation. Thus industry aided and abetted a militarisation of its operations which came to be the hallmark of the Nazi regime more generally. As the well-known sociologist and economist Goetz Briefs observed shortly before his emigration to the United States, a 'strictly liberal notion of property combined with a military ideology of leadership and command [to produce] a company militarism'. The second point is that, where rulings from the top went unheeded, it was always possible under the Hitler dictatorship to call in the Gestapo to deal with 'saboteurs' and 'subversives'.

Nevertheless, it would be wrong to deduce from all this that from 1933 German industrialists ruled as absolute monarchs in their domain. The Hitler regime sent them a number of people who were supposed to supervise various welfare provisions for the workforce. Thus the Nazis had built up, well before their assumption of power, a trade-union-like organisation of their own, the Nationalsozialistische Betriebszellenorganisation (NSBO). Its functionaries did not appear on the shop floors for long after 1933, though. It was feared that the NSBO, by attracting new members from the banned Free trade unions, would become a fifth column organisation and a refuge for Communists and Social Democrats. So the NSBO failed to gain official approval. However, the former works councils were replaced by 'councils of trust' (*Vertrauensräte*). Its members were nominated by the Trustees of Labour (Treuhänder der Arbeit), who appeared on the scene from May 1934 onwards. These 'trustees', most of whom had previously worked in industrial associations and hence could be relied upon to be broadly sympathetic towards management, were also charged with receiving complaints and participating in the fixing of wage levels.

Finally, there were the representatives of Robert Ley's German Labour Front (DAF) to contend with, and they frequently proved more awkward than the Trustees of Labour. The DAF was not an ersatz union. Rather, it was supposed to propagandise the ethics of work and efficiency which the regime held up to the Germans as the foundation of their future position in Europe and the world. The DAF had no powers to intervene directly in management affairs. However, its officials could influence employers and their treatment of the workforce indirectly by pressing for improvements in the factory environment and for the introduction of welfare schemes. Thus DAF functionaries liked to encourage the establishment of canteen facilities and company sports clubs; they advocated improvements in the layout of the shop floor, of ventilation and washing facilities; they promoted accident prevention and the idea of vacation homes and package holidays, many of them run by the DAF-sponsored 'Strength-through-Joy', programme. All this was part of the general 'aestheticisation of politics' (W. Benjamin) designed to give the working population a sense of participation when in fact they had been divested of their political and economic rights by a brutal dictatorship.

Although the sight of DAF officials pompously enquiring into the well-being of employees must have been irritating to many employers, they were often also used as lightning-conductors for grievances or to reassure the rank and file that they were not being forgotten about. No doubt they were easier to deal with than Social Democratic or Christian works council chairmen or trade-union secretaries during the Weimar days. Moreover, there is some evidence that DAF reports on conditions in the factories in the 1930s were not only used to pressurise employers into making improvements to work conditions but also had some effect, however marginal given the massive rearmament programme of the Nazi regime, on wages and social policies. The Nazi leadership, traumatised by the defeat of 1918 and the demoralising impact of inevitable austerity on the home-front in the First World War, appears to have been conscious of the need not to depress the economic situation of the population too sharply.

Given the depth of the recession at the time of the Nazi seizure of power, Hitler's programme of huge public investments in armaments production initially avoided austerity and in fact strengthened the prestige of the Hitler government. Many people regained their jobs, and this alone raised their living standard. So they had little reason to grumble about their immediate economic situation. However, in the long term the wage freeze proclaimed in 1933 spelt danger for the regime once inflation, powerfully fuelled as it was by arms production and the neglect of consumer goods, began to make itself felt. Soon the index for weekly nominal wages rose faster than that of hourly wages, although it had started at a lower point on the scale in 1933. This meant that working longer hours had become the main way of achieving a higher income. Accordingly, average weekly working time rose from 42.9 hours in 1933 to 47.0 hours in the first half of 1939. Worse, by this time the fruits of harder labour were increasingly eaten up by higher price rises, especially for food and clothing, two items which took up about half of the weekly budget of a working-class household.

No amount of Nazi propaganda succeeded in distracting from these realities, which together with a desperate shortage of skilled labour, in a curious way, actually increased the leverage of the working class *vis-à-vis* the regime and the employers. Their organisations and formal channels for exerting their weight had been destroyed. But this did not mean that the German working class had lost its power completely. In view of the old Nazi trauma of home-front demoralisation, and also in view of the fact that, contrary to contemporary impressions, the Hitler dictatorship remained highly unstable and racked by internal conflict, workers retained some influence, especially in the vital armaments industries, which reached the government through alarmist reports of the DAF about growing shop-floor dissatisfaction. The message was that the regime should do everything to avoid imposing unbearable burdens on the workforce. Although it would be far-fetched to call all this a system of industrial relations, it nevertheless appears that there were a few limits to the brutal exploitation which the regime was on the whole engaged in.

For the same reasons, the Hitler government also refused to depress living standards sharply at the beginning of the Second

World War. The pretence was that the lightning campaigns did not require any economic sacrifices on the part of the population and that the conflict would be brought to a quick and victorious end. Thus, lest they suffer a decline in their living standards, high benefits were paid to the families of those breadwinners who had been drafted into the Wehrmacht. Business as usual, was the official propaganda line. Pressures on the workforce were stepped up to total-war levels only when it became clear towards the end of 1941 that Germany might lose the war. Thenceforth real wages began to drop and the regimentation of labour reached unprecedented levels.

However, it should also be borne in mind that the change of the tide in military fortunes provided the regime with two further levers against 'shirkers' and opponents: apart from an even more ruthless use of police surveillance and repression, the fear of defeat, skilfully exploited by the Goebbels propaganda machine, rallied people and made them willing to accept utmost austerity. The threat of being drafted into the army also acted as a deterrent against not fulfilling Speer's higher production targets. In fact, the Wehrmacht's manpower requirements rose so steeply that of the males who had been in employment in 1939 only 55 per cent were still working in the economy in 1944. However, the gap was not made up, as in Britain for example, by the recruitment of women into industry. Their number increased by a mere 300,000 between 1939 and 1944. On the other hand, in the meantime the number of foreign slave workers and POWs increased from 1.2 million in May 1940 to 7.5 million in September 1944. The treatment of these men and women, most of whom were taken to the Reich by force, represents one of the darkest chapters in German history. Most of the German industrialists who accepted these workers at starvation wages treated them without much pity and most of the companies concerned have refused to this day collectively to face the responsibility which industry bears for the exploitation and death of countless *Fremdarbeiter*. Nor have many German workers who viewed the foreigners from the East as 'sub-humans' looked back to these realities. No doubt, the presence in the factories of people even more wretched than themselves helped them psychologically to overcome their own sense of deprivation.

If the interactions that developed between German employers, German workers and slave labourers are to be called 'industrial relations' at all, the wartime experience had at least one salutary effect on the Germans: these were conditions to which none of them ever wished to return after the end of the war. This was certainly also the attitude of most industrialists. In the early years of the Nazi dictatorship many of them had welcomed the dynamism of the Hitler movement. Was not this regime creating conditions which allowed them to manage again — or so, at least, it seemed? It was also a relief to be rid of the Weimar system of industrial relations and to have the Gestapo to cope with the threat of disruptive and costly spontaneous strikes. But as time went on, government intervention in, and regimentation of, the economy increased, finally to reach its climax under Speer in the Second World War. The Hitler government also restructured the network of business associations and system of representation. On 19 June 1933 the RDI and VdA were merged to form the Reichsstand der Deutschen Industrie. The complex structure of regional and branch-specific associations was also drastically simplified. The chamber system took on a different shape. Indeed, it was a very peculiar type of capitalism that had evolved in Germany by the early 1940s — one which soon caused many employers to long for the end of the Hitler regime and for a return to 'normalcy'. The Nazi experiment had become a nightmare and people began to wonder if the Weimar system had really been as bad as it had been assumed to be.

6
The Re-emergence of an Industrial Relations System after 1945

6.1 Introduction

When the Allied armies finally defeated the Wehrmacht in May 1945 and the Nazi dictatorship was destroyed, the occupying powers and those Germans fortunate enough to be alive and fairly healthy were confronted with the seemingly unmanageable task of reconstruction. This is not the place to count the horrendous costs of the Second World War and to deal with the re-emergence of social, economic and political life in postwar Germany in any comprehensive way. Our brief is to examine the re-establishment of a system of industrial relations in the three Western zones of occupation and in the Federal Republic which was fashioned out of these three zones in 1949. In particular, we shall have to trace the genesis of two pieces of legislation, the 1951 Coal and Steel Co-determination Act and the 1952 Works Constitution Act, both of which contributed in a major way to giving West German industrial relations its peculiar shape. Both laws became cornerstones of the West German 'model', which remains significant to this day. However, while the immediate postwar roots of this 'model' are of considerable interest in themselves, the wider historical background which has been outlined in the previous chapter must always be borne in mind. In this sense the Nazi experience presented the negative image of a system to which neither the employers nor the re-emerging working-class movement wanted to return. On the other hand, as tends to happen in times of national crisis, only a minority of people wanted to embark upon something completely new. Instead, most Germans turned to the pre-1933 period in search of traditions and ideas from which they might derive inspiration. As will be seen in a moment, many proposals in the field of industrial relations therefore referred back to discussions and institutions which had developed before the Nazi seizure of power.

6.2 Allied Industrial Policies and the Re-establishment of Business Associations and Trade Unions

Although the early postwar period saw a continuation of the wartime Allied debate about the level of industrial activity at which the Germans would be allowed to operate, Britain and the United States and even the French government (which had belatedly been allocated a zone in the south-west of Germany) soon took measures to revive their respective zonal economies. This required great organisational effort as well as considerable material and manpower resources. As these were scarce and the taxpayers back home were not to be burdened with even higher occupation costs, the military authorities quickly tried to enlist German expertise. Closely supervised by them, the Allies cleared the way for a rebuilding of the administrative infrastructure and the reopening of the factories. The general approach was not to permit any centralisation in German hands. This suited those workers who had seized the initiative themselves, especially in those companies where the owners or directors had compromised themselves by their close association with Nazism. In other places the managers and workers made a joint and concerted effort to get production going again. This even applied to many bigger companies as it was not until the autumn of 1945 that the British and American authorities began to arrest large numbers of prominent industrialists, especially in coal and steel.

The 'grassroots' approach of the Allies to a rebuilding of the country's infrastructure also explains why the chambers of commerce were among the first industrial and commercial associations to be allowed to resume operations. These associations, as will be remembered, had fulfilled certain public functions, and in an attempt to revive these as supporting struts of the local economic bureaucracies, the British and the French even brought back the chamber laws of the Weimar days. Only the Americans insisted that the chambers of their zone should be no more than organisations in private law, and this they remained until 1957, when they too regained their former public functions. Soon the chambers were back in operation in most cities to act as foci for the local business community and to regulate, for example, the examining of apprentices. On the other hand, it took until 1949 for the Deutscher Industrie- und Handelstag (DIHT) to emerge as the successor organisation of the former DHT.

Industrial associations which united particular branches of industry under one roof were similarly readmitted by the British and American authorities only a few months after the collapse of the Third Reich. Thus, in October 1945, some 200 entrepreneurs of the Rhenish chemicals and pharmaceuticals industry met in a warehouse of the Duisburg Tropon-Werke to found a regional association. The Bavarian chemicals industry began to form their own association at about the same time. The end of October 1945 also saw the constitution of the Economic Association of the Iron, Sheet-Metal and Metal Manufacturing Industries, whose first chairman was Fritz Berg. Thereafter contacts between different branches intensified at the zonal level. With the creation of the Anglo-American Bi-Zone on 1 January 1947, attempts were made to establish inter-zonal associations. The Arbeitsgemeinschaft Eisen und Metall, founded in February 1948, was already, in effect, a roof organisation for the whole of West German industry, as it included not only all branches of the metal industry but also electrical engineering and optics. On the other hand, it took until January 1950 for the Bundesverband der Deutschen Industrie (BDI) to be formally established, its immediate predecessor (founded in October 1949) still and somewhat coyly calling itself Ausschuss für Wirtschaftsfragen der industriellen Verbände (Committee for Economic Questions Relating to Industrial Associations). For all practical purposes the BDI was the successor of the RDI of the Weimar days.

It took industry and commerce also quite long to persuade the Allies to allow the re-formation of employers' associations. They, too, first began to operate at local and regional level, charged with representing the employers in the collective bargaining system which had been reconstituted. If it took until 1949–50 for a national employers' federation, the Bundesvereinigung der Deutschen Arbeitgeberverbände (BDA), to emerge, this delay was partly due to the policies of the occupation authorities; but it was also due to the unwillingness of the regional and branch associations which had meanwhile sprung up and which had entrenched themselves in the collective bargaining process with the trade unions to subordinate themselves to a powerful peak association. In the end, agreement could only be reached by allowing the regions and branch organisations to retain their cherished autonomy.

The rebuilding of trade unions also experienced a number of twists and turns before the Deutscher Gewerkschaftsbund (DGB) was finally constituted as a national umbrella organisation in October 1949. Long before the end of the war, the Allies had been clear that democratic unions were essential in a future Germany, and General Dwight D. Eisenhower had made an announcement to this effect in December 1944. With the war barely over, trade unions quickly proliferated at a local and regional level all over the country. Thus only a few weeks after the British authorities had issued the required licences, some 94,000 workers had joined trade union organisations in Lower Saxony. By July 1946 the trade unions of the British zone counted a total of 1.2 million members. Given these growth figures and many unresolved organisational and programmatic issues, it is not surprising that disagreements soon arose between the Allies and those trade-union leaders who had returned from exile or re-emerged from an underground existence in the Third Reich anxious to apply what they saw as the lessons of the past. Many of them blamed the unions' failure to resist and combat the Nazi threat more effectively on the lack of unity in the Weimar period. They were therefore particularly keen to overcome the old divisions into Free, Catholic and Hirsch-Duncker unions and to create an *Einheitsgewerkschaft*, a unitary structure. Such a centralised organisation was to weld all industrial and white-collar unions together into a single movement. Only in this way, the leaders believed, would it be possible to build up a power position and to achieve their far-reaching political and economic objectives formulated in the wake of the Nazi experience. Yet the proposed concentration of union power was bound to worry the occupation authorities. They tended to see the trade unions as one of the pillars of a future German democracy, to be established from the bottom up.

Soon, however, Allied beliefs in the principle of democracy came into conflict with Allied fears of a grassroots radicalism.

Might this radicalism not use the available democratic channels to build up political positions which were unacceptable to the Allies? We shall see in a moment that these fears were not entirely unjustified and that quite powerful anti-capitalist aspirations began to articulate themselves among the rank and file of the working-class movement. Accelerated by growing tensions between the West and the Soviet Union and by worries about the strength of the communist vote, the conflict was soon resolved in favour of those in the Allied administration who had been more sceptical of their colleagues' 'bottom-up' strategy from the start. Rather than allowing the 'base' to call the tune and to experiment with what looked to the Allies like syndicalism, it seemed wiser to them to encourage a 'top-down' development in which a less radical trade-union hierarchy guided the reconstruction and reorganisation effort. It is not difficult to see that, their other disagreements notwithstanding, the views of the occupation authorities would converge on this point with those of the union moderates at the top of the *Einheitsgewerkschaft*. These moderates were no less concerned than the Allies about signs of a grassroots radicalism and preferred control from above.

Disagreement between the Allies and the trade-union leadership persisted over the degree of centralisation to be attained. In particular the Americans, whose weight in the councils of the Western occupation powers had grown steadily since 1945, favoured a federal solution along the lines of the American Federation of Labor (AFL). In the end a compromise was forged between the Allies and the trade-union leadership at the cost of the 'base'. Grassroots democracy lost out against centralisation, which in turn was mitigated by the federal principle and the right of parliamentary-democratic control through representative assemblies elected by the rank and file members. Individual unions retained a large measure of autonomy *vis-à-vis* the umbrella organisation, first created at a zonal level, before it was transformed into a national DGB after the founding of the Federal Republic. Finally, while the idea of a *centralised* unitary structure foundered, the notion of *Industriegewerkschaft*, which the British occupation authorities promoted, triumphed. This was the concept, already analysed above (see pp. 41f.), that no more than one single union should operate in a particular

171

enterprise. Depending on what branch of industry the company belonged to, all members would be organised in that one union. To be sure, membership was on a voluntary basis, and closed-shop arrangements were illegal. Both the federal principle and the *Industriegewerkschaft* principle were to shape the future of industrial relations in West Germany in important ways and have been dealt with in the first part of this book.

6.3 Genesis of Co-determination and Workers' Participation

While much of the energies of the first two years after the end of the war were taken up, as far as the unions were concerned, with organising the workers after years of labour repression and with determining the constitutional framework of trade-union action, substantive issues, which were obviously at no point insignificant, gradually gained in importance. Ultimately they, too, were settled after much passionate ideological and political argument in the late 1940s and early 1950s.

If German entrepreneurs, not least because of their involvement in the Nazi economy, were in a state of ideological confusion in 1945 and at most capable of a defensive response to Allied policies and to the often quite radical social and economic ideas circulating among the German population at this time, the trade unions did not suffer from a lack of programmatic planks. Their concepts must be seen against the background of a general feeling that the failure of capitalism after 1929 had been a major factor in the rise of Nazism up to 1933 and twelve years of ruthless dictatorship thereafter. There were also quite a few Germans who believed that the industrial elites had been a pillar of the Hitler regime and had welcomed or condoned the destruction of the working-class movement in 1933. Reflections of these early postwar sentiments could even be found in the Christian Democratic Union, the main middle-class party founded in 1945. In February 1947 the Christian Democratic Union approved the so-called Ahlen Programme, which contained the following introductory sentences:

> The capitalist economic system has failed to do justice to the vital political and social interests of the German people. Following the

terrible political, economic and social collapse as a consequence of criminal power politics, only a fundamental renewal is conceivable. Capitalist striving for profit and power can no longer constitute the essence and objective of this social and economic renewal; it will have to be the well-being of our nation. By adopting a cooperative economic order (*gemeinwirtschaftliche Ordnung*), the German people shall obtain an economic and social constitution which is commensurate with the rights and dignity of man, serves the spiritual and material reconstruction of our nation and secures peace at home and abroad.[1]

If such demands could be heard from within the camp of the middle-class parties, the pressure for fundamental reforms was bound to be even stronger on the left of the political spectrum. Under the leadership of its chairman Kurt Schumacher, who had spent most of the Nazi period in a concentration camp and who, for this reason alone, possessed great moral authority among his followers, the reconstituted Social Democratic Party advanced a programme which aimed at the establishment of a 'democratic socialism'. The Social Democrats argued that there was only one lesson to be learnt from the past: the realisation of genuinely democratic principles both in the sphere of politics and of the economy. As a first step towards economic democratisation, the Social Democratic Party proposed to take into public ownership the large combines in coal and steel as well as the big financial institutions. Although one must be careful not to identify the programmatic positions of the re-emerging trade-union movement too closely with those of the Social Democratic Party, socialisation was a demand which also enjoyed widespread support on the shop floor. While socialisation was assumed to solve the problems of power and control in certain industries, large areas of business remained which, in the view of the trade unions, required a new institutional framework. Within this framework the unions were to have a major voice in matters of economic management, be it at company level or above. The aim was to achieve parity between capital and labour in these areas of industry with a national Economic Council (Wirtschaftsrat) at the top of the power-sharing pyramid.

---

1. Quoted in O.K. Flechtheim (ed.), *Die Parteien der Bundesrepublik Deutschland*, Hamburg, 1973, p. 157.

The trade unions also had no doubt that they should be the only legitimate representatives of the workforce when it came to establishing equal participation at company level and above. Hence the demand for *überbetriebliche Mitbestimmung* in matters concerning the macro-economic planning and management of industry, where unions and employers would meet either for bilateral discussions or in a trilateral arrangement involving government officials. As Hans Böckler, the chairman of the DGB in the British Zone, put it in March 1946: 'We must be represented in the economy on completely equal terms, and not just in individual organs, not just in the chambers, but in the economy as a whole'.[2] Similarly, the Fourth Inter-Zonal Conference of May 1947, at which Social Democratic, Christian and Communist union representatives were present, passed a motion calling for a 'reformation of the economy' involving the 'establishment of a system of a planned and directed economy' with 'organs of economic self-administration'. At the local and regional level the chambers were thought to constitute a suitable infrastructure for the implementation of the parity principle. At the inter-zonal (or national) level the above-mentioned Economic Council was envisaged which would lay down broad guidelines for the overall management of the economy. Whatever the details of this pyramid of economic agencies, it is not difficult to see that its origins went back to the efforts to create a similar peacetime planning machinery after the First World War.

The idea of union participation at supra-company level must be distinguished from that of *betriebliche Mitbestimmung*, — that is, an involvement in the affairs of individual companies. The fact that in many places workers had had a major share in the reopening of factories immediately after the defeat had no doubt given a boost to this concept of participatory management. Moreover, many companies had also introduced works councils through which employees were able to participate. Not surprisingly, therefore, the idea of 'economic democracy' at company level had a special appeal among the organised working class. To be sure, it was not just a matter of collective bargaining and negotiations with the management on the basis of equality which the unions wanted. They aimed at nothing less than

2. Quoted in V.R. Berghahn, *The Americanisation of West German Industry, 1945–1973*, Leamington Spa–New York, 1986, p. 210.

parity on the Supervisory Boards of all larger companies not earmarked for nationalisation. Furthermore, they demanded a direct say on the Management Board, which under German company law was charged with the executive tasks of running the company. Here a so-called labour director (*Arbeitsdirektor*) was to look after all matters relating to employment and social policy. Again, to understand the peculiarities of *paritätische betriebliche Mitbestimmung* it is important to remember the debates in the ADGB during the 1920s and the divergent concepts of economic democracy developed at that time.

However, the ultimate shape of the new system fell far short of what the trade unions were pushing for in the late 1940s. First, the nationalisation programme fell by the wayside, despite initial high hopes that it would succeed. These hopes were founded in the fact that most of the major coal and steel firms were situated in the Ruhr area which the British had taken over as part of their zone. In 1945 a Labour government had come to power in London which was itself committed to a domestic programme of nationalisation. It was also important that the British had a good deal of sympathy for the trade-union leaders of their zone, a number of whom had lived as exiles in London during the war. As late as 25 October 1946, the Foreign Secretary, Ernest Bevin, had told the House of Commons that the German people were to be given ownership of the basic industries and that German plans in this direction could count on British support. Less than ten weeks later, however, the administrative merger of the British and American zones was announced. Her own exhaustion and postwar problems had almost forced Britain into the arrangement with the Americans, who had emerged from the war as the dominant power. By 1946 it had become clear that, on top of reconstructing her own international and domestic position, maintaining several million Germans in the Ruhr and other urban centres went beyond Britain's financial resources. Only the Americans were strong enough to help out; but they agreed to do so only after having wrung concessions from London on how to handle certain fundamental questions of occupation policy in the Bi-Zone. Thenceforth Washington and the Office of Military Government US (OMGUS) under General Lucius D. Clay took the driver's seat in matters of economic policy-making, and all the British

were able to do was to put on the brakes and to delay developments with which they were unhappy.

As far as the aspirations of the German trade unions were
concerned, nationalisation of the basic industries was the first
casualty of American hegemony in the Bi-Zone. This was an
issue on which Washington and OMGUS had particularly strong
views, even if the policy adopted was given a sugar-coating in
public: the Germans — so the Americans argued — would have
to decide for themselves whether they wished to take banks and
heavy industry into public ownership. Such a decision could
only be taken after a national parliament had been elected.
Postponement rather than outright rejection was henceforth the
strategy of the United States occupation authorities. A growing
fear of Communism, with all its political and economic associations, strengthened the hand of the opponents of nationalisation further.

Meanwhile, the Marshall Plan was proclaimed which held out
to the Germans the prospect of economic aid only a few months
after they had experienced, 1946–47, a particularly cold winter
with mass misery and starvation. This was the sugar-coating on
the pill which the trade unions were asked to swallow. As late as
August 1947 the DGB of the British Zone had ratified, at a
conference at Nienburg, its 'Principles . . . for a Re-ordering of
the Basic Industries'. Yet, only a few weeks later Böckler made a
speech in London in which he said that, if faced with 'the
alternative between socialisation of the mining industry or a
reconstruction of the economy', the trade unions would prefer
'postponement to starvation'. Given the rapidly changing international situation and the shifting balance of domestic forces in
western Germany, nationalisation now receded more and more
into the background. It was only as a result of an elaborate
compromise, concluded between the Catholics and the Social
Democrats during the drafting of the Basic Law (the constitution
of the future Federal Republic), that the *possibility* of nationalisation was enshrined in Articles 14 and 15, provided parliamentary majorities could be found in the Bundestag. Such majorities
have not existed to this day and are unlikely to come about in
the foreseeable future.

The establishment of parliamentary democracy, first at the
level of individual states and later at federal level, also cut the

ground from under the idea of economic democracy at supra-company level (*überbetriebliche paritätische Mitbestimmung*). With legislative assemblies becoming the centres of control and decision-making, the hierarchy of elected economic councils, which the trade unions envisaged, was bound to lose much of its power-political *raison d'être*. It was difficult to defeat the argument put forward by the parliamentary democrats that a council system as a means of democratic control over economic matters was no longer required when popularly elected parliaments had been given a comprehensive legislative mandate and hence could also pass laws pertaining to the regulation of the economy. As a result of this constitutional development, the whole elaborate structure devised by the unions for gaining parity representation on councils and chambers at supra-company level had suddenly become demoted to the position of a sub-structure which might proffer advice to the parliamentary bodies, but did not possess independent powers of decision-making. In other words, the early aspirations of the trade unions to gain participatory power and control had been decisively undermined.

The net effect of these developments, which were heavily influenced by the United States but welcomed by the employers, was that the unions were pushed back into the field of industrial relations in the strict sense. Increasingly, they began to concentrate on the question of parity at company level. While the Americans were not keen on this type of participation either, Böckler and his colleagues could count on the support of the British occupation authorities. In the autumn of 1946 they indicated a preparedness to experiment with a parity model of co-determination and did so not only because the Attlee government was sympathetic towards the German trade unions and more concerned to control the latent power of German industry than the Americans, but also because they were worried about the above-mentioned grassroots radicalism in the factories, which had once more become evident in the recent works councils elections. Clearly, it was preferable to have reliable and moderate union functionaries to cope with instead of shop-floor communists whose political aims were anathema to the British Labour Party. As it had been decided to reorganise the coal and steel industries of the Ruhr irrespective of vigorous opposition

177

by German management, giving the unions parity of representation might kill two birds with one stone: it would strengthen the hand of the union leadership *vis-à-vis* shop-floor radicals and it might win over the DGB to support the deconcentration plans that were being prepared for heavy industry by the North German Iron and Steel Control (NGISC) under William Harris-Burland.

These appear to have been the considerations behind an invitation which Böckler received towards the end of 1946 to enter into negotiations with a view to establishing *paritätische Mitbestimmung* in the Ruhr steel industry. It is perhaps also significant that the formation of the Bi-Zone was looming on the horizon and that the Steel Trustees, a group of German experts appointed by the British to develop deconcentration plans, had completed their first assessment of the Ruhr steel industry. The group of experts was headed by Heinrich Dinkelbach, a former board member of the Vereinigte Stahlwerke, before 1945 Europe's largest steel trust. Dinkelbach had gained the confidence of the British, not least, it appears, because he himself favoured a deconcentration of heavy industry. There is also some evidence that he had come under the influence of Catholic social thought and was more open to cooperation with the unions than his former colleagues.

In December 1946 Dinkelbach met a delegation under the leadership of Böckler to explain his plans for deconcentration. He added that he was also inclined to put employee representatives on the Supervisory Boards and the Management Boards of the steel companies in question. Böckler responded quickly, and by the middle of January 1947 the details of union representation had been agreed in respect of the first four steel trusts singled out for deconcentration: the Supervisory Boards were to consist of eleven members, five of whom were to be delegated by the shareholders and five by the works council as representatives resp. union delegates. The 'neutral' eleventh member and chairman was to be appointed from among the Steel Trustees. The Management Board was to be made up of a technical director, a director in charge of the commercial and financial side and a labour director. The latter was to be nominated, like his two colleagues, by the Supervisory Board. However, no labour director could be nominated against the wishes of the company's works council and of the unions. The much-debated West German model of co-determination (*paritätische betriebliche Mitbestimmung*) had been born (see also pp. 117ff.).

Only now did Dinkelbach inform the employers of the bargain that he had struck with Böckler. It took the employers a mere twenty-four hours to respond. On 18 January 1947 Karl Jarres, the chairman of the Klöckner Supervisory Board, and the Gutehoffnungshütte directors Hermann Reusch and Hilbert, sent two letters to the *Einheitsgewerkschaft* in Cologne. In them they offered union participation on the Supervisory Boards of their companies, but not on the basis of complete parity. Nor did they mention the future composition of the Management Board. It was obvious that these offers fell short of what Dinkelbach had put on the table. It was also clear that, if Böckler had made common cause with Jarres, Reusch and Hilbert, any deal would still have required the approval of the NGISC. As the employers' side must have been aware of these difficulties, the question arises as to how far the two letters should be seen as a tactical move rather than an offer on which they would be taken up. Not surprisingly, Böckler refused to drop the Dinkelbach agreement. Thenceforth Gutehoffnungshütte and a number of other steel companies grudgingly began to adopt co-determination on the basis of the above-mentioned parity model at Supervisory Board level; a labour director was put on the Management Board.

What must have looked like a major victory for the unions, had one major flaw whose seriousness was probably not appreciated at the time: the model had come about against the will of the employers, and it was not based on legislation ratified through parliamentary channels. It had been introduced by an Allied fiat which put its durability under a cloud. The employers were likely to press for abolishing the Böckler–Dinkelbach accord and could certainly be expected to oppose a co-determination bill, should an attempt ever be made to have the new system confirmed by a future West German parliament.

Such a parliament, the Bundestag, came into being in 1949, after the Western Allies had approved the formation of a West German state based on a parliamentary-democratic constitution and after elections had been held in the three Western zones of occupation. The results of these elections paved the way for the formation of a coalition cabinet made up of ministers from a number of bourgeois parties. On 20 September 1949 the head of this new government, Chancellor Konrad Adenauer, presented his programme to the Bundestag. This programme contained a reference to the need to put the relations between employers and employees in industry and commerce on a 'modern' footing. Six weeks later the Bundestag majority mandated the Adenauer Cabinet to draw up a Works Constitution bill. Although not even the experts may have appreciated all the ramifications of this proposed piece of legislation at the time, the central question was from the start as to how much weight the employees and the unions were to have in the decision-making bodies (Supervisory Board and Management Board) of larger companies. Should the unions and the workforce be given parity or no more than a minority representation? Would there be a labour director on the Management Board or would the interaction between the management and the works council, which everybody expected to continue to operate, be without a labour director as an intermediary?

Adenauer realised that these were very contentious issues, even within the parties of his own government coalition, and rather than forging ahead with the drafting of a Works Constitution bill, he therefore thought it wise to stimulate preliminary discussions between the two sides of industry. If an accord could be hammered out between the BDA and the DGB, the passage through the Bundestag of a bill which incorporated this compromise would obviously have been smoothed. The BDA and DGB responded to these suggestions and held a first meeting before Christmas 1949. It was agreed to hold detailed negotiations at the beginning of January in the town of Hattenheim near Rüdesheim on the Rhine.

This first round of talks was full of ambiguities. To begin with, there were psychological problems. Although trade unionists and employers had more than once met around the table at local and zonal level since the end of the war, this was the first time since the 1920s that formal discussions involving major issues took place at top level. All representatives were old enough to have memories of the Weimar Republic and the post-1918 system of industrial relations, but also of the conflicts that broke out in the late 1920s and early 1930s. On the employers' side there was Gerhard Erdmann, a ZAG veteran, who had been general secretary of the VdA and who had just resumed that position in the BDA. Erdmann was in favour of top-level cooperation with the unions, but he loathed the idea of 'economic democracy' as first promoted by the ADGB in the Weimar Republic. The DGB representatives could not but have at the back of their minds the experience of the working-class movement under Nazism which industry had done nothing to ameliorate. On the other hand, and with some of their colleagues still being imprisoned as war criminals, the employers were very conscious of what had happened to them after 1945 under Allied occupation. Nor were they oblivious of the broader power-political aspirations of the unions and their demand for participation in industry. At the same time, many employers realised that a fresh start had to be attempted and that there were great benefits in concluding a lasting social peace when all energies were to be devoted to industrial reconstruction. To be sure, there were some who saw a future Works Constitution bill as an opportunity for curbing union power and for rolling back some of the advances that had been made by the DGB after 1945. They were particularly hostile to the idea of union representation and at company level wanted to deal with representatives of the workforce alone. Behind this attitude there lurked a more general inability of many employers to accustom themselves to the idea of unionisation, which they had so comfortably done without before 1945.

It was with these and a number of other assumptions and perceptions about each other that the two sides came face to face at Hattenheim. The unions were asked to present their case and started off with the question of co-determination at regional and national level, proposing, rather vaguely, that the two sides of industry should be involved in a system of social and economic 'self-administration and self-responsibility'. But no specific proposals were made. The union spokesman then explained the need for employees to be involved in the economic and social affairs of individual companies which could only be achieved in 'close contact with the unions'. The employers responded by signalling their basic preparedness to develop a system of cooperation and participation at supra-company level. Considering that a parliamentary system had now been established, it was not particularly risky to offer further discussions on this aspect.

A national Economic Council, proposed by the unions, would have had no more than advisory powers. As regards participation at company level, the employers asked for details on how the unions proposed to run the system. The subsequent discussion, the minutes of which are now available, brought out some of these details, but also led to the first serious differences of opinion. Thus participation had an all-embracing meaning for the union representatives; the employers, on the other hand, were only prepared to concede some say in matters of welfare and personnel management while insisting that there must be no interference with the managerial prerogative to make the final decision concerning the economic operation of the company. The right to manage was to be upheld at all cost. However, these differences notwithstanding, both sides were eager not to break off the top-level contacts that had only just been established. It was agreed to hold a further round of talks at Hattenheim, which were convened for 30–31 March 1950.

In preparation of this meeting the DGB sent the employers a set of detailed proposals. The actual discussions on 30 March were this time led off by Viktor Agartz, the economic adviser of the DGB. He explained the union views on a future Economic Council and how it would differ from the Reich Economic Council of the Weimar days. He then outlined the DGB's positions relating to a reform of the system of chambers and other regional bodies of economic self-administration, adding that in order for this system to function properly the unions expected to obtain parity of representation with the employers. But the real shock came when Agartz next elaborated the DGB's ideas on participation at company level. Referring to the model which had been introduced in the Ruhr steel industry in 1947–8, he made clear that the unions were hoping to extend this model to large-scale enterprises in all other branches of industry and commerce. Without going into the exchanges that followed this statement, it was over this point that the Hattenheim talks ultimately became deadlocked. An extension of the Dinkelbach model was totally unacceptable to the employers both because of the parity principle and because of the role to be given to union representatives within it. On 4 April Walther Raymond, the BDA president and leader of the employers at Hattenheim, informed Adenauer that there was no room for compromise and that the chancellor's strategy of the autumn of 1949 had therefore failed.

On 14 April 1950 the DGB defiantly published its 'Proposals for the Re-ordering of the German Economy', which demanded parity at the level of large-scale enterprises and above. The problem had now been thrown back into the public and parliamentary arena. There was a possibility that the DGB proposals might find their way into the Bundestag and that the Social Democratic Party might form a united front with those Christian Social deputies in the Christian Democratic Union who were likewise in favour of a major reorganisation of industrial relations in West Germany. Other deputies from the Christian Democratic Union and the more right-wing Free Democratic Party were also busy devising alternative legislative proposals which envisaged much more modest forms of employee participation. If their ideas became law, the Dinkelbach model would have to be dismantled because it would have lacked a legal basis. Adenauer was highly alarmed by the hectic activity of all these countervailing forces. His coalition government was too unstable to survive a major parliamentary conflict between the Christian Democratic Union's Christian Social wing on the one hand, and the rest of the party and the Free Democratic Party on the other. Nor could he afford to alienate the unions and thereby undermine the prospect of industrial peace so vital for the success of his government. The economy was still in a precarious state, and strikes were the last thing the chancellor wanted.

In this situation Anton Storch, Adenauer's Labour Minister and a man close to the Catholic trade-union movement, made a last-ditch attempt to engineer a compromise between the two sides of industry. Under his chairmanship, talks were started at the Maria Laach Monastery north-west of Koblenz at the end of June 1950. There were several meetings, but at the beginning of July Storch had to admit defeat. Thenceforth the situation became increasingly polarised and the conflict drifted towards its dramatic climax of January 1951.

By the autumn of 1950 rumours were circulating in Bonn that a ministerial draft had been completed for the introduction of a Works Constitution bill which made no mention of the parity principle and of existing arrangements in the steel industry. If such a bill was ratified, the Dinkelbach model would have become obsolete. Faced with the threat of being disenfranchised in this way, the Metal-Workers Union (I.G. Metall) polled its members on whether they would be prepared to go on strike in that eventuality. At the end of November no less than 97.87 per cent of the members voted in favour of strike action. Given this result, Adenauer was now being pulled in two directions. On the one hand, the hardliners in industry, who had never reconciled themselves to the advances made by the unions after the war and who detested the Dinkelbach model, urged him to stand firm and not to give in to union 'blackmail'. On the other hand, the chancellor, encouraged by some of his advisers and by a number of more far-sighted industrialists, felt that a defeat of the DGB was both counter-productive and, in view of the contribution the unions had made to postwar stabilisation, historically unfair. Around Christmas 1950 Adenauer made a further move to bring the two sides together. The compromise which was now beginning to emerge was an ingenious one. If it was clear that the unions lacked the muscle to extend the parity principle beyond heavy industry, but also that the Dinkelbach model could be dismantled only at great political cost, the miracle solution suddenly appeared to be to take the 1947 steel model as a separate legislative item *in advance* of the Works Constitution Bill. This solution would appease the unions and avoid a major and damaging strike. The employers, on the other hand, would be reassured that parity would not be extended beyond heavy industry. A model which was less radical could then be adopted via a Works Constitution bill at a later date.

On the basis of these premises Adenauer succeeded in bringing the two sides of industry back to the negotiating table. The documents show that there arose dramatic scenes in the course of these negotiations, and more than once were they on the brink of collapse. But, with the chancellor keeping himself in readiness as a mediator, agreement was finally achieved on 25 January. The essentials of the Dinkelbach model were to be preserved for all steel-producing companies with over 1,000 employees and to be extended to mining enterprises of equivalent size. On 29 January the unions approved the guidelines which had emerged from the previous negotiations. Subsequently, a draft bill was put to the Bundestag and accepted by a clear majority. Thenceforth, coal and steel in West Germany

Figure 6.1 Co-determination in the mining and the iron- and steel-producing industries

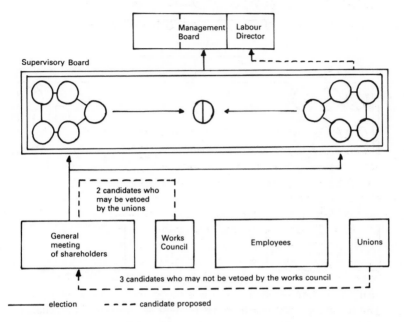

had the structure illustrated in Figure 6.1 (until May 1981, when the changes were made which have been described on p. 119).

It is illuminating to juxtapose this model with the structure of participation in large-scale enterprises outside coal and steel which was laid down by the 1952 Works Constitution Act. Figure 6.2 highlights the much simpler structure of the 1952 Act. There was no employee or union representative on the Management Board. The workforce had a minority representation on the Supervisory Board and there was no direct trade-union input. Whatever union influence there existed was wielded through the works council, which all joint-stock enterprises and limited companies with more than fifty employees were obliged to have. Its elected members were to represent the workforce *vis-à-vis* the management, which was under the obligation to consult with the works council on matters of personnel planning, manpower policy and welfare. Finally, the management was legally bound to inform the works council of any major

185

Figure 6.2 Employee participation under the Works Constitution Act, 1952

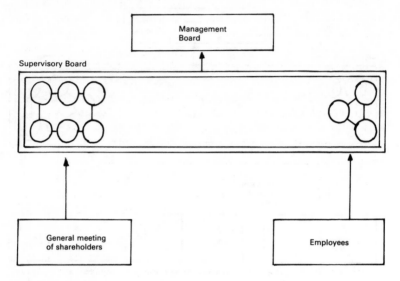

structural changes it was proposing to make in the company. The works council, for its part, was given primarily a mediating role between management and workforce. Accordingly, it was not supposed to assume a mobilising function, for example, in the preparation of a strike.

This is not the place to trace the parliamentary debates relating to the 1952 Works Constitution Bill. It is clear that, although the DGB and the Social Democratic Party tried to reintroduce the idea of parity into the debate once the 1951 Co-determination Act had been ratified, they failed to gain the necessary parliamentary majorities for their proposals. Nor did the unions achieve a privileged constitutional position in the works council itself or in the selection of the works council members for service on the Supervisory Board. All in all, participation outside coal and steel therefore never amounted to co-determination and power-sharing. It was more in the nature of consultation and moderation. On the other hand, the significance of the platform gained by employees and, indirectly, by the unions should not be underestimated. It was an institutionally secured base from which important initiatives for improved welfare benefits could be launched and negotiated at company level or, if necessary, could be transmitted to parliament or the regular collective-bargaining rounds between the regional employers' associations of a particular branch of industry and their counterpart organisation on the union side.

It is important to emphasise these points because they provided the workforce with levers, not to transform the capitalist system and to weaken the dominant position of the employers in any decisive way but to wring concessions which certainly contributed to the long-term improvement of the material position of the working population in West Germany and, in turn, to the relative industrial peace and low incidence of strikes. It also facilitated the flow of information about a company's problems. Unlike their counterparts in Britain, West German workers do not hear of such problems for the first time through the newspaper but learn about them well in advance through the works council. Thus the construction of a social welfare 'net' (to be referred to in the next chapter) is unthinkable without the constitutional framework devised in the early 1950s. Finally, it is worth reiterating that the developments discussed in this chapter amounted to a reconstruction also in an institutional sense. The industrial relations edifice which was created in the late 1940s and early 1950s contained quite a number of 'building bricks' which dated back to the 1920s and which were once more combined, with some variations, to form the basis of the post-war system of union–employer interaction.

6.4 Practice of Industrial Relations in the 1950s

The creation of an institutional framework, however deeply linked to historical antecedents, did not guarantee that those who were expected to operate the new rules would also make them work. Even if a particular system of industrial relations lives up to the original hopes and expectations in the long run, there may be a longer 'running-in' period when the two sides involved have to adapt themselves to the new game and to each other. Looking at the experience of co-determination in coal and steel, the long-term impact of the 1951 model would appear to have been beneficial. This emerges not only from the analysis presented in the first part of this book, but also from a study undertaken at Princeton University in the mid-1950s. Its author, W. Michael Blumenthal, concluded that all in all:

> codetermination in steel companies proved to be much less radical than expected. It did not disrupt the enterprises, nor ruin the industry . . . . Codetermination did not solve as many problems as predicted, nor did it create as many as prophesied. . . . Labor's presence on the company boards inaugurated a spirit of cooperation and understanding of mutual needs quite uncommon in German labor relations. Codetermination was of considerable educational value to the unions. It forced them to develop and train a group of leaders who would have a high level of understanding of the problems of workers as well as of companies. Furthermore, since these men became involved in the management process, they came to have a stake in the well-being of the enterprises.[3]

Finally, Blumenthal also found 'a convincing body of direct and indirect evidence that the incidence of strikes and work stoppages declined under codetermination'. Some fifteen years later, January 1970, a Commission of Experts under the chairmanship of Kurt Biedenkopf submitted a report on its own exhaustive investigations into the experience of co-determination. Its assessment of the 1951 Act was also surprisingly favourable and in fact gave a further stimulus to the revised industrial relations legislation of the 1970s (see pp. 137ff.).

Blumenthal's reference to strikes and open labour conflicts points to an area of union–employer interaction which, like the operation of the 1951 and 1952 Acts, required collective learning and mutual adjustment. Given the legacies of the Nazi dictatorship and its disruptive effect on industrial relations in Germany, this too was a process which did not happen overnight. As to the unions, their defeat in 1952 over the question of participation and works councils representation led some of their leaders to change their strategy. With the economy booming, they began to concentrate not on extending their constitutional power position but on wages and working conditions of their members. This implied that the DGB and its affiliated unions

---

3. W.M. Blumenthal, *Codetermination in the German Steel Industry*, Princeton, 1956, pp. 107ff.

slowly abandoned earlier aspirations of a fundamental transformation of the existing socio-economic order. They acknowledged that the type of liberal capitalism which had emerged by the early 1950s was there to stay and gaining in popularity. It was hence more important to try and improve the lot of the working population and to create a market economy cushioned by increased welfare provision. On the whole, this alternative strategy has been remarkably successful.

It was also in this context that the unions learned to cope with and to manipulate a system of collective bargaining which was increasingly characterised by legally prescribed procedures. Supervised by a system of labour courts, whose roots went back to the Weimar period, the juridification of West German industrial relations set in. Occasionally, the lesson was learnt the hard way, as in the case of I.G. Metall, which following a four-month strike in Schleswig-Holstein, was told by the Federal Labour Court to pay huge sums in damages. The union had been found guilty of having called for a strike ballot before the wage negotiations had officially been declared to have been broken down. This move was deemed to have been a violation of the legally required *Friedenspflicht* of the collective bargaining partners — a duty discussed in the first part of this book (pp. 82f.).

It also took the unions — which after all had not had an opportunity to organise strikes since the Weimar days — some time to discover that traditional strike tactics were not necessarily adequate to the new postwar situation. Successes, it turned out, could just as effectively, but more cheaply, be won by avoiding the time-honoured all-out strike and by adopting a regional or local approach (*Schwerpunktstreik*) in one selected industry or individual companies. Finally, as has been seen (p. 51), it tended to pay off to use as trend-setters those unions, like I.G. Metall, which were well organised and had more clout at the bargaining table. However, up to the late 1950s the strategy of the unions remained ambiguous. The problem was that some leaders, though favouring an activist and expansionist wage policy, did not see this approach as exclusive. Otto Brenner of I.G. Metall, especially, did not share the moderation of his colleagues in other branches and continued to press for a redistribution of economic power as Böckler had done. His speeches were more aggressive and more frightening to the employers, and it was only after his humiliation in the Federal Labour Court after the strike in Schleswig-Holstein that the intra-union balance of power clearly began to tilt towards those who advocated a 'social partnership' approach rather than confrontation and conflict. Thenceforth the Keynesian demand managers and Social Democratic reformists won the upper hand in the DGB, and the period of ambiguity came to an end.

On the other side of the fence, West German industrialists had to make even greater mental and psychic adjustments to the changed postwar situation. There was not merely the obstacle of the 1951 Co-determination Act, which many of them refused to see as anything else than a diktat by the unions; they also had great difficulties recognising the unions as legitimate bargaining partners in wage negotiations where this partnership was legally never in doubt. For men like Hermann Reusch, the influential director-general of the Gutehoffnungshütte, or Berg, the first president of the BDI, union leaders across the negotiating table remained what they had always been regarded as by heavy industry in the Weimar Republic and under the Hohenzollern monarchy: 'socialists' who needed to be opposed uncompromisingly. The BDA, on the other hand, developed a more conciliatory line and began to play an important educational role inside the employers' camp. Its presidents, Raymond and Hans Constantin Paulssen, assisted by the ZAG veteran Erdmann, were wedded to the idea of social partnership with the unions. Their exhortations to view the unions as *Ordnungsfaktoren* (factors of stability) rather than as destroyers of capitalism and parliamentary democracy were primarily beamed at their own colleagues. Thus Paulssen declared at the BDA Annual Congress in Bad Godesberg near Bonn at the end of November 1956: 'We must get away from sterile juxtaposition and opposition. We must find ways of jointly shaping our social order [to make it] the opposite of the methods of communist coercion in the East.'[4]

If the older generation of industrialists in particular continued to resist such appeals, this was partly because, contrary to later impressions, the industrial picture of the 1950s was at no point tranquil and free from latent or open conflict. Above all, how-

4. Quoted in Berghahn, p. 241.

ever, it was because of the inability of men like Reusch to abandon their authoritarian view of industrial relations which Heinz Hartmann in his well-known study of *Authority and Organization in German Management*[5] found to be deeply implanted in their mind. Finally, there was the fact that the Federal Republic underwent structural changes of both its economic and its political system which became clearly visible in the early 1960s and which prevented a stabilisation of the system of industrial relations which the moderates in the DGB and BDA had begun to bring about during the 1950s.

5. Princeton, 1959.

7
Structural Change and Industrial Relations Politics, 1960–76

7.1 Introduction

Although a constitutional framework for the operation of industrial relations had been constructed by the mid-1950s, it took somewhat longer for the two sides of industry to learn to handle the various laws and rules and to accept the underlying assumptions of the post-Hitler system. Yet even now, as this system began to solidify and to develop its unique features, it remained subject to constant change. Indeed, while mentalities were trailing behind and pulled the system back in one direction, the dynamic transformation of the West German capitalist economy likewise tugged at the existing legal structures. These pressures took two forms. First, Allied deconcentration policies had barely come to an end when a reconcentration of economic power was set in train. This movement was accompanied by a shift away from the hitherto dominant heavy industries towards manufacturing engineering, electrical engineering and chemicals. Second, there was the pressure resulting from changes in the balance of political power within the parliamentary system of the Federal Republic which, in turn, were a consequence of changing voting behaviour. As we shall see, both the changes in the economy and those in the political system were to exert a profound influence on the operation of co-determination and on industrial relations in general.

7.2 Economic Concentration and Its Effects on Co-determination and Wealth Distribution Policies

While the trade unions gradually abandoned their earlier ideas of a far-reaching transformation of the West German economy and concentrated increasingly on collective bargaining and an

Table 7.1 Concentration ratios in West German industry, 1954–60

Branch	1954	1960	Change
Oil	72.6	91.5	18.9
Tobacco	68.8	84.5	15.7
Ceramics	28.5	37.5	9.0
Vehicles	58.6	67.0	8.4
Mining	34.6	42.0	7.4
Iron and steel	51.6	57.8	6.2
Glass	45.7	51.7	6.0
Chemicals	37.5	40.6	3.1
Timber and paper	38.5	41.5	3.0
Leather	36.5	37.3	0.8
Non-ferrous metals	44.0	44.7	0.7
Electrics	37.8	38.4	0.6
Rubber and asbestos	60.7	59.7	–1.0
Precision mech./optics	25.3	25.2	–0.1
Foundries	25.3	22.4	–2.9
Plastics/fibres	27.9	20.5	–7.4

Source: J. Huffschmid, *Die Politik des Kapitals*, Frankfurt, 1969, p. 47

extension of a welfare-state capitalism, industry and finance began to reconcentrate. Table 7.1 shows the concentration ratios in various branches of industry and thus provides a first impression of what was happening during the late 1950s.

Between 1960 and 1966 (and calculated in this instance in terms of the eight largest enterprises in the branches concerned) concentration continued as follows: in chemicals it rose by 10.3 per cent, in heavy industry by 9.3 per cent, in vehicle manufacture by 8.9 per cent and in electrical engineering by 7.2 per cent. Banking likewise experienced a concentration movement. But a really remarkable merger movement began in the late 1960s, which is reflected in Figure 7.1.

Some of this concentration, to be sure, occurred within a particular product area. Thus August-Thyssen-Hütte (ATH), under the leadership of Hans-Günther Sohl, expanded into the largest steel trust in Western Europe, specialising in a relatively small range of products. But with mining in decline and the traditional vertical link between iron and steel (known in Germany as *Verbundwirtschaft*) weakening, many of the other steel combines — Krupp, Flick, Gutehoffnungshütte and Mannesmann among them — diversified horizontally and bought up

Figure 7.1 Merger movements in the West German economy, 1958–75

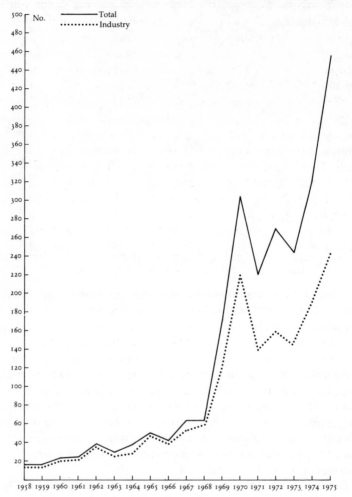

Source: J. Cable, *Merger Development in West Germany*, Warwick, 1979, p. 6

companies elsewhere, particularly in manufacturing engineering. Thus Krupp and Flick went into vehicle manufacture. Gutehoffnungshütte concentrated on machine-tools, and Mannesmann became one of the biggest pipeline manufacturers in Europe and also took over the hydraulics firm of G.L. Rexroth.

Chemicals and electrical engineering also adopted diversification strategies. Of course, an end to this process is still not in sight, with the large German trusts meanwhile having turned themselves into multinationals with participations and subsidiaries all over the world. The important point here is that by comparison with the industrial structures that were emerging by the 1960s, those of the early 1950s, when the legal framework of West German industrial relations was being created, were in fact quite simple. Or to put it the other way round, the existing framework increasingly turned out to be inadequate to cope with the dynamic economic change brought on by industry itself. It is important to emphasise this point as it casts union policy in a different light. Contemporaries tended to have the impression that the trade unions were constantly taking the offensive on the industrial relations front. In fact, however, they were responding to the above-mentioned structural changes and their destabilising effect on the social and political institutions.

There can be little doubt that the concentration movement was greatly helped by the boom of the 1950s. Returns on capital in joint-stock companies between 1951 and 1959 hovered between 10.9 per cent and 14.0 per cent. With inflation rates running low, real growth in the economy, including a meagre 3.7 per cent in 1958, averaged no less than 7.9 per cent during the 1951–9 period. High wage settlements resulting from a successful application of the new union strategy tended to fuel inflation. However, savings as a percentage of disposable income rose from 5.8 per cent in 1956 to 8.7 per cent in 1958, thus helping to restrict inflationary pressures, while providing additional capital for industry through the German system of 'universal banks' prepared to commit themselves to investment on a long-term basis.

It is not difficult to see how this favourable economic climate stimulated concentration and diversification. Often concentration occurred in several intermediate stages, culminating in fully fledged mergers only at the end of the process. However, we are primarily concerned with how these developments affected industrial relations. Changing approaches to collective bargaining and the emergence of the *Schwerpunktstreik* must obviously also be seen against this background. However, the impact was most dramatic on the constitutional framework

195

which had been established in 1951–2; for, as Ruhr combines such as Gutehoffnungshütte and Krupp, began to move out of coal and steel into manufacturing, the question was bound to arise as to whether the 1951 parity model still applied or whether, from a certain point onwards, they came under the 1952 Works Constitution Act, with important repercussions for the problem of union and works council representation on the Supervisory Board and the Management Board.

In practice the issue first surfaced in the context of the rise of the holding company. Holdings acted, so to speak, as roof organisations of a cluster of companies. Its directors were not merely involved in the administration of various participations; rather, they also tended to intervene directly in the management of the individual companies under their control. If this dependent company was in coal or steel and was hence governed by the 1951 Co-determination Act, did this imply that the holding should also be brought into the purview of this Act? Or could the holding directors circumvent union influence on the boards? The trade unions, seeing their position threatened, began to argue that the holding should also be governed by the parity principle. The holdings, on the other hand, insisted that the milder rules of the 1952 Works Constitution Act applied. Otherwise, so the employers feared, the holding might become the thin end of the wedge leading to the belated extension of the parity principle to other branches in which holding companies also had a stake. From the point of view of the conservatives in the Ruhr, the task was not an extension but a rolling back of the 1951 Act.

This conflict between the unions and the employers came into the open in 1953 when an expert appraisal was submitted to the Annual Meeting of Mannesmann shareholders which argued that holdings were subject to the Works Constitution Act even if the subordinate companies fell under the 1951 Co-determination Act. A tug-of-war ensued over this issue between the unions and the employers which was finally settled in 1956 with the passage of the Co-determination Supplementary Act (*Mitbestimmungsergänzungsgesetz*). This law stipulated that if the majority of a holding company's controlling interests were in co-determined enterprises, the 1951 Act would also apply to the umbrella organisation, but with the following variations: the

196

Supervisory Board was to be made up of fifteen members, seven each from the two sides of industry meeting under the chairmanship of a neutral fifteenth member. The election of the seven employee representatives was governed by a complex system of electors which need not concern us here.

The 1956 Act offered no more than a temporary solution, and further adjustments of the law were made in 1967 and 1981. Structural change also affected the position of the labour directors. As co-determined enterprises in coal and steel lost their independence as joint-stock companies and were incorporated into larger combinations, formerly autonomous Management Boards were demoted to the status of executive teams of works or works groups for which there existed no legal requirement to have a labour director among them. It is a reflection of this dynamic transformation of entire branches that the number of labour directors saw a marked decline. The 1951 Act was fast becoming an empty shell and the relatively greater militancy of the Metal-Workers Union (I.G. Metall) under Brenner was to some extent also due to the fact that it was determined to resist the process of disenfranchisement by slow attrition. By the late 1950s a number of steel firms had become so worried about the implications of this development for industrial peace that they seized the initiative where the legislator was apparently unwilling or unable to act. In 1959 Hoesch, Ilseder Hütte and Klöckner concluded the so-called Lüdenscheid Accord with I.G. Metall. This was an agreement in private law whereby the steel companies undertook to retain the labour director, even if the Management Board lost its independence and became a team of executives within a larger corporation. However, except for Krupp, no other heavy industrial enterprise in this category joined the Lüdenscheid Accord. Consequently, the number of labour directors continued to shrink in the 1960s.

In these circumstances it was almost to be expected that the unions would sooner or later try to reverse the tide by demanding an *extension* of the 1951 Act to large-scale enterprises in all branches of industry. It could also be anticipated that a renewed attempt would be made to gain a direct influence on the composition of the works councils and to revise the 1952 Works Constitution Act. Even before these possibilities hardened into a legislative programme propounded by the Social Democratic

Party (SPD) in the Bundestag, a number of left-wingers in the Christian Democratic Union (CDU) had apparently begun to develop a strategy which they hoped would stop a revival of DGB aspirations in the field of co-determination. As the Christian Democratic leader, Rainer Barzel, formulated it later, the idea was to anticipate the threat of an extension of 'co-determination by law' through an 'extension of co-determination as a result of co-ownership'. In other words, if employees gained a stake in 'their' company as shareholders, they would lose interest in gaining a stake through works councils and worker representatives sitting on the Supervisory Board.

Of course, the idea of a 'people's capitalism' was not a new one; nor was it a concept which was confined to West Germany. In other countries, too, the demand could be heard at this time that if mergers were inevitable, at least the shares in the emergent giant companies should be distributed more widely. By the late 1950s and in the wake of a continued boom with high returns on capital, the demand for a broader distribution of wealth gained a new urgency when another set of figures became available. For however successfully average living standards had been raised throughout the 1950s, wealth remained very unevenly distributed in West German society. In fact, the gap between the rich and the rest of the population of modest means increased all the time. Between 1950 and 1963 the distribution of wealth by occupational groups developed as shown in Table 7.2.

It was the social and political implications of these figures which began to worry politicians and economists alike. As the well-known liberal economist Moritz Bonn had put it as early as the 1920s, capitalism in the age of democracy was constantly threatened by the political power of the non-capitalists. For if these non-capitalists no longer took a benevolent interest in the existing economic order, so Bonn had warned, its future stability would be called into question. A generation later, and with the crisis of the 1930s behind the industrialised West, it was not thought to be sufficient anymore to provide greater, though unevenly distributed, 'prosperity for all'. Wealth formation (*Vermögensbildung*) in the hands of the mass of the population became the new catchword. It was also an idea with which Ludwig Erhard, Adenauer's minister of economics and reputed

Table 7.2 Distribution of wealth by occupational group, 1950–63

	Wealth in milliard marks	% of total nat. wealth	No. of households	% of all households
Workers	27.1	17	6.6 mill.	33.7
White-collar employees	21.6	13	2.8 mill.	14.3
Civil servants	11.1	7	1.2 mill.	6.1
Pensioners	26.5	16	5.9 mill.	29.8
Total	86.3	53	16.5 mill.	83.9
Farmers	12.4	8	1.1 mill.	5.4
Self-empl.	63.9	39	2.1 mill.	10.7
Total	76.3	47	3.2 mill.	16.1

father of the postwar German 'economic miracle', began to toy in the late 1950s.

One of his first schemes designed to promote wealth formation was the partial privatisation of the state-owned Volkswagen Corporation. Shares were initially taken up by many small savers, who were given preferential treatment at an attractively low issue-price, and hopes ran high that this might be the beginning of a 'people's capitalism'. But within a short time of the company being quoted on the stock market, shares soared beyond the 1,000-mark level. The original small shareholders could not resist the temptation of making a considerable profit and sold. The big investors moved in and 'people's capitalism' crumbled.

While Erhard kept on experimenting with privatisation, a few private companies began to develop profit-sharing schemes enabling employees to obtain a stake in 'their' company. The idea caught on among some of the more conservative union leaders. In 1964 an agreement was signed between the construction industry and the I.G. Bau Steine Erden under the leadership of Georg Leber which provided for a programme of wealth formation for building workers. The ratification of the 312-Marks Act, a tax-deductible savings programme, and the encouragement of home-ownership through *Bausparkassen* (building societies) savings plans were motivated by similar political considerations of putting the existing socio-economic system on a more popular basis. However, it is also highly significant that all these attempts to create a legal basis for wealth formation ran into the vigorous opposition of the majority among the employers. They suspected that all coordinated planning in this direction was the beginning of a new collectivism. It was therefore not merely the mechanisms of the market but also this opposition which caused Erhard's 'people's capitalism' to run into trouble. The net result of his largely unsuccessful initiatives, which failed to change the distribution of wealth in West Germany in any significant way, was that Barzel's extension of employee 'co-determination through co-ownership' as a means of *anticipating* fresh demands for 'co-determination by law' foundered. The former concept could not stop the re-emergence of the latter, and by the mid-1960s both were competing against each other. Ultimately, the strategy, adopted by the unions, of extending 'co-determination by law' remained victorious in the conflict that ensued.

7.3 Origins of the Revised Industrial Relations Acts of 1972 and 1976

The late 1960s and early 1970s were a dramatic period in West German domestic politics. As far as industrial relations were concerned, the issue which generated a great deal of debate and conflict was the revival of the idea to extend the 1951 Act to large-scale enterprises outside heavy industry. This, so the unions argued, was the only way to respond to the structural changes in industry which have been analysed in the previous section. Accordingly, the DGB ratified another *Grundsatzprogramm*, the first since the programme of 1949, which demanded that parity be established on the Supervisory Boards of all large corporations. Moreover, a labour director was to be put on all Management Boards. What the *Grundsatzprogramm* did not contain, though, was a call for immediate action. This demand appeared two years later, and significantly it was articulated by I.G. Chemie Papier Keramik, the union whose members had become directly affected by rapid concentration, rationalisation and technological change in the chemical industry. By extending co-determination to this branch, the union also hoped to achieve increased protection against the social consequences of structural change. A little later, Ludwig Rosenberg, the chairman of the DGB, threw his weight behind these proposals arguing that the on-going technological revolution required a constant adaptation of the country's social institutions.

The employers' response to these ideas was predictably even more hostile than it had been to the concept of wealth formation. Virtually all the big names in industry and banking spoke out against an extension of the 1951 model. They were supported in this by the newspapers of West Germany's 'press tsar', Axel Springer. Thus Ferdinand Fried, a veteran right-wing intellectual of the Weimar days, asserted in Springer's *Die Welt* (10 May 1965) that for the first time the unions were shaking 'the foundations of the economic constitution'. Harking back to Naphtali and the debate on economic democracy of the 1920s, he warned against 'socialisation through the backdoor' and drew comparisons with the situation in France on the eve of the 1789 Revolution. The 'Storming of the Bastille', he thought, was imminent. Not surprisingly, the moderates in the employers' camp were alarmed by the strident tone of these responses. Otto Wolff von Amerongen, the new DIHT president, cautioned his colleagues not to poison the atmosphere. It was indeed a strange sight. On the one hand, Rosenberg declared that he did not think the unions had taken a dogmatic stand on the question of co-determination. Rather, they wished to have continuous and open discussions with everyone who was 'likewise searching for new ways'. The conservatives in industry, on the other hand, bluntly rejected all exploratory talks.

Perhaps it was in recognition of the dangers of a purely negative stance that the BDA, led by the Daimler-Benz director Hanns Martin Schleyer, constituted a 'working circle' to study the problem of co-determination. He was seconded by Otto A. Friedrich, a former board chairman of the Phoenix Rubber Company before he joined the Flick management in 1966. Conscious of the need to maintain popular support for the existing liberal-capitalist system, he had been toying with wealth-formation plans for some time. In 1964 he produced a first draft of what was to become known as the 'Friedrich Plan'. Thenceforth a tacit alliance developed between Schleyer and Friedrich, with Schleyer advocating careful study of the Friedrich Plan. He also proposed an expansion of the 312 Marks Act as well as improved educational and training facilities for blue-collar workers. It seems that this faction tried to build up wealth-formation into an antidote to co-determination as espoused by the unions. As a memorandum of the Deutsches Industrie-Institut put it in the summer of 1968, the wealth-formation debate had been propelled by the discussions over co-determination and was seen by many industrialists as a 'social-policy alternative' to an extension of the 1951 Co-determination Act. There is also the statement by Erwin Häussler, a Bundestag deputy committed to the idea of wealth-formation. Writing in *Der Industriekurier* (11 May 1968), he argued: 'It is not yet too late. But it is high time to adopt an effective savings policy and to pass legislation without delay for organising profit-sharing schemes. Then the fascination exerted by the ideology of co-determination would fade away as quickly as it has been built up.'

The ultimate aim of these counter-moves had been outlined by Schleyer a few months earlier. In May 1968 he had lectured to his colleagues in the Verband baden-württembergischer Metallindustrieller on 'ways of integrating our fellow workers into society in conjunction with an extension of cooperation within the factory on the basis of partnership'.[1] The problem was that the unions were no longer prepared to accept manifestly ineffective savings schemes at a time when the structures and technologies of industry were experiencing rapid change which actually undermined both job security and union power. In these circumstances the DGB was increasingly attracted by a renewed demand for a greater say in management questions. Worse from the employers' point of view was that, with the re-establishment of political democracy in West Germany, the 'masses' were, theoretically at least, furnished with a legislative lever which could also be deployed for the establishment of greater economic democracy in industry. It was a threat which had haunted the employers since the days of the Weimar Republic and which they continued to fight vigorously, arguing that the demand for economic democracy could not be derived

1. Quoted in V.R. Berghahn, *The Americanisation of West German Industry, 1945–1973*, Leamington Spa–New York, 1986, p. 315.

from the successful operation of democracy in the sphere of politics. As *Der Industriekurier*, a paper with close links to the Ruhr industry, put it in October 1965: 'The democratisation of the economy is just as nonsensical as the democratisation of schools, garrisons or penitentiaries'.

But whatever dams the employers tried to erect against an extension of co-determination, they could not stop a slow shift in the balance of forces in the parliamentary sphere and prevent the Bundestag, mandated by the verdict of the voter, from becoming an engine of institutional change through legislation. All the employers could hope to do was to delay the introduction of legislation relating to industrial relations issues. The first signs of changes in the balance of political forces came towards the end of 1966 when Erhard fell from power and the SPD joined the CDU/CSU to form the so-called Grand Coalition. The new chancellor, Kurt-Georg Kiesinger, was a CDU man. But Willy Brandt, the leader of the Social Democrats, became his deputy and took charge of the foreign ministry. The Grand Coalition gave the Social Democrats an opportunity to demonstrate that they were quite capable of responsible conduct in high office, while the Free Democratic Party (FDP), now a small opposition party, regrouped under the leadership of its left wing. Fresh elections were held in 1969 in which the CDU/CSU remained the largest party, but failed to obtain an overall majority. This constellation made it possible for the SPD to link up with the Free Democrats to form a coalition government led by Brandt. It was for the first time since 1930 (!) that a Social Democrat chaired a national cabinet in Germany.

At the time of the Grand Coalition, the government — at the insistence of the SPD's parliamentary party and the Christian trade unionists within the ranks of the CDU — had already taken on board not only Friedrich's wealth-formation plans but also the demands for co-determination advanced by the unions. While the more ambitious wealth-formation schemes, including the one by Friedrich, got ground to pieces between the mill-stones of the conservative opposition in the employers' camp and the objections raised by the unions, Kiesinger appointed a commission of experts chaired by Professor Kurt Biedenkopf to study the experience of co-determination in coal and steel and to make proposals for further discussion. When the Biedenkopf

Commission finally reported in January 1970, it recommended that there should be 'a relative increase in employee representation on the Supervisory Boards of those enterprises on which employee representatives have held one-third of the seats up to now'.[2] Biedenkopf added that the representatives of the shareholders should retain a clear majority. The employee representatives were to be elected by the employees of the company concerned, although the unions operating in that company were to be given the right to nominate candidates from outside the enterprise. The idea of labour directors was not taken up by the commission. However, it recommended that a board member should be specifically charged with personnel matters and should be legally obliged to cooperate closely with the company's works council.

If these ideas were not immediately translated into legislative action by the Brandt Government, it was primarily because of the FDP, in which industry continued to wield considerable influence. For, whereas the FDP leadership agreed with the SPD that a number of reforms were to be tackled in a variety of fields, the 1969 coalition compromise also contained an accord that the question of co-determination would not be touched by the Bundestag in the current session. This agreement explains why the revised Co-determination Act was not ratified until 1976. The shift in the balance of political power in 1969, on the other hand, paved the way for a revision of the 1952 Works Constitution Act, after the Biedenkopf Commission had identified the works councils as the institutional counterparts of the board member charged with personnel matters. The bill, whose clauses have been discussed in the first part of this book (pp. 120ff.), passed through the Bundestag in November 1971 by 264 to 212 votes and reached the statute book in the spring of 1972.

Meanwhile, the 1969 coalition accord not to introduce a revised co-determination bill before the next national elections did not of course prevent the issue from being discussed in public and schemes from being proposed. In fact, all parties juggled with a variety of models concerning the composition of the Supervisory Board. At the one end of the political spectrum the CDU advocated a straight 7 : 5 split between shareholders and

2. Bericht der Sachverständigenkommission zur Auswertung der bisherigen Erfahrungen bei der Mitbestimmung (Bundestag-Drucksache VI/334), Bochum, 1970, p. 96.

employees. The SPD/DGB model, on the other hand, envisaged a 4 : 4 ratio, with both groups electing a fifth member and all ten members then agreeing on a neutral (eleventh) chairman. Meanwhile, the FDP advanced two schemes which, on the side of the employees, tried to differentiate between ordinary employee representatives and the representatives of the upper white-collar management (*leitende Angestellte*). The models, invented by two prominent FDP politicians, suggested the following ratios.

Riemer model:

Shareholders		Employees		Upper management
6	:	4	:	2

Maihofer model:

Shareholders		Employees		Upper management
4	:	4	:	2

The next step came after the SPD–FDP coalition won an impressive victory in the national elections of November 1973. With the Brandt cabinet continuing in power, the co-determination issue was certain to figure on the legislative agenda for the coming parliamentary session. But the differences between the above-mentioned SPD and FDP proposals also explain why the 1976 Co-determination Act fell short of the 1951 Act. Above all, the parity principle had not been achieved by the unions. On the other hand, labour directors did appear on all Management Boards of larger companies.

7.4 The West German Experience of Tripartism

The formation of the Grand Coalition in 1966 ushered in a shift in the balance of parliamentary forces which culminated in the SPD–FDP era of reformism in the 1970s. One of the fruits of this left-liberal reformism was a modification of the institutional framework in which West German industrial relations had been operating since the early 1950s. However, there is another important factor to be considered. The Grand Coalition arose from a profound sense of crisis which spread throughout West

German society in the mid-1960s. On the surface the crisis was a governmental one, resulting from the break-up of the CDU—FDP coalition and the consequent fall of the Erhard cabinet. But Erhard's downfall need not have led to the formation of the Grand Coalition, had it not been for the fact that the country was hit by a cyclical recession which, in turn, gave rise to radical political movements. These movements promoted, through their propaganda, solutions to the crisis which transcended and hence threatened the existing political system. On the left-wing it was the emergence of a vociferous neo-Marxist critique of liberal capitalism and parliamentary democracy which gave rise to concern among the established parties and groups. Even more alarming to them was the growth of a radical right-wing anti-capitalism and anti-republicanism articulated by the Nationaldemokratische Partei Deutschlands (NPD).

Feeding on the discontent of many provincial voters, this party achieved a spectacular breakthrough in the elections to the Hesse Diet in November 1966, polling 7.9 per cent and obtaining seven seats. Two weeks later the NPD achieved the same result in the Bavarian Diet elections, thenceforth being represented by fifteen deputies in the Diet at Munich. Was this a repetition of the Weimar experience when, under the impact of the Slump, many voters had similarly turned towards the extreme right? It was this nightmarish possibility which brought the leaders of the two main parties together. Their aim was to use the broad parliamentary majorities which they could muster, to ratify a speedy programme of economic and political stabilisation before it was too late. The programme of the Grand Coalition was an undoubted success in the sense that stability was restored and the NPD disappeared as quickly as it had risen to prominence. In the 1969 national elections the party's share dropped to 4.3 per cent, and it thereby failed to obtain seats in the Bundestag owing to a 5 per cent hurdle which had been erected in the 1950s against splinter parties.

More importantly, by 1969 the national economy was booming again and unemployment was below 1 per cent of the working population. Although the recovery of the late 1960s was export-led, it is doubtful whether it would have succeeded so quickly had it not been for the application of Keynesian methods of demand management and a systematic manipulation of the economy. In 1967 real growth had been reduced to –0.2 per cent. The Grand Coalition under the leadership of its Keynesian Minister of Economics, Karl Schiller, a Social Democrat, completely reversed the tide within a year. In 1968 real growth was back to 7.3 per cent, rising to 8.2 per cent a year later. Apart from restoring business confidence and applying a variety of technical devices of fiscal and economic management, Schiller's achievement was in no small part also due to the fact that he successfully launched the 'Concerted Action' of 1967: the round-table talks of unions, peak associations of industry, economic experts and ministerial officials under the chairmanship of the economics minister.

As these tripartist gatherings touch upon industrial relations in the strict sense, it is worthwhile looking at their origins and subsequent development. We have seen how difficult it was for the two sides of industry to evolve a stable relationship outside the framework of collective bargaining with its tendentially confrontationist procedures. However firmly the institutionalisation of labour conflict may have established itself at the level of regular negotiations between employers and unions over wages and conditions, the conservatives in industry, steeped in the authoritarianism and anti-unionism of the pre-1945 period as they still were, found it difficult to accord the unions a place in industrial politics which went beyond the arena of collective bargaining and recognised them as societal *Ordnungsfaktoren*. Although the BDA under Raymond and Paulssen tried hard to persuade their members to change their negative view of the role of unions in advanced industrial societies, it was only in 1961 that formal *Ordnungsfaktor* recognition was extended for the first time, and in this instance only by the construction industry, whose tradition of cooperation went back to the Wilhelmine period. A statement to this effect was to be found in the so-called Augsburg Accord, signed with Leber's I.G. Bau Steine Erden. Meanwhile, the rest of the labour movement had to make do with informal entrepreneurial expressions of appreciation or to note with some satisfaction the appeals which Paulssen addressed to his colleagues urging them to overcome their deep-seated reservations and to tackle all major issues of the national economy in cooperation with the unions.

A joint approach appeared to him to be all the more desirable

207

when it became more generally accepted that the state also had an increasingly important role to play in the management of the economy. In a way it was a variation on Rathenau's post-1918 argument. Originally, the neo-liberalism of Ludwig Erhard had been based on the assumption that there should be as little government regulation as possible in order to allow a liberal market economy to develop its inherent dynamism. To him state intervention was to be reduced and confined to the setting of a legal framework within which a competitive capitalism, subject only to the forces of the market, would be able to thrive. Hence Erhard's stubborn fight for a West German anti-cartel law, which he regarded as the 'Economic Basic Law' of the Federal Republic and which represented to him the best safeguard of competition. However, at no point was his *laissez-faire* philosophy purist and dogmatic. Erhard accepted that the state had to provide a welfare net, especially in the postwar period when millions had been impoverished by the war or had come to West Germany as penniless refugees from the East. Nor was he in principle opposed to his civil servants consulting with industry or to their being informed of employers' attitudes towards specific items of proposed economic legislation. In fact, in this latter respect a close relationship developed in the 1950s between the peak associations of industry and commerce and the ministrial bureaucracy.

Many of Erhard's civil servants had been members of the Reich Economics Ministry before 1945 and were at least familiar with many of the names in industry, some of whom they had met on the war production boards. In this way the old bilateral relationship between industry and the state, which the Nazi system had strengthened, was revived. Similar traditional ties between the bureaucracy and the trade unions did not exist or had been disrupted by the Nazi experience. Unlike in Britain or in the United States, where unionists had served on various war production boards in an atmosphere of patriotism and mutual trust, German trade-union leaders had spent the Second World War either in exile or in prison. Nor did the early postwar programmatic positions of the *Einheitsgewerkschaft* chime in well with the political and economic attitudes of the emergent West German civil service. In short, although there were occasional contacts, the relationship between the DGB and the Erhard ministry lacked warmth and intimacy for a whole variety of historical and other reasons. Closer cooperation might have come about if a *Bundeswirtschaftsrat*, promoted by the DGB, had been created. But as we have seen, the idea of councils with real power was undermined by the victory of the parliamentary principle (see pp. 176f.).

However, from the mid-1950s, if not before, things began to change on this front as well. Industrial concentration and structural change made a greater coordination of macro-economic policy-making unavoidable. The reorientation of the unions away from the idea of economic democracy towards cooperation within the existing system facilitated the forging of links between the DGB and the ministrial bureaucracy. Thus, with Paulssen working hard to reinforce links with the unions on his front, the contours of a trilateral framework began to emerge. The government recognised the importance of large functional groups in society and became interested in institutionalising a triangular collaboration on an informal basis. The concentration and centralisation of economic decision-making and the adoption of economic management methods and selective state intervention at the national level furthered the slow growth of more formal links between the government and the two sides of industry often defined as 'liberal corporatism'. By the early 1960s the hitherto informal advice from academic experts which the Erhard ministry had begun to seek also became formalised. In 1963 the Council of Economic Experts was formed, whose members tended to urge the government to develop medium-term fiscal projections and more generally to adopt methods of modern macro-economic management such as other advanced industrial countries were also using by this time.

All this is meant to indicate that Schiller's 'Concerted Action' of 1967 was not a completely new departure. Its roots are to be found in the Erhard period and to some extent even in the Weimar Republic, even if the earlier framework still lacked the ideological underpinnings of Keynesianism. With Schiller, Keynes's methods were, for the first time in German history, officially and publicly pursued by an elected government. To this extent it was an unusual sight to have industrialists like Berg sitting around the table with leading DGB officials and under the chairmanship of a Social Democrat to hammer out a coordinated policy for dealing with the 1966–7 recession. At the first meeting Schiller took the lead and proposed a strategy which expected the unions to reduce their wage claims in order to facilitate a planned revival of the economy. Later, Schiller added, once the expected upturn of the economy had been achieved, the temporary 'social asymmetry' was to be rectified in favour of the employees. Ground lost in previous years on the wages front could then be recovered.

It would be an exaggeration to say that the DGB subscribed to Schiller's strategy with enthusiasm; however, the unions did not openly oppose it. As a result, the West German economy emerged from the recession with remarkable speed. However, what put the unions under pressure were not so much the high growth rates achieved in 1968 and 1969; the main bone of contention became the eye-catching discrepancy between the increases in the incomes of the self-employed, on the one hand, and those of the employees, on the other. In 1968 the former enjoyed a rise of no less than 17.5 per cent, while the latter trailed by more than 10 per cent behind! It did not take long for these discrepancies to be translated into political action. Unrest spread at the shop-floor level, which finally exploded in a wave of spontaneous unofficial strikes in September 1969. Dissatisfaction in the factories was fanned by the left-wing student movement which had proliferated in the wake of the Grand Coalition, but must also be seen as part of the world-wide upsurge in youth protest against the Vietnam War accompanied by a neo-Marxist critique of the international capitalist system.

The 1969 strikes caught the union leadership off guard. In fact, they were directed as much against the moderation which the top functionaries had shown in the context of the 'Concerted Action' as they were aimed at the employers. At the beginning of 1969 the DGB chairman, Rosenberg, had published a book in which he stated:

> The trade unions — once the standard bearers of revolutionary solutions — supported without qualification the parliamentary democracy of the Weimar Republic, and they do so even more today. The development of the past century has created a new world. This [new environment] offers the preconditions for mastering those

problems peacefully which hitherto neither force nor a total reversal of [existing] structures of domination has been able to solve.[3]

A few months later, it looked as if Rosenberg's assessment might be overtaken by events.

The response of the union leaders to the incipient rank-and-file radicalism was a traditional one: they put themselves at the head of the movement in an attempt to channel it. Yet their decision made it unavoidable that they abandoned some of their earlier moderation. In particular, they now turned their attention to wages and working conditions. Soon employee incomes began to outpace those of the self-employed, eventually completely reversing the trend of the late 1960s. At the same time and with sympathetic Social Democratic ministers in the Brandt cabinet to support them, they pushed harder for an extension of co-determination and a revision of the 1952 Works Constitution Act.

It cannot be said that this strategy by the union leadership was an immediate success and that it was able to reassert its control and monopoly of representation against grassroots pressures. The wave of strikes continued, and the year 1971 saw a further increase in the number of workers who downed their tools. The south–west German metal industry experienced a particularly bitter confrontation in which the employers resorted to a mass lock-out. All in all some 4.4 million working days were lost during that year, by far the highest number since the founding of the Federal Republic. But Bonn was not Weimar, and the system of industrial relations which had slowly established itself in the 1950s and 1960s was not demolished. On the contrary, the peculiar collective-bargaining framework proved viable even in the face of two oil shocks and the resultant world recession. The revised system of co-determination and worker participation may also be said to have contributed to stabilising the pattern of industrial relations which has been described in the first part of this book. This pattern survived various crises and even the end of the 'Concerted Action'.

The unions remain a powerful factor in West German industry to this day, but they continue to use their power rationally

3. Quoted in *Die Zeit*, 6 May 1969.

and in ways which have promoted technological and social modernisation and a further overall rise in living standards. Thus the task of the remainder of this book is to draw a number of general conclusions from the analysis of the previous chapters.

Conclusion

Although the primary objective of this study has been to provide straightforward empirical information on industrial relations in West Germany for students and practitioners, it seemed useful to widen our perspective at the end of our analysis and to raise a number of larger issues which can be found to lie behind the evidence presented so far.

The first eye-catching feature of the West German industrial relations picture is the low incidence of strikes (see Table A.12, p. 235). This is in marked contrast not only to other industrialised nations, but also to the Weimar Republic (see Table A.8, p. 231). There are, of course, quite a number of factors which explain the relative industrial peace which the country has enjoyed during the last four decades after a very rocky start in the first half of this century. Some of these factors are to do with Germany's history and the lessons learnt by both sides of industry from the conflicts of the past. Others relate to the constitutional and legal arrangements devised after 1949. Another area to be discussed in this concluding section concerns the relative power balances between the major forces operating within the West German industrial relations framework. Finally, there is the remarkable economic growth which allowed a rapid increase in the standard of living. This also permitted an expansion of the welfare state and the safety net provided by it, which must be assumed to have made a tangible contribution to the relative calm and stability of the recent period. All this is not to say that there have been no strikes or sharp confrontations; nevertheless, the overall effect of the above-mentioned factors has been to create an overwhelming consciousness among the leaders and the rank-and-file membership of the two sides that gradual adaptation and improvement is preferable to the push and pull of roll-back strategies on the side of the employers and demands for radical change by the unions. However, before coming back to these notions of adaptation and improvement, some elaboration of these peace-making factors is called for.

Given the upheavals which German industry and society underwent in the first half of this century, it should not be too difficult to understand why there was such a strong desire for domestic peace and cooperation after 1945. This feeling was particularly explicit in the sphere of party politics. On the left of the political spectrum there was considerable grassroots pressure to overcome the split between the Social Democrats and the extreme Left which had occurred at the end of the First World War. It was this split which had contributed not only to the bitter struggles of the 1920s but also to the paralysis of the left in the face of National Socialism. Both the SPD and the Communists found it impossible to unite against Hitler, although it was clear that they would be among his first victims after his seizure of power. After 1945, with the experience of twelve years of persecution behind them, there was a marked tendency, especially among the ordinary members of the two working-class parties, to form a united front — until the Cold War, irreconcilable differences over strategy and tactics and the division of Germany flouted this particular idea. Another bridge-building operation in the party-political sphere may be said to have been more successful: the overcoming of the old denominational divisions between the Catholic Centre Party and the predominantly Protestant middle-class parties on the right which had been a major feature of Wilhelmine and Weimar politics. When the Christian Democratic Union (CDU) was founded after 1945, it explicitly comprised Protestants from the north and Rhenish Catholics under one roof.

To be sure, many of the older political and ideological divisions remained. In the parliamentary sphere they were reflected in the welter of small parties which participated in the early national elections and which succeeded, thanks to the system of proportional representation, in gaining parliamentary seats and even ministerial posts in the cabinets of Chancellor Konrad Adenauer. However, by the late 1950s, the party system had begun to consolidate itself and, like other Western political systems, that of the Federal Republic was characterised by three or four large parties which did not appeal to particularist economic interests, as so many Weimar parties had done, but presented themselves as 'catch-all parties'.

As we have seen, there was also a great willingness among trade unionists who emerged from inner emigration or external exile to avoid both the old sharp divisions into 'Free' and 'Christian' trade unions as well as the competition among different unions within one and the same company. One result of this yearning for unity was the creation of the *Einheitsgewerkschaft* (see pp. 43f.), another the introduction of the *Industriegewerkschaft* principle (see pp. 41f.). On the side of the employers there was likewise a strong desire for unity and centralisation, even if there was also a stronger tradition of this than among the unions. Nor had this tradition been disrupted by the policies of the Third Reich. Knowledge of the history of industrial associations in Germany appears to have been a major factor accounting for the lack of even-handedness with which the Western Allies treated industrial associations in relation to trade unions. They deliberately promoted the growth of viable and large unions as a counterweight to employers' organisations and, for the same reason, initially retarded the reconstruction of powerful and centralised industrial pressure groups.

The unions tried to exploit this favourable situation beyond the organisational task. They tried to enhance their concepts of nationalisation and economic democracy and aimed for parity between labour and capital in the decision-making processes at all levels of the economy. As we have seen, the stopping of the nationalisation programme at the insistence of the United States and the establishment of parliamentary-democratic channels of decision-making put paid to these early attempts at industrial reconstruction along syndicalist lines. The only exception to this rule was the introduction of co-determination in the iron- and steel-producing industries in 1947 in accordance with plans developed by Dinkelbach's office and against the vigorous opposition of the employers.

Subsequent events showed that the durability of this solution was precarious. The Allies, and the United States in particular, were keen to see the principles of collective bargaining, freedom of association and of organisational pluralism established and written into a catalogue of basic rights; but they and the majority of the German drafters of the Basic Law of 1949 were unwilling to go beyond this and to incorporate the principle of parity in the industrial relations sphere into the constitutional document.

215

This outcome is not surprising in view of the fact that the developments in the constitutional sphere were accompanied by the re-establishment of a liberal-capitalist economy, again under the aegis of the Americans. In 1945–6 many people may still have been searching for an alternative economic constitution to the one which emerged a few years later; but once the basic decision on ownership and nationalisation had been made, ideas about the building of a 'democratic socialism' were quickly pushed into the background and only found their way into Articles 14 and 15 of the Basic Law, which left nationalisation open as a vague possibility for the future. In the end, the 1951 Co-determination Act was the only tangible remnant in the economic sphere from the early postwar period when all kinds of alternatives to, and variations of, the liberal-capitalist model were being seriously debated. Otherwise, as is indicated by the substance of the Works Constitution Act 1952, the balance of rights had again tipped towards the employers and against the unions and the unorganised employees.

What was true of the formal economic constitution and the pieces of legislation underpinning it, applies even more so to what German constitutional lawyers call the *Realverfassung*, which is less concerned with codified rights than with the actual and often hidden power realities. Hindsight has helped to clarify these particular realities. At least there are not many political scientists and political economists today who would uphold in its pure form the theory of pluralism which became so popular in the Anglo-Saxon world after 1945. Its early protagonists had asserted:

> that there are a number of loci for arriving at political decisions; that businessmen, trade unions, politicians, consumers, farmers, voters and many other aggregates all have an impact on policy outcomes; that none of these aggregates is homogeneous for all purposes; that each of them is highly influential over some scopes, but weak over many others; and that the power to reject undesired alternatives is more common than the power to dominate over outcomes directly.[1]

The conclusion drawn from this was that 'there are, in Western societies, no such [things as] predominant classes, interests or

1. R.A. Dahl quoted in R. Miliband, *The State in Capitalist Society*, London, 1973, p. 5.

groups. There are only competing blocs of interests, whose competition . . . ensures that power *is* diffused and balanced.'[2] Not least it is therefore the function of parliamentary-democratic systems to sanction and guarantee inter-group competition and thereby to make certain that 'no particular interest is able to weigh too heavily upon the state'. The state is thus not seen by the pluralists as 'a rather special institution whose main purpose is to defend the predominance in society of a particular class'. Ultimately, their theory was therefore a response to Marxist interpretations of Western capitalist societies, all of which postulated, in one way or another, the existence of a ruling class wielding its power over the rest of the population through its ownership of the means of production and, indirectly, by using the allocative and repressive functions of the modern state for the stabilisation and perpetuation of their dominant position in economy and society.

The problem with both the pluralist and the instrumentalist-Marxist analysis was that the loopholes in the argument became more and more evident with the passage of time. Pluralism seemed to be as starry-eyed about observable reality in Western societies as Marxist reductionism looked utterly cynical. There were too many cases which could not be fitted into either of the two frameworks. Nor did critics of both approaches find it easy to accept the view that the government and the 'state' as the third factor in the equation were supposed to be no more than respondents to outside pressures, be they those of a plurality of interests or those of a dominant ruling class. It was from this critique that a third position was formulated which, to begin with, allocated to the state a more active role in the mediation of interests and in particular in the mediation between trade unions and employers as the two key blocs in modern capitalist-industrial societies. The state, in this view, is not a passive instrument, rather it actively tried to incorporate the two blocs into a compromise structure which is worked out, with active contributions from the government, within the triangle of unions, employers and the state. Thus American notions of an open and diffuse pluralism and Marxist concepts of a power monopoly by the capitalists are being tied together 'in the

2. Ibid., also for the following.

middle' by the adherents of neo-corporatist theory to produce an *oligarchical* system of active tripartist economic management and negotiated compromise.

To be sure, the debate did not end there. In particular, the neo-corporatists have argued among themselves as to whether the *capitalist* state would be bound to favour the employers over the unions, whatever the tripartist bargaining constellation may be. Certainly, the *Marxisants* among them would postulate this to be a systemic condition. While these arguments are likely to continue, neo-corporatism, though not a fully fledged theory of power and decision-making in capitalist countries, nevertheless constituted an advance over earlier approaches in one respect which is crucial to the study of West German industrial relations: it took on board not only the older pluralist and Marxist notions of the institutionalisation of industrial conflict as reflected in the emergence, since the late nineteenth century, of trade unions and employers associations meeting around the table to talk about wages and conditions; no less importantly, neo-corporatism conceptualised the new role of the state, next to the two sides of industry, as an active manager of the economy. It abandoned the notion that it was either the mechanism of the free market or the systemic contradictions of capitalism which moved Western industrial societies forward. Once politicians had adopted welfare-state policies and Keynesianism, such notions were at variance with industrial practice and clearly needed adjustment. This is where the neo-corporatists came in.

The debate concerning the 'relative autonomy' of an activist state *vis-à-vis* civil society and vested interests was recently given another boost by the British-American political economist Jonathan Zeitlin in a stimulating essay, 'Shop Floor Bargaining and the State'. He asserted:

> the state's distinctive interests in domestic order, external security and the extraction of resources place it in a highly ambivalent relation to the cleavages and antagonisms of civil society. Its desire to maintain public order and to assure the steady flow of revenue often leads the state, as Marxists have always insisted, to support the existing structure of social and economic relations against potentially disruptive challenges from subordinate groups. Similarly, when their own

resources are constrained, states will naturally resist any demands from below which appear to threaten their own financial solvency, as workers employed in the public sector have frequently discovered. Where states do not themselves control economic activity, they will often need to reach accommodations with the possessors of key economic resources in order to achieve their own political and military ends, as Block's account of the dynamic of business confidence suggests.[3]

On the other hand, Zeitlin continued, 'the state's broader interest in the preservation of domestic order may also prompt it to strike bargains with subordinate groups which restore social peace at the expense of propertied elites'. It was for this reason, he concluded, that 'dominant classes, from seventeenth-century Prussian Junkers to twentieth-century American corporate executives, have characteristically preferred to limit as far as possible the state's autonomy and access to resources, provided that they can fend off challenges from below independently and are not threatened by imminent foreign invasion.'

Without wishing to support some of the more far-reaching general conclusions which Zeitlin erects upon these statements, it is worthwhile to compare the substance of the above quotations with the material presented in this volume. Looking at the experience in postwar Germany in the strict sphere of industrial relations and economic management, a good many examples may be found to show that the state posed as the active promoter of the interests of the dominant groups in West German society. But we have also seen that the vagaries of universal suffrage and parliamentary democracy produced governments which struck bargains with subordinate groups against the vigorous opposition of industry and the propertied classes.

There are two further points to be added to Zeitlin's reinterpretation as far as the German case is concerned. To begin with, the legacies of the past, and especially those of the 1930s and 1940s, delayed the emergence of a system of industrial relations in the Federal Republic which deserved its name; that is, one in which the two sides of industry recognised each other and their important role in society unequivocally and in which

3. In S. Tolliday and J. Zeitlin (eds.), *Shop-Floor Bargaining and the State*, Cambridge, 1985, pp. 1ff., also for the following.

the balance between the two factors was not totally uneven. We have seen that the older generation of industrialists found it difficult to abandon earlier authoritarian attitudes and beliefs. Conversely, the unions also took some considerable time to make their transition towards the adoption of strategies which operated from within the existing liberal-capitalist system and did not try to transform it into socialism.

The labour unions' gradual acceptance of their functional role in a market system was enhanced by some other factors. Most important is a remarkable economic success: after the poverty during and immediately after the war, Germans experienced a prosperity which they themselves perceived as a 'miracle'. This economic success was largely credited to a decision in favour of a market system which was taken in 1948 by Ludwig Erhard, the later popular first minister of economic affairs. He had pushed for abandoning the planned bureaucratic economy with rationing, fixed prices and ubiquitous shortages in favour of a concept called 'social market economy' (*soziale Marktwirtschaft*). The theoretical basis of the system is the neo-liberal idea that economic processes should be regulated by market forces rather than by state control. The market forces, however, can only operate to the best advantage if they are harnessed by a legal framework which secures the compatibility of the individual economic interest with the welfare of society. As the market forces attribute income only to those who also contribute to production, a social policy has to supplement the system. The liberal tradition sees these social objectives best served by a two-tier approach: state policy has to secure economic growth, prosperity, full employment and stable prices; this is to be supplemented by a general redistribution of income and wealth and by specific welfare measures in support of economically weak persons and groups.

There is no doubt that the Federal Republic was very successful in the first area, prosperity and growth — at least for the first twenty-five years of its existence (see Tables A.1, A.6, pp. 225, 229). Also, the individual welfare measures were expanded considerably. Important achievements in this context are:

(1) reforms of the system of compulsory insurance. With few exceptions, dependent workers are members of the four statutory insurance schemes: health insurance, accident insurance,

unemployment insurance and old-age insurance. Therefore they are protected against the most important hazards of life. All four schemes have improved their benefits; most importantly, the old-age insurance was reformed in 1957, when the 'dynamic pension' (*dynamische Rente*) was created. Since then, old-age pensions increase in step with the level of current wages.

(2) In 1969 the 'General Continuation of Wages in Case of Illness' (*Lohnfortzahlung im Krankheitsfall*) was legally introduced. For six weeks all workers who fall sick receive from their employer their average net wage; after that period the worker is entitled to payments from the compulsory insurance schemes. This accomplishment is attributable to the unions who had included such arrangements in collective agreements earlier.

(3) In 1969 a law (*Kündigungsschutzgesetz*) was enacted which protects all employees against socially unjustified dismissal if they have been employed for at least six months. In addition, special provisions protect pregnant women and handicapped people.

(4) Sizeable reductions of working hours were accomplished. By now the regular weekly working time is about forty hours for all employees. Almost all workers are entitled to thirty working days of paid leave; as there are also — depending on the Land — between ten and twelve public holidays, a German works about 220 days per year.

In addition, there are child allowances and tax-subsidised wealth-formation schemes; there is free education on all levels; tenants enjoy specific protection, and so on. Many firms have supplementary company-pension schemes, pay Christmas bonuses and an extra month's salary to their employees. Workplace security has been improved, progress has been made in the 'humanisation' of work, and social compensation plans aim at protecting the employees in case of a major restructuring of their company. The fact that the Basic Law refers to the Federal Republic of Germany as a 'social state' (Art. 20), is interpreted to oblige legislators, administration and the judiciary to take due consideration of the social effects of all their actions. In fact, there is little doubt that the Federal Republic is indeed a 'social state'.

Altogether, workers are entitled to many social benefits either by law or by collective agreement. Many of these benefits were introduced in response to trade-union pressure, and in so far as all weaker groups in society were to benefit, the unions accomplished this in conjunction with other groups. The only field where little if anything was achieved was that relating to a more equitable distribution of wealth. But, everything considered, these developments give testimony to the considerable strength of the unions not only in collective bargaining, but also as a social pressure group which defends the cause of under-privileged groups.

The general public attributed much of the economic success to the concept of the 'social market economy'. In fact, this system was so popular that the Social Democratic Party in its 1959 Godesberg Programme advocated a very similar concept. Since then, all larger political parties subscribe to a market system, although there is some differentiation mainly regarding social policy. It is not surprising, therefore, that the trade unions also gave up all intentions of radically transforming the economy into a socialist system. They concentrate now on pushing for piecemeal improvements of existing structures.

The fact that socialist alternatives lack appeal for the Germans in the Federal Republic is partly attributable to the deterrent provided by 'real socialism' in the German Democratic Republic. Trade unionists in the Federal Republic, in particular, learnt from this example that free trade unions can exist only in a liberal-democratic society.

All these developments and institutional arrangements may help to understand the behaviour of the trade unions: their cooperative attitude contributed to the success of the economy and consequently of the unions — and this in turn further strengthened the cooperative attitude. It is understandable that this mechanism worked well in a period of prosperity. Until now, the system also withstood the strain of high long-term unemployment and of a recent perceptible roll-back of the welfare state.

We have now reached the point at which we can come back to the question raised at the beginning of this Conclusion. No doubt West Germany has enjoyed a surprisingly long period of social and industrial peace. But by now it should also be clearer which major factors contributed to this development. More importantly, what looked at first glance like mere stabilisation amounted in fact to an infrastructural modernisation of the West German political economy. All in all, the balance of power continues to be tilted in favour of the employers, who on issues of principle will find the majority of bureaucrats, politicians and judges on their side. On the other hand, it would be wrong to underestimate the political and economic muscle of West Germany's trade unions and of the forces which they are capable of mobilising in society.

Over the past thirty years they have made a major contribution to the modernisation of German industry and they are likely to go on advocating social and constitutional change in the face of the rapid technological and economic transformations affecting the world economy during the Third Industrial Revolution. Conversely, they will not countenance attempts by sections of industry to put the clock back. Employers who intend to ignore the unions' contribution to what has evolved in the sphere of industrial relations — and worse, who underestimate the existing balance of power — will do so at their own peril. Similar dangers of misjudgement also lurk behind an attitude of 'presentism', which is unaware of the history of today's system. It is for this reason that this volume has tried to provide not only an up-to-date summary of current industrial relations law and practice, but also of the deeper historical roots of the current framework.

Appendix A: Statistics

Table A.1 Real growth of the West German economy, 1951–1984 (%)

Year	%	Year	%
1951	10.4	1968	7.3
1952	8.9	1969	8.2
1953	8.2	1970	5.8
1954	7.4	1971	3.0
1955	12.0	1972	3.4
1956	7.3	1973	5.1
1957	5.7	1974	0.4
1958	3.7	1975	−2.7
1959	7.3	1976	5.8
1960	9.0	1977	2.7
1961	5.4	1978	3.3
1962	4.0	1979	4.5
1963	3.4	1980	1.8
1964	6.7	1981	−0.2
1965	5.6	1982	−1.0
1966	2.9	1983	1.3
1967	−0.2	1984	2.6

Sources: Die Zeit, 29 August 1975; W. Voss, *Die Bundesrepublik Deutschland*, Stuttgart, 1980, p. 69; Statistisches Bundesamt (ed.), *Datenreport 1985*, Bonn, 1985, p. 232.

Table A.2 Unemployment, 1900–85 (annual averages)

Year	No. (000s)	% of working pop.	Year	No. (000s)	% of working pop.
1900[a]	183	1.9	1933	4,804	25.9
1901	631	6.7	1934	2,718	13.5
1902	272	2.9	1935	2,151	10.3
1903	268	2.7	1936	1,593	7.4
1904	211	2.1	1937	912	4.1
1905	166	1.6	1938	429	1.9
1906	128	1.2	1939	119	0.5
1907	175	1.6	1940	52	0.2
1908	319	3.0			
1909	307	2.9	1950[b]	1,869	8.1
1910	211	1.9	1955	1,074	4.2
1911	215	1.9	1960	271	1.0
1912	239	2.0	1965	147	0.5
1913	348	3.0	1971	185	0.7
			1975	1,110	4.1
1921	346	1.8	1978	993	
1922	215	1.1	1980	865	3.8
1923	818	4.1	1981[c]	1,210	5.5
1924	927	4.9	1982[c]	1,810	7.5
1925	682	3.4	1983[c]	2,360	9.1
1926	2,025	10.0	1984[c]	2,370	
1927	1,312	6.2	1985[c]	2,440	
1928	1,391	6.3			
1929	1,899	8.5			
1930	3,076	14.0			
1931	4,520	21.9			
1932	5,603	29.9			

(a) Statistics for 1900 to 1913 for industry only, excl. handicrafts and only as far as recorded by trade unions. Actual figures probably much higher.
(b) 1950 to 1985, Federal Republic.
(c) Average for January to May.
Sources: P.C. Witt, *Die Finanzpolitik des Deutschen Reiches von 1903 bis 1913*, Lübeck, 1970, p. 384; W. Abelshauser et al. (eds.), *Sozialgeschichtliches Arbeitsbuch, 1914–1945*, Munich 1978, p. 119; W. Voss, *De Bundesrepublik Deutschland*, Stuttgart, 1980, p. 83; *Die Zeit*, 12 September 1980; *Die Zeit*, 20 June 1986.

Table A.3 Social welfare budget, 1950–83, in marks and in
percentage of GNP

Year	Marks (thou. millions)	% of GNP
1950	16.8	17.1
1960	62.8	20.7
1970	174.7	25.7
1975	347.0	33.7
1980	476.7	32.1
1983	537.2	32.3

Sources: W. Müller-Jentsch, *Soziologie der industriellen Beziehungen*, Frankfurt, 1986, p. 255; *Die Zeit*, 13 January 1984.

Table A.4 Structure of the labour force in occupational groups, 1875–1983 (000s)

Sector	1875	1885	1895	1905	1913	1925	1935	1955ᵃ	1970	1983
Agriculture	9,230	9,700	9,788	9,926	10,701	9,778	9,030	4,257	2,262	1,371
Mining	286	345	432	665	863	743	525	637	551	502
Industry and handicraft	5,153	6,005	7,524	9,572	10,857	11,708	11,011	10,265	12,436	10,012
Transport	349	461	620	901	1,174	1,472	1,461	1,327		
Commerce/banking	1,116	1,457	1,970	2,806	3,474	3,864	4,056	3,777	7,688	7,389
Insurance, hotels, domestic services[b]	(1,490)	1,488	1,571	1,541	1,542	1,357	1,211	638		
Other services	589	659	894	1,159	1,493	1,969	2,645	2,386	2,978	4,005
Defence	430	462	606	651	864	142		303		
Total	18,643	20,577	23,405	27,221	30,968	31,033		23,590		

(a) Federal Republic.
(b) Incl. restaurants etc.

Sources: W.G. Hoffmann et al. (eds.) *Das Wachstum der deutschen Wirtschaft seit der Mitte des 19. Jahrhunderts*, Heidelberg, 1965, p. 206; *Die Zeit*, 26 April 1985.

Table A.5 Numbers of foreign workers in West Germany, 1973–83 (000s)[a]

Citizenship	1973	1976	1978	1980	1982	1983[b]
Greek	250	173	147	133	116	109
Italian	450	279	289	309	259	239
Yugoslav	535	387	369	357	313	306
Portuguese	85	62	59	59	51	46
Spanish	190	108	93	86	76	72
Turkish	605	521	515	591	554	540
Other	480	392	397	537	415	402
Total	2,595	1,921	1,869	2,072	1,784	1,714

(a) Excl. other family members.
(b) As of 30 June 1983.
Source: Kursbuch Deutschland 85/86, Munich, 1985, p. 413.

Table A.6 Indices of monthly wages and salaries per employee and of prices, 1950–83 (1950 = 100)

Year	Gross wages and salaries nominal	Net wages and salaries nominal	real	Cost of living[a]
1950	100	100	100	100
1960	211	203	168	121
1970	474	420	271	155
1980	1,026	825	329	251
1983	1,158	911	313	291

(a) Based on cost of living of four-person employee household.
Source: W. Müller-Jentsch, *Soziologie der industriellen Beziehungen*, Frankfurt, 1986, p. 187.

Table A.7 Average hours of work per week in major branches of
industry, 1895–1983

Year	Total	Coal-mining	Metals	Chemicals	Textiles
1895	64	51.5	63	60	65
1900	62	53	63	60	62.5
1905	60	46		60	61
1910	59	48.5			59
1914	57	50	60	58	
1919	48		48	48	47
1925	50.5	42			
1930	44	40	45.5		43
1935	44.5	41.5	47	44	41
1940	50	47.5			
1950	48	42	51	48.5	47
1955	49	38.5	51	49	46.5
1959	45.5		45	47	44
1961	46.2[a]				
1965	45.2[a]				
1969	44.9[a]				
1975	41.2[a]				
1979	42.4[a]				
1983	39.6[a]				

(a) Average for male, industrial workers, incl. overtime.
Sources: W.G. Hoffmann et al. (eds.), *Das Wachstum der deutschen Wirtschaft seit
der Mitte des 19. Jahrhunderts*, Heidelberg, 1965, p. 214; *Die Zeit*, 27 April
1984.

Table A.8 Strikes and lock-outs, 1900–32, based on trade union
statistics (A) and Reich statistics (B)

Year	No. of strikes and lock-outs		No. of employees (000s)		Working days lost (000s)	
	A	B	A	B	A	B
1900	852	1,468	115.7	141.1	1,234.0	3,712.0
1901	727	1,091	48.5	68.2	1,194.5	2,427.0
1902	861	1,106	55.7	70.7	964.3	1,951.0
1903	1,282	1,444	121.6	135.5	2,622.2	4,158.0
1904	1,625	1,990	135.9	145.5	2,120.1	5,285.0
1905	2,323	2,657	508.0	542.6	7,362.8	18,984.0
1906	3,480	3,626	316.0	376.3	6,317.7	11,567.0
1907	2,792	2,512	281.0	286.0	5,122.5	9,017.0
1908	2,052	1,524	126.9	119.8	2,045.6	3,666.0
1909	45	1,652	131.2	130.9	2,247.5	4,152.0
1910	3,194	3,228	369.0	390.7	9,037.6	17,848.0
1911	2,914	2,798	325.3	385.2	6,864.2	11,466.0
1912	2,825	2,834	479.6	493.7	4,776.8	10,724.0
1913	2,600	2,464	249.0	323.4	5,672.0	11,761.0
1915		141		15.2		46.0
1916		240		128.9		245.0
1917		562		668.0		1,862.0
1918		532		391.6		1,453.0
1919		3,719		2,132.5		33,083.0
1920		3,807		1,508.4		16,755.0
1921		4,485		1,617.2		25,874.0
1922		4,755		1,895.8		27,734.0
1923		2,046		1,626.8		12,344.0
1924		1,973		1,647.1		36,198.0
1925		1,708		771.0		2,936.0
1926		351		97.1		1,222.0
1927		844		494.5		6,144.0
1928		739		775.5		20,339.0
1929		429		189.7		4,251.0
1930		353		223.9		4,029.0
1931		463		172.1		1,890.0
1932		648		129.5		1,130.0

Sources: G. Hohorst et al. (eds.), *Sozialgeschichtliches Arbeitsbuch, 1870–1914,*
Munich, 1975, pp. 132f.; W. Abelshauser et al. (eds.), *Sozialgeschichtli-*
ches Arbeitsbuch, 1914–1945, Munich, 1978, p. 114; J. Bergemann (ed.),
Beiträge zur Soziologie der Gewerkschaften, Frankfurt, 1979, p. 54.

Table A.9 Strikes and lock-outs in Federal Republic, 1950–85[a]

Year	No. of strikes and lock-outs	No. of employees	Working days lost
1950	1,344	79,270	380,121
1951	1,528	174,325	1,592,892
1952	2,529	84,097	442,877
1953	1,395	50,625	1,488,218
1954	538	115,899	1,586,523
1955	866	597,353	846,647
1956	268	25,340	263,884
1957	86	45,134	2,385,965
1958	1,484	202,483	782,123
1959	55	21,648	61,825
1960	28	17,065	37,723
1961	119	21,052	65,256
1962	195	79,177	450,948
1963	791	316,397	1,846,025
1964	34	5,629	16,711
1965	20	6,250	48,520
1966	205	196,013	27,086
1967	742	59,604	389,581
1968	36	25,167	25,249
1969	86	89,571	249,184
1970	129	184,269	93,203
1971	1,183	536,303	4,483,740
1972	54	22,908	66,045
1973	732	185,010	563,051
1974	890	250,352	1,051,290
1975	201	35,814	68,680
1976	1,481	169,312	533,696
1977	81	34,437	23,681
1978	1,239	487,050	4,281,284
1979	40	77,326	483,083
1980	132	45,159	128,386
1981	297	253,334	58,398
1982	40	39,981	15,106
1983	114	94,070	40,842
1984	1,121	537,265	5,614,360
1985		78,000	35,000

(a) 1950–7 excl. Saar and West Berlin; 1957–9 excl. West Berlin; 1960–78 incl. West Berlin.
Source: W. Müller-Jentsch, *Soziologie der industriellen Beziehungen*, Frankfurt, 1986, p. 172.

Table A.10 Distribution of strikes by federal state, 1951–80

Fed. state	Participating workers (%)			Working days lost (%)		
	1951–60	1961–70	1971–80	1951–60	1961–70	1971–80
Schleswig-Holstein	4	1	1	25	4	1
Hamburg	2	0	2	3	0	2
Niedersachsen	6	3	4	11	6	2
Bremen	3	2	5	8	1	8
Nordrhein-Westfalen	58	34	27	17	23	25
Hessen	8	6	5	15	4	4
Rheinland-Pfalz	1	1	1	1	3	0
Baden Württemberg	6	43	48	2	40	53
Bayern	11	5	3	17	4	3
Saarland		6	1		14	1
Berlin/West		0	4		0	2
	100	100	100	100	100	100

Source: W. Müller-Jentsch, *Soziologie der industriellen Beziehungen*, Frankfurt, 1986, p. 176.

Table A.11 Distribution of strikes by branch of industry, 1951–80

Branch	Participating workers (%)			Working days lost (%)		
	1951–60	1961–70	1971–80	1951–60	1961–70	1971–80
Mining	36	19	0	6	15	0
Construction	2	1	1	6	14	1
Textiles	4	2	1	14	3	0
Metal manuf.	25	61	56	59	47	61
Iron and steel	11	12	11	5	6	18
Printing	4	1	9	3	5	6
Chemicals	0	3	4	0	7	4
Public services	16	0	18	4	0	9
Others	3	1	1	4	3	1
	100	100	100	100	100	100

Source: W. Müller-Jentsch, *Soziologie der industriellen Beziehungen*, Frankfurt, 1986, p. 175.

Table A.12 Number of working days lost through industrial stoppages, per 1,000 employees in all sectors, incl. agriculture

Year	West Germany	France	Italy	Holland	Belgium	Luxem-burg	United Kingdom	Ireland	Denmark
1970	4	110	1,427	6	482	—	489	1,406	56
1971	119	272	999	2	409	—	613	376	11
1972	3	229	1,315	3	116	—	1,081	285	11
1973	26	233	1,549	14	281	—	318	280	2,007
1974	48	198	1,251	2	183	—	647	732	96
1975	3	228	1,722	0	195	—	265	390	53
1976	19	292	1,588	3	290	—	146	1,032	107
1977	1	211	1,017	57	215	—	448	571	116
1978	115	126	625	1	325	—	413	765	63
1979	18	209	1,602	73	197	—	1,257	1,752	83
1980	3	95	920	13	69	—	521	480	90
1981	3	86	589	5	—	—	195	503	315
1982	1	133	1,108	50	—	—	370	506	45
1983	2	76	802	27	—	—	170	382	38

Source: Eurostat (Employment and Unemployment), 1985, p. 225.

Table A.13 Trade union membership, 1890–1978 (000s) and SPD
membership, 1905–70 (000s)

Year	Free	Christian	Hirsch-Duncker	Total	SPD
1890	278	—	63[a]	357	
1895	259	5	67	327	
1900	680	77	92	849	
1905	1,345	192	116	1,653	384[b]
1910	2,017	316	122	2,455	720
1913	2,549	343	107	3,024	983
1914	2,076	283	78	2,437	1,086
1915	1,159	176	61	1,396	
1916	967	174	58	1,199	
1917	1,107	244	79	1,430	
1918	1,665	405	114	2,184	249
1919	5,479	858	190	6,527	
1920	7,890	1,077	226	9,193	1,180
1921	7,568	986	225	8,779	
1922	7,895	1,049	231	9,175	
1923	7,138	938	216	8,292	
1924	4,618	613	147	5,378	940
1925	4,156	588	158	4,902	
1926	3,977	532	163	4,672	806
1927	4,150	606	168	4,924	
1928	4,654	647	169	5,469	867
1929	4,906	673	169	5,740	
1930	4,822	659	198	5,679	1,021
1931	4,418	578	181	5,177	
1949					736
1950	5,450[c]				
1955	6,105				
1960	6,379				649
1965	6,574				710
1970	6,713				780
1975	7,365				
1978	7,752	249			
1979					
1980	7,883				
1981	7,958				
1982	7,849				
1983	7,746				
1984	7,660				

(a) Figure for 1891.
(b) Figure for 1906.
(c) From 1950 = DGB.
Sources: D. Groh, *Negative Integration und revolutionärer Attentismus*, Frankfurt,
1973, p. 734; K. Schönhoven, *Expansion und Konzentration*, Stuttgart
1980, p. 101; W.L. Guttsman, *The German Social Democratic Party*, London, 1980, p. 153; H. Kaack, *Geschichte und Struktur des deutschen
Parteiensystems*, Opladen, 1971, p. 496; W. Müller-Jentsch, *Soziologie der
industriellen Beziehungen*, Frankfurt, 1986, p. 91.

Table A.14 DGB member organisations and their membership strengths and structures, 1984

Trade union	Blue-collar workers	White-collar workers	Civil servants	Males	Females	Total	Share (%)
I.G. Metall	2,114,849	382,884	—	2,137,433	360,300	2,497,733	32.6
Gew. Öffentliche Dienste, Transport und Verkehr	568,708	513,035	86,511	826,531	341,723	1,168,254	15.3
I.G. Chemie-Papier-Keramik	516,888	121,288	—	519,029	119,147	638,176	8.3
I.G. Bau-Steine-Erden	474,455	42,561	—	490,706	26,310	517,016	6.8
Deutsche Postgewerkschaft	140,422	42,999	272,265	317,558	138,128	455,686	5.9
Gew. der Eisenbahner Deutschlands	180,871	7,686	175,484	345,862	18,179	364,041	4.8
Gew. Handel, Banken und Versicherungen	48,435	314,829	—	156,372	206,892	363,264	4.7
I.G. Bergbau und Energie	313,112	46,981	223	353,221	7,095	360,316	4.7
Gew. Nahrung-Genuss-Gaststätten	209,170	54,806	—	176,729	87,247	263,976	3.4
Gew. Textil-Bekleidung	235,260	24,905	—	109,663	150,502	260,165	3.4
Gew. Erziehung und Wissenschaft	—	52,709	143,979	103,054	93,634	196,688	2.6
Gew. der Polizei	8,984	16,825	139,065	151,060	13,814	164,874	2.2
Gew. Holz und Kunststoff	136,798	10,379	—	127,544	19,633	147,177	1.9
I.G. Druck und Papier	109,468	32,866	—	108,628	33,706	142,334	1.9
Gew. Leder	46,381	2,760	—	27,625	21,516	49,141	0.6
Gew. Gartenbau. Land- und Forstwirtschaft	36,459	2,842	2,614	36,482	5,433	41,915	0.5
Gew. Kunst	—	29,590	—	18,341	11,249	29,590	0.4
DGB total (on 31 Dec. 1984)	5,140,260	1,699,945	820,141	6,005,838	1,654,508	7,660,346	100.0

Source: W. Müller-Jentsch, *Soziologie der industriellen Beziehungen,* Frankfurt, 1986, p. 81.

Figure A.1 Degree of unionisation of DGB, DAG[a] and DBB[b], 1950–80 (%)

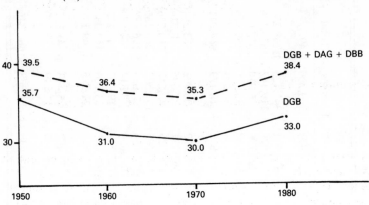

(a) White-collar union
(b) Civil service union
Source: W. Müller-Jentsch, *Soziologie der industriellen Beziehungen*, Frankfurt, 1986, p. 93.

Appendix B: Documents

Document I: The 1981 Basic Programme of the German Trade-Union Federation (DGB) — Extracts[1]

Preamble

Imbued with a feeling of responsibility towards its members and all German people, the German Trade-Union Federation and its member unions express strong support for the inalienable rights of men to freedom and self-determination. They strive for a society in which the dignity of men is respected and they demand the full realisation of human rights in all parts of the world as they are spelt out in the declaration of the United Nations.

. . .

The trade unions' untiring struggle for equal political and social rights of workers succeeded in so far as important elements of the trade unions' demands are guaranteed today as basic rights of citizens in democratic constitutions and are recognised by public opinion. There remains the task of the trade unions to work towards the further development of the social and constitutional state and the democratic structure of society and to continue their struggle for equal rights of workers in all fields.

Thus the trade unions have become a decisive integrating element of democracy and are an indispensable force for a further democratic development of economy and society.

Free and independent trade unions are a prerequisite of any democratic society. Trade unions had to fight for their existence, their sphere of action and their rights. Any attack on their autonomy and their freedom of action is an attack on the basis of democracy. In defending democracy, the trade unions also defend the basis of their own existence.

. . .

The general increase in the standard of living, which is mainly due to the creative capacity and the industriousness of the workers and also attributable to the trade unions' struggle for social and economic

1. Deutscher Gewerkschaftsbund, *Grundsatzprogramm des Deutschen Gewerkschaftsbundes, beschlossen auf dem 4. ausserordentlichen Bundeskongress Düsseldorf 12.–14. 3. 1981.*

reforms, has opened up new ways of living for many workers. But insecurity of the workplace, unjust distribution of income and wealth, unequal educational opportunities and dependency on economic power have not been overcome. Further burdens result from the deterioration of environmental conditions as well as from increasingly demanding work, mainly due to technological and organisational innovations which are orientated towards the interests of capital only.

. . .

The trade unions strive for expansion of workers' co-determination in order to initiate a reorganisation of economy and society which will bring equal participation of workers in all economic, social and cultural decisions.

. . .

Aware of their responsibility towards their members and towards all workers, and in the spirit of international solidarity, the trade unions of the German Trade Union Federation profess adherence to the following basic positions:

1 *Rights of Workers*

. . .

The trade unions' right to strike is inviolable. The lock-out, an arbitrary measure of the employers, is unconstitutional in any form and has to be prohibited. The trade unions fight against the lock-out in full solidarity because it is an attack on their scope of action and their existence.

The autonomous regulation of working conditions by concluding collective agreements is the task of the trade unions and the employers and their associations. No governmental interference with the autonomy of collective bargaining is permissible. This also applies to any form of compulsory mediation.

2 *Employee–Employer Relationship*

The personality of the worker and his dignity as a human being are to be respected also at his place of work. His labour is not to be considered a commodity. . . .

. . .

3 *Humane Working Conditions*

. . .

Technological developments and organisational changes do not necessarily result in humane working conditions. Rationalisation and automation shall not endanger employment, qualification, health or income of workers. Advances in productivity which can only be reached by more demanding work must be opposed. Technological and organisational innovations should only be implemented after due consideration of the workers' interests and after those leading to unacceptable social consequences have been excluded. In the planning, preparation and implementation of measures of rationalisation, the co-determination of workers and their trade unions has to be ensured.

. . .

4 *Principles of Economic Activity*

The economic system envisaged by the trade unions shall:
— guarantee to each worker a maximum of freedom, responsibility and social security;
— secure equal participation of workers in economic life;
— guarantee to each worker adequate employment under humane conditions;
— allow a qualitative, adequate and steady growth of the economy;
— bring about a just distribution of income and wealth;
— restore and maintain ecological equilibrium;
— prevent any abuse of economic power and guarantee democratic control of economic power;
— duly consider the problem of finite resources;
— apply both competition and planning for the attainment of economic goals;
— further the understanding of economic relations by making all required information accessible.

5 *Full Employment*

. . .

An important, though not sufficient, precondition for full employment is adequate and steady economic growth.

. . .

The trade unions have a positive attitude towards technological development as a decisive factor in increasing the standard of living and the easing of human work. Technological developments should secure employment and help to realise humane working conditions. Advances in productivity which result from technological innovations shall not lead to social hardship. The workers and their families have to be protected against the adverse social effects of structural change.

Appendices

. . .

6 *Just Distribution of Income and Wealth*

. . .

7 *Control of Economic Power*

. . .

8 *Co-determination*

. . .

9 *Competition and Planning*

. . .

10 *Framework Planning of Economic Development*

. . .

11 *Investment Guidance*

. . .

Misallocations of capital and labour impair the standard of living in the same way as unemployment and forgone opportunities for economic growth do. Therefore investments both in the private and the public sector have to be co-ordinated with structural and stability requirements of the economy.

. . .

12 *Public Finance, Taxes and Monetary Policy*

Government budgets have to satisfy needs of society, further social justice and create and secure employment. Public finance is to be subordinated to these goals. They have priority over considerations of short-term stability and private profitability. Full employment has priority over other goals. . . .

. . .

242

13 *Public and Free Co-op Economic Activities*[2]

. . .

14 *Energy Policy*

. . .

— All possibilities of energy saving should be utilised.
— Much stronger efforts should be made in the development of non-nuclear, mainly renewable, sources of energy.
— The use of domestic sources of energy, mainly coal, has priority.
— The use of nuclear energy is to be extended only if this is unavoidable. . . .

. . .

15 *International Economic and Social Co-operation*

. . .

16 *Further Development of Social-Security Systems*

. . .

17 *Health Policy*

. . .

18 *Social-Welfare Benefits*

. . .

19 *Financing Social Security*

. . .

20 *Self-government of Social-Security Institutions*

2. The German Federation of Trade Unions advocates a concept of 'co-op enterprises' (*gemeinwirtschaftliche Unternehmen*). These are companies which — unlike capitalist firms — do not primarily strive for high profits but aim for the provision of particular needs. Typical examples are public-utility companies, but the unions advocate a wider application of this principle.

. . .

21 *Jurisdiction in Social, Administrative and Labour Courts*

. . .

22 *Housing Policy*

. . .

23 *Environmental Protection*

. . .

24 *Principles of Education and Educational Planning*

. . .

25 *Vocational Training*

. . .

26 *Further Education*

. . .

27 *Schools, Universities and Other Institutions of Learning*

. . .

Education shall not be a means of social selection. The educational system must further all gifted children and compensate social disadvantages.

. . .

28 *Science and Research*

. . .

The trade unions advocate freedom of science, research and teaching. These have to serve the universal development of man and the improvement of working and living conditions. This is only possible if science and research meet their social responsibilities independently of the interests of private business. This is a specific task of the public support of science. The co-operation between universities and trade unions is to be extended.

. . .

29 *Press, Broadcasting and Television*

. . .

The freedom of information of the press as well as the independence of journalists and their freedom of opinion must be guaranteed. This implies, in particular, the protection of the press against economic dependency.

. . .

30 *Arts and Culture*

. . .

The trade unions oppose all attempts to subject culture to criteria of profitability. . . .

. . .

Document II: Constitution of the Metal-Workers Union (I.G. Metall) — Extract[3]

Para. 2: *Tasks and Aims of I.G. Metall*

I.G. Metall has the task of promoting the economic, social and cultural interests of its members. While safeguarding its independence from governments, administrations, employers, churches and political parties, it professes its loyalty to the free democratic basic order of the Federal Republic of Germany and advocates the protection and further development of the social constitutional state and the further democratisation of economy, state and society.

I.G. Metall safeguards and defends the free democratic basic order as well as the basic rights of democracy. To defend these rights as well as the autonomy and the existence of trade unions, the Executive Board may, if necessary for this purpose, call on its members to stop working (the right to resist according to article 20, para. 4 of the Basic Law).

The tasks and aims of I.G. Metall are:

3. I.G. Metall, *Satzung, Beschlossen auf dem 14. ordentlichen Gewerkschaftstag in München, Gültig ab 1. Januar 1984.*

(1) Effecting solidarity amongst all who are employed in metal industry, in metal crafts and other metal working firms with the purpose of united actions.

(2) Reaching better conditions of pay and work through conclusion of collective agreements.

(3) Democratisation of the economy with the exclusion of neo-fascist, military and reactionary elements.

(4) Achieving and safeguarding of the workers' rights of co-determination at plant and company level and in the economy at large by establishment of economic and social councils; nationalisation of key industries and other companies which dominate or control markets or economic sectors.

(5) Co-determination in vocational education including schools and universities.

(6) Improvement and uniform structuring of a democratic law of labour and of social affairs.

(7) Securing the legal preconditions of the trade unions' freedom of activity, in particular by a prohibition of lock-outs.

(8) Improvement of preventive health care and of measures of workplace safety with the purpose of a better protection of workers.

(9) The education and training of its members in trade unionism.

(10) Imparting of legal advice on social, administrative, financial and labour matters to its members.

(11) Promotion and implementation of leisure and holiday activities, in particular by maintaining holiday, recreation and youth homes.

(12) Financial support of members if the financial situation permits this.

(13) Cooperation with the trade unions which are members of the German Trade-Union Federation and international organisations, in particular the International Metal-Workers Federation and the Federation of European Metal-Workers Unions.

Document III: Resolution No. 12 of the 12th Union Congress of I.G.Metall in Düsseldorf, 18th to 24th September 1977[4]

The 12th Union Congress of the I.G. Metall agrees that despite the increasingly acrimonious wage disputes due to the deteriorating economic situation, considerable improvements have been gained for the

---

4. Published in English in I.G. Metall, *The Strike in the Iron and Steel Industry, 1978/1979,* Frankfurt n.d. (reproduced with minor modifications of terminology).

worker through collective bargaining.

The I.G. Metall continues to insist on the principle of unrestricted autonomy of collective bargaining (Tarifautonomie) as an indispensable precondition for a successful wage policy. It therefore rejects all directives, guidelines and wage and salary freezes, aimed at linking earnings to productivity growth, and regards any attempts by political agencies to influence public opinion in this direction as irreconcilable with the autonomy of collective bargaining.

The right to strike is inalienable. The lock-out is unethical and contrary to the principle of equality between the conflicting parties. (Compulsory arbitration in any form cannot be accepted.)

All attempts by the employers and their associations to exploit the present economic situation to the disadvantage of the workers must be countered with a constructive wage policy, aimed at consolidating the workers' living and working conditions, particularly as regards income, employment conditions and employment stability.

The I.G. Metall therefore puts forward the following demands:

(a) increased wages, salaries and training rates with the object of improving real earnings

(b) a form of collective agreement under the terms of which these increases in wages, salaries and training rates can be negotiated and implemented in various forms and combinations. This means that all collective agreements containing wage contracts must be terminated, and that such contract clauses must be excluded from future agreements

(c) provision for monthly remuneration for workers as well as for salaried employees

(d) a guaranteed annual income, consisting of basic compensation rates and a different system of supplementary earnings
— differential pay
— incentive bonuses
— other supplements (standard allocations and bonuses)
— other standard contributions (e.g. special payments, savings and
    investment scheme, increased vacation pay)

(e) collective agreements with equal conditions for all employees (workers and salaried personnel) as regards both work and compensation

(f) new standard regulations on wage differentiation for all employees (workers and salaried personnel)

(g) provisions for shorter working hours, to be enforced through new regulations on retirement age, hours of work per year, week, day or shift, as may be deemed most appropriate, without loss of earnings

(h) 6 weeks' minimum vacation for all employees

(i) improved arrangements on vacation entitlement and increased vacation pay

(j) introduction of the 35-hour week

(k) 6 minutes' rest period per hour for all employees, 12 minutes' rest period per hour for all employees on night shift

(l) 3 minutes' minimum personal time off per hour for all workers, 6 minutes' minimum personal time off per hour for all workers on night shift

(m) agreement on reasonable conditions for night work and shift work

(n) collective agreement provisions whereby the workers' social status is maintained in the event of technical or structural reorganisation

(o) collective agreement provisions on maintaining differentiation levels

(p) a minimum of 13 months' wages for all employees

. . .

(r) standard provisions on employment protection and security of earnings to be improved and their field of application to be extended

(s) standard provisions for the protection of trade union shop-floor representatives

(t) humanisation of working conditions as regards working hours, workshop conditions, work systems and working environment
— definition of work systems to allow opportunities for advancement, job satisfaction or job transfer, with corresponding wage-level classifications
— humanisation of plant and procedures, work systems and processes, and of the work place in general
— cash compensation for abnormal working conditions or health hazards will not be accepted; their causes must be removed
— unavoidable hardships may be compensated through appropriate paid time off; additional pay must be agreed on for the use of the prescribed safety measures and installations

(u) standard regulations on health and safety at the workplace

(v) collective agreements must contain provisions for improved vocational training.

The order in which the demands have been formulated does not imply a scale of priorities. The unions' decision-making bodies will put forward individual demands when opportune.

I.G. Metall wage negotiations will be conducted at regional or national level, according to the requirements of each particular case.

Constant briefing and discussion among rank-and-file members is imperative, if these wage-policy goals are to be achieved. For this reason all members and officials must be informed in good time when a demand is about to be put forward, in order to prepare the ground for an eventual wage drive.

Document IV: The Federal Constitutional Court's Judgment on the Co-determination Act[5]

1 *Statement by the Public Relations Office of the Federal Constitutional Court*

The First Panel of the Federal Constitutional Court today pronounced its judgment in the two proceedings linked together for a joint hearing and decision on the Co-determination Act of 4 May 1976.

Nine firms and 29 employers' associations lodged a constitutional appeal against the provisions governing the selection of companies covered by the Act (Article 1, para. 1), the membership of the Supervisory Board comprising an equal number of shareholders' members and workers' members (Article 7, para. 1), the election of the chairman of the Supervisory Board (Article 27), the voting procedure in the Supervisory Board (Article 29), the appointment of members responsible for the legal representation of a company (Article 31) and the appointment of a labour director as a full member of the authority responsible for the legal representation of the company (Article 33). The complainants proceeded on the assumption that these provisions would introduce parity co-determination or, in some case, supra-parity co-determination. They held that this infringed the fundamental rights of property as set out in Article 14, para. 1 of the Basic Law, their freedom to form associations (Article 9, para. 1 of the Basic Law), the right freely to choose their trade, occupation or profession (Article 12, para. 1 of the Basic Law), the right to free development of personality (Article 2, para. 1 of the Basic Law) and the right to form associations (Article 9, para. 3 of the Basic Law). The employers' associations argued that they were subjected to the influence of the opposite contracting party through the change in their internal structure caused by the change in the internal structure of their more important member firms prescribed in the contested provisions and that they were thus impaired in their activities as associations protected by Article 9, para. 3 of the Basic Law. Furthermore, the German Protective Association for Security Holders lodged a constitutional appeal against the final rulings which had been

5. Federal Minister of Labour and Social Affairs, *Co-determination in the Federal Republic of Germany*, Bonn, 1980 pp. 38–45 (reproduced with minor modifications of terminology).

handed down in a legal case on the question as to which statutory provisions were to govern membership of the Supervisory Board and which affirmed the compatibility of the Co-determination Act with the Basic Law. Finally, a decision had to be given pursuant to a resolution on the submission of the case by the Regional Court of Hamburg as to whether membership of the Supervisory Board consisting of an equal number of shareholders' and workers' members including two or three trade-union representatives (Article 7, paras. 1 and 2) in conjunction with the provision on the appointment and revocation of the members of the authority responsible for the legal representation of a company (Article 31) infringed Article 9, para. 3 of the Basic Law. In accordance with the judgment delivered by the Federal Constitutional Court, the extended co-determination for workers introduced by the Co-determination Act is consistent with the basic rights of companies, shareholders and employers' associations.

(1) The decision subjects solely the contested provisions of the Co-determination Act submitted for examination to constitutional scrutiny. It does not voice an opinion on whether other provisions in the Co-determination Act are consistent with the Basic Law.

(a) To begin with, the decision clarifies the extent of workers' influence in companies pursuant to the Act, which is taken as the basis for further examination by the Court. Neither from the legal standpoint nor in any other way connected with the Act is their influence equal to that of the other side or indeed more than equal. Under the statutory provisions, one cannot proceed on the assumption of parity co-determination because of the second vote accorded to the chairman of the Supervisory Board, who is normally elected by the shareholders, and because of the non-homogeneous composition of the employees' side comprising workers, salaried employees and top managerial staff. That also holds true if one includes the partially equal rights of co-determination for the works council. The basic assumption of the complainants that this non-equal representation in reality conceals a fundamentally equal or even more-than-equal representation, which the legislators actually envisaged or wished to facilitate, does not lead to any other judgment, either. There is nothing to indicate that the material substance of the case, which is fundamentally authoritative for an examination of its constitutionality, and the actual impact of the contested normative provisions are divergent in any way.

(b) There is no certainty about what effect this slightly sub-parity co-determination will produce in future. Particular importance attaches to cooperation in individual firms — a cooperation

250

which the law itself can only facilitate and encourage by providing the machinery. If both sides are willing to engage in loyal cooperation, co-determination for employees will produce a different effect than a situation in which the atmosphere in companies is dominated by mutual distrust or even enmity. Another factor which may prove significant is whether there is a willingness outside the companies to welcome co-determination in its present form in the interest of these individual firms as well as of the economy as a whole. Unlike the complainants, the legislators proceeded on the assumption that the effects envisaged by the Act would actually occur and that they would not involve any disadvantageous consequences for the viability of the individual companies and for the economy as a whole. The Federal Constitutional Court could only proceed from another assumption if the prognosis made by the legislators about the future effects of the law did not accord with the requirements of the Constitution. This was not the case, as the legislators had based their opinion on an objective and justifiable assessment of the available material.

(c) The Federal Constitutional Court has now reaffirmed the view which it had hitherto adopted on the question of whether the contested provisions in the Co-determination Act, as interpreted in content and on the basis of the justifiable prognosis of the legislators, are consistent with the Basic Law. The criteria governing the constitutional examination are those individual, fundamental rights which mark out the constitutional framework and limits of the legislators' dispositive rights in introducing extended co-determination. The Basic Law does not contain any direct stipulation about guaranteeing a certain economic system or concrete constitutional principles for the arrangement of economic life. On the contrary, it leaves the organising of the economy to the legislators, who have a free right to decide on this within the limits imposed by the Basic Law without this requiring any further legitimation than that provided by the customary democratic process. This dispositive right on the part of the legislators cannot be further restricted by means of an interpretation of the Basic Law such as individual rights would call for. At the same time, the latter have the same importance as in other contexts. Pursuant to their history and their current content, they are primarily individual human and civic rights designed to protect concrete and particularly endangered areas of human freedom. The question of the constitutionality of those laws which contribute towards an orderly economic system — considered from the standpoint of fundamental rights — is primarily one of preserving the freedom of the individual citizen and not one (as alleged by the complainants) of the 'institutional implications of the country's economic system' as substantiated by an independent confirmation which enhances the content of fundamental rights in their capacity as individual human rights.

(2) On the basis of these criteria, the Court held that Articles 7, 27, 29 and 31 of the Co-determination Act are consistent with the Basic Law:

(a) The provisions infringe neither the property of the shareholders nor that of the companies; on the contrary, they define the content and limits of property in pursuance of the powers conferred upon the legislators under Article 14, para. 1, sentence 1 of the Basic Law. Admittedly, the powers of the shareholders as members of the Supervisory Board have been reduced — though not by half — inasmuch as the shareholders as a whole retain their decisive influence in the company. However, this restriction remains within the ambit of the commitments of property-owners to society in general and these commitments increase in scope, the closer the relationship between the property in question and its social environment as well as its social function. As a rule, the personal relationship conferred by shareholdings covered by the Co-determination Act is less pronounced in its impact upon the law affecting membership of the Supervisory Board. On the other hand, the shareholdings embrace a wide-ranging social relationship and a significant social function, above all because the use of this property always requires the cooperation of the employees whose fundamental rights are affected by such use. To the extent that the property of corporations which hold an interest in the companies affected by the Act is concerned, one cannot assume pursuant to the relevant prognosis made by the legislators that extended co-determination will render companies unworkable or produce conditions similar to such a situation. If the changes in the organisation and the procedure for decision-making in the Supervisory Board of companies result in certain de facto complications, these remain within the framework of the social commitment for larger companies inherent in property.

(b) Nor has the fundamental right to form associations been impaired. It may even appear doubtful whether the protected right set out in Article 9, para. 1 of the Basic Law and the substance of this provision permit an application of the guarantee even to larger joint-stock companies because, unlike the type of association and society which the Basic Law has hitherto primarily wished to safeguard and which it still wishes to safeguard, the personal element in such large companies dwindles to the point of insignificance. However, this issue can remain unresolved since the contested provisions do not infringe Article 9, para. 1 of the Basic Law even if we proceed in principle from the assumption that it is applicable in this case. The provisions do not clash with the axiom of free association nor do they impair, in a manner contrary to the Basic Law, the viability of the companies. By the same token, they do not constitute any inadmissible interference with the self-determination of companies in regard to their internal organisation and decision-making processes. Nor is the situation altered by the fact that the employees representatives in the Supervisory Board must include two or three representatives of the trade unions. This rule does not, in principle, contradict the hitherto valid company law nor is it immaterial, since it facilitates the sending of particularly well-qualified representatives by the employees, too, and helps to mitigate the 'parochial' attitude sometimes inherent in extended co-determination.

(c) Furthermore, the contested provisions do not infringe either Article 12, para. 1 nor Article 2, para. 1 of the Basic Law inasmuch as this fundamental right safeguards the freedom of economic activity. In view of the size of the firms falling within the scope of the Co-determination Act, freedom of choice in regard to trade, occupation or profession in such firms largely lacks the personal element forming the real core of the guarantee in this fundamental right. To this extent, freedom of choice in regard to trade, occupation or profession in companies which can only practise such freedom with the help of the employees may be deemed to have a social relationship and a social function. Hence, the contested provisions of the Co-determination Act prove to be admissible provisions in the exercise of one's trade, occupation or profession. To the extent that this still leaves scope for Article 2, para. 1 of the Basic Law, that fundamental right cannot be considered as infringed, either. There are no reasons to show that the criticised provisions fail to leave adequate scope for the development of entrepreneurial initiative and therefore affect the substance of companies' or shareholders' freedom of activity.

(d) Finally, the Court held that Articles 7, 27, 29 and 31 of the Co-determination Act are consistent with Article 9, para. 3 of the Basic Law. Pursuant to the rulings regularly handed down by the Federal Constitutional Court, this fundamental law protects the crucial part of the right of free association. This also includes the general guarantee of autonomy in negotiating collective agreements — a guarantee which accords the legislators wide scope for interpretation. The provisions do not impinge upon this crucial part of the right of free association. They leave untouched freedom to found and join associations and also the guarantee of non-State interference in the activities of the latter. The legislators have not offended against the Constitution by adding to collective wage bargaining another type of promoting labour and economic conditions. Nor have there been any improper restrictions on the principle of the independence of the right of free association, irrespective of the opposite side, whereby the employers' associations must also be enabled to represent effectively and continuously the interests of their members in the field of labour and social legislation. An examination of the constitutionality of the case must proceed on the assumption that the representatives of co-managed companies in the employers' associations adhere to the statutory requirement prohibiting them to look after the interests of the opposite side. Inasmuch as an influence by the employees on the employers' associations has to be taken into account, such influence must fall below the sub-parity influence of the employees in the companies and moreover it cannot fundamentally question the independence of the employers' associations. Finally, we cannot assume in the light of the justifiable prognosis made by the legislators, that the contested provisions of the Co-determination Act will result in the autonomy of concluding collective wage agreements becoming unworkable. If the existing statutory provisions should nevertheless prove insufficient to ensure the fundamental independence of the associations in respect of the opposite side, it is a matter for the legislators to provide a remedy.

(3) The provision on the labour director (Article 33 of the Co-determination Act) contested by the complainant firms and employers' associations is subject to an independent examination only from the standpoint of an infringement of the constitutional rule of adequate definiteness. No such infringement is discernible, since both the duties and the function as well as the procedure for the appointment of the labour director are clearly and specifically defined in the text of the law. The selection of the companies in question by virtue of their legal form and the number of employees (Article 1 of the Co-determination Act) is not in default of the subject-matter of the Act.

(Judgment of 1 March 1979 — 1 BvR 532 und 533/77, 419/78 und 1 BvL 21/78.)

Karlsruhe, 1 March 1979

Select Bibliography

1 Industry and Workers Prior to 1945

Abraham, D., *The Collapse of the Weimar Republic*, 2nd edn, New York, 1986

Carsten, F.L., *Revolution in Central Europe*, London, 1972

Feldman, G.D., *Army, Industry and Labor in Germany, 1914–1918*, Princeton, 1966

——, *Iron and Steel in the German Inflation, 1916–1923*, Princeton, 1977

Gillingham, J., *Industry and Politics in the Third Reich*, London, 1985

Grebing, H., *The History of the German Labour Movement*, Leamington Spa, 1985

Hunt, R.N., *German Social Democracy, 1918–1933*, New Haven, 1964

Kele, M.H., *Nazis and Workers*, Chapel Hill, 1972

Maier, C.S., *Recasting Bourgeois Europe*, Princeton, 1975

Michels, R., *Political Parties: A Sociological Study of the Oligarchical Tendencies of Modern Democracy*, (1915), New York–London, 1962

Morgan, D.W., *The Socialist Left and the German Revolution*, Ithaca, 1975

Moses, J., *German Trade Unionism from Bismarck to Hitler*, 2 vols., London, 1981

Schweitzer, A., *Big Business in the Third Reich*, Bloomington, 1964

Spencer, E.G., *Management and Labor in Imperial Germany*, New Brunswick, 1984

Sweezy, M.Y., *The Structure of the Nazi Economy*, Cambridge (Mass.), 1941

Turner, H.A., *German Big Business and the Rise of Hitler*, Oxford, 1985

2 Industry, Unions and Politics since 1945

Backer, J.H., *Priming the German Economy, 1945–1948*, Durham, NC, 1971

Bendix, R., *Work and Authority in Industry*, New York, 1956

Berghahn, V.R., *The Americanisation of West German Industry, 1945–1973*, Leamington Spa–New York, 1986

Blumenthal, W.M., *Codetermination in the German Steel Industry*, Princeton, 1956

Braunthal, G., *The Federation of German Industry in Politics*, Ithaca, 1965

Cawson, A. (ed.), *Organised Interests and the State*, London, 1985

Cox, J. and H. Kriegbaum, *Growth, Innovation and Employment: An Anglo-German Comparison*, London, 1980

Dahrendorf, R., *Democracy and Society in Germany*, London, 1968

Doeringer, P.B. et al. (eds.), *Industrial Relations in International Perspective*, New York, 1981

Dyson, K. and S. Wilks (eds.), *Industrial Crisis*, Oxford, 1983

Federal Minister of Labour and Social Affairs (ed.), *Co-determination in the Federal Republic of Germany*, Bonn, 1980

Flanagan, J., W. Soskice, and L. Ullman, *Unionism, Economic Stabilization, and Incomes Policies. European Experience*, Washington DC, 1983

Gimbel, J., *The American Occupation of Germany*, Stanford, 1968

Gourevitch, P. et al., *Unions and Economic Crisis*, London, 1984

Hartmann, H., *Authority and Organization in German Management*, Princeton, 1959

I.G. Metall (ed.), *The Strike in the Iron and Steel Industry (1978/1979)*, Frankfurt, n.d.

Lawrence, P., *Managers and Management in West Germany*, London, 1980

Maitland, I., *The Causes of Industrial Disorder: A Comparison of a British and a German Factory*, London, 1983

Markovits, A., *The Politics of the West German Trade Unions*, Cambridge, 1986

―――― (ed.), *The Political Economy of West Germany*, New York, 1982

Miller, J., *British Management versus German Management*, Farnborough, 1979

Milward, A., *The Reconstruction of Western Europe*, London, 1984

Paterson, W., and G. Smith (eds.), *The West German Model*, London, 1981

Spiro, H.J., *The Politics of German Codetermination*, Cambridge, Mass., 1958

Streeck, W., 'Co-determination: the fourth decade', in B. Wilpert and A. Sorge (eds.), *International Perspectives on Organizational Democracy*, London, 1984, p. 391

―――― , *Industrial Relations in West Germany*, London, 1984

Thim, A.L., *The False Promise of Co-Determination*, Toronto–Uxington (Mass.), 1980

Tolliday, S. and J. Zeitlin (eds.), *Shop Floor Bargaining and the State*, Cambridge, 1985

Tokunaga, S. and J. Bergmann (eds.), *Industrial Relations in Transition: The Cases of Japan and the Federal Republic of Germany*, Tokyo–Frankfurt, 1984

Vogl, F., *German Business after the Economic Miracle*, London, 1973
Wangenheim V. von, *Industrial Relations in West Germany*, London, 1984
Windmuller, J.P. and A. Gladstone (eds.), *Employers' Associations and Industrial Relations*, Oxford, 1984

Index

Most technical terms in this subject index will be listed in their German version on the assumption that readers will come across this version in the first instance and now wish to look up the relevant detail.